The
Syriac World

The Syriac World

In Search of a
Forgotten Christianity

FRANÇOISE BRIQUEL CHATONNET

AND MURIEL DEBIÉ

Translated by

JEFFREY HAINES

Yale UNIVERSITY PRESS/NEW HAVEN & LONDON

Published with assistance from the foundation established in memory
of Philip Hamilton McMillan of the Class of 1894, Yale College, and with
assistance from the Ronald and Betty Miller Turner Publication Fund, and with
support from the Fund established in memory of Oliver Baty Cunningham, a
distinguished graduate of the Class of 1917, Yale College, Captain, 15th United
States Field Artillery, born in Chicago September 17, 1894, and killed while on
active duty near Thiaucourt, France, September 17, 1918, the twenty-fourth
anniversary of his birth.

Yale University Press books may be purchased in quantity for educational,
business, or promotional use. For information, please email sales.press@yale.edu
(U.S. office) or sales@yaleup.co.uk (U.K. office).

Set in 11/14.5 Minion type by Newgen North America.
Printed in the United States of America.

Library of Congress Control Number: 2022945252
ISBN 978-0-300-25353-5 (hardcover : alk. paper)

A catalogue record for this book is available from the British Library.

This paper meets the requirements of ANSI/NISO Z39.48-1992
(Permanence of Paper).

10 9 8 7 6 5 4 3 2 1

Contents

Maps

Introduction

S yriac was a major cultural language in Syro-Mesopotamia from
approximately the 2nd to the 13th century AD. Although it
stretched from the Mediterranean to East Asia, it was never the
language of a state or a particular people in a national or ethnic
sense; instead, it was a language of encounter and cultural contact. Its
legacy is primarily religious: it was the process of Christianization that
has made this particular dialect of Aramaic last up to the present day,
and it is still the classical literary and religious language of the members
of the Oriental churches and their Catholic and Protestant offshoots in
the Middle East, India, and, increasingly, in the diaspora.

Next to Latin and Greek, Syriac is the third most important branch
of ancient Christianity. As the heir to Greco-Latin antiquity, the Western
world is largely unaware of this Christian tradition, which is anchored
in Hellenism but also descended from a Near Eastern and Semitic past.
In parallel with the Greco-Latin tradition in the West, it spread to the
East in the first centuries of Christianity, eventually reaching as far as
India and China. Compared with other branches of Christianity, Syriac
Christianity has also undoubtedly had the greatest contact with Islam,
with which it continues to coexist.

It is in Edessa, to use its Greek name, or Urhay, to use its Aramaic
name (today Urfa or Şanlıurfa in southeastern Turkey)—"the mother

of all the cities of Mesopotamia," as it styled itself on its coins—that the story of Syriac begins. Syriac was originally the dialect of Aramaic that was spoken and written in Edessa, the capital of the vassal kingdom of Osrhoene, which was situated on the frontiers of the Roman Empire in the 2nd century AD after briefly becoming part of the Parthian Empire. If it had not been for the Christianization of Edessa, Syriac would have stayed a local language, used largely for funerary inscriptions and administration like other dialects of Aramaic in other cities. Instead, after becoming the written language of Aramaic-speaking Christians, it spilled over the borders of Osrhoene and spread to the eastern shores of the Mediterranean, Arabia, and East Asia.

Syriac Christianity is unique because of its Semitic roots, its close proximity to Judaism, and especially its theology, which diverged from the Greek-speaking "Orthodox" church following the councils of Ephesus and Chalcedon in the 5th century. These two councils crystallized the relationship between Syriac Christianity and the other denominations, and marked the point when the Syriac churches slowly started separating into their own bodies, each with their own patriarch (such churches are known as "autocephalic"). They include an eastern church (meaning east of the Tigris River), known as the Church of the East or the Church of Persia, which was sometimes called by others by the pejorative name Nestorian (now called the Assyrian Church of the East or—for the Roman Catholic branch—the Chaldean Church), and three western churches (west of the Tigris): the Miaphysite or Syriac Orthodox Church (sometimes called Jacobite; the Roman Catholic branch is called Syriac Catholic), the Maronite Church (a Chalcedonian branch, also in communion with the Roman Catholic Church), and the Melkite Church, which is also Chalcedonian and uses both Greek and Arabic in worship. Religious membership, together with language, still plays a major role in defining Syriac identity. Even today in Iraq, for example, the Assyro-Chaldean-Syriacs, as they call themselves, have not been able to come to a single unified name that would include the membership of all the churches—whether Assyrian, Chaldean, Syriac Orthodox, or Catholic—even as they claim to be freed from ecclesiastical power.

After the first two centuries of the Christian era, Syriac was never the official language of a state, and perhaps it is precisely that fact that allowed it to become a universal Christian language and permitted its expansion across political borders into Asia. Syriac missionaries traveled along the Silk Road and established monasteries and churches at the same time that Manichaeans and Buddhists were spreading their own messages, centuries before the first Latin missionaries arrived in East Asia. In the 7th century, Syriac Christians had set up a "pope" in Tibet and spread the Syriac language as far as the famous Xi'an stele in northern China and to the edge of the deserts of Central Asia, where Syriac manuscripts have been recovered. Syriac Christianity also established a foothold along the sea routes in the Persian Gulf and India, where communities known as "St. Thomas Christians" still live and where there are still seven churches of the Syriac tradition.

Syriac Christianity should also be understood as being in dialogue not only with other churches and Christian traditions in the southern and western Mediterranean but also with other religions of the Middle East and Asia: paganism, Judaism, Manichaeism, Zoroastrianism, and Islam, and to a lesser extent with Buddhism, Taoism, and Hinduism in their respective forms. It owes a great deal to the interpretations of Judaism in northern Mesopotamia where it developed, and in its turn, it played a major role in the beginnings of Islam. Through the clergy and the literary and liturgical connections that it maintained with the Arab Christian communities in Yemen, on the periphery of the Persian Gulf, and in northeastern Arabia, it created a religious and theological foundation for the Qur'an that is just now beginning to attract more attention. Syriac writers, who continued to read, translate, and comment on Greek philosophical and scientific works, transmitted Hellenic and Sasanian culture into Muslim thought, especially in 9th-century Baghdad. Syriac doctors, astronomers, philosophers, and secretaries were an essential part of Muslim courts until the medieval period.

Syriac can perhaps primarily be characterized as a culture of intermixture from the beginning: the heir, despite the ruptures, of Mesopotamian culture and the ancient Aramean world; steeped in Greek language and culture that had predominated following the founding of the Hellenistic kingdom of the Seleucids after the conquests of Alexander the Great in the 4th century BC; a participant in the political and military culture of the Roman Empire that replaced the Seleucids; imbued with Iranian culture, Parthian, and then Sasanian, and marked by that of the Arabs who lived throughout the region. The birth of Syriac in Osrhoene, the kingdom of which Edessa was the capital, contributed to the creation of a distinct (As)Syrian and Aramaic identity that continued to evolve through its contact with Roman, Persian, and Arab Muslim religions and powers, as well as with the Franks, Mongols, and Turks who would come later. Syriac Christians were always a religious and political minority in states where the official religion was different from their own, even if demographically they were not always a minority, and these various powers were the ones who created the cultural, religious, and civic categories in the vast geographical territory in which Syriac Christianity developed, evolved, and spread. This is partly why Syriac developed as a language of intercultural exchanges; translations first in Greek, and subsequently in Latin, Armenian, Georgian, Ethiopic, Middle Persian, Arabic, Sogdian, Uighur, Turkish, and Malayalam (a language from the south of India) bear witness to the centrifugal force of Syriac culture.

These encounters were not always a matter of peaceful commercial, religious, or intellectual exchange. As the populations of borderlands almost by definition—situated between the two great Roman and Persian Empires until the seventh century, then different Muslim powers, and today between countries of the Near and Middle East, such as Turkey, Lebanon, Syria, Iraq, and Iran, as well as southeastern India—Syriac-speaking communities underwent countless massacres, invasions, sieges, destructions, and occupations, culminating in a genocide in Turkey in 1915. This litany of catastrophes has left its mark on their philosophy and their theology of their history. This story of loss coincided with the disappearance of local archives, the destruction of buildings, and the irreparable loss of manuscripts. Texts, which were the major product of Syriac culture, are thus nearly the only means by which their history can be written (along with, to a lesser extent, archaeology). Syriac culture is especially unique in its written culture; its material culture is similar to others of various languages and religions in the environment where it developed. Its uniqueness lies in the fact that it was transmitted and in great part carried on by clerics of a high rank.

Heirs of Mesopotamian poetry and archival practices, of Jewish interpretation, of both Christian and secular Greek literature, Syriac writers blended their Greek and Semitic roots to create a unique Christian literature based on typological, symbolic, and literary imagery. If one had to choose a few key points of this tradition, the role of poetry, the place given to women, and the religious dimension and importance of writing and teaching deserve to be highlighted.

Poetry is the quintessential form of Syriac writing. Everything can be said in *memre* (metrical discourses), *madrashe* (strophic poems), and *sogyata* (dialogue poems): theology, exegesis, lives of saints, history, grammar, and even astronomy. Symbolic interpretation and images constitute their own form of language alongside the discursive dimension. Sung in church with alternating male and female choirs, *madrashe* and *sogyata* are meant to be beautiful forms of worship as well as a catechetical tool; they also play a major role in internal distinctions between Christian denominations and between the Greek and Syriac traditions, as well as external distinctions, such as with Jews, Manichaeans, and Zoroastrians, or later Muslims. The *memre* spoken during the liturgy are also both a literary medium for theological ideas and a way to frame biblical references in poetic imagery for ordinary believers.

Another notable distinction of the Syriac Christian tradition is the place given to women: poems give words to women who are silent in the Bible, and Syriac Bibles themselves are rearranged in such a way as to give greater prominence to the "books of women" (Ruth, Suzanne, Esther, and Judith, along with in some manuscripts the story of Thecla, the disciple of Paul). Theologians experimented with feminine imagery of the divine. The "Daughters of the Covenant," who were consecrated for service in the divine liturgy, received a basic education, an almost unknown phenomenon in the ancient world, and it was specifically for women that the greatest Syriac poet, Ephrem, composed his *madrashe* in the fourth century.

Syriac literature is made up for the most part of Christian literary genres: exegesis, homiletics, patristic commentary, and hagiography. Religion is the lens by which Syriac authors read the world and the relationship between humanity and God. At the same time, an intense

interest in asceticism and mysticism did not prevent a similar enthu-
siasm for magic, astrology, history, philosophy, logic, or science, especially medicine and astronomy. But all of these are nearly entirely the
domain of monks and clergy, including bishops and patriarchs, who
formed these disciplines, practiced them, translated them, and wrote
them down.

Another characteristic of Syriac culture is the valorization of
teaching and the role of (religious) schools, including the codification of
grammar and orthography—which created an overarching homogene-
ity in academic culture despite differences between West and East Syriac
(west and east in relation to the Tigris, as always), and a standardization
of language over the *longue durée*. The importance of written culture is
notable, tied to the tradition of written culture in the Edessan chancellery and the tradition of Christian theology developed in Antioch that
depicted God as the ultimate teacher of humanity.

This book invites you into the discovery of this unique language
and culture.

Note on Terms

Dates that were originally written according to the Seleucid calendar used by Syriac writers, which begins on October 1, 312 BC (known as the Greek Era, which corresponds to the foundation of the Seleucid Empire), or according to the Muslim (Hijri) calendar, have been transposed into the Gregorian calendar. Since the years do not always exactly correspond, however, dates are sometimes given with a double year.

As for the dates for a specific person, dates without any other marker indicate birth and death; *r.* indicates the dates of the rule of a king, while *d.* indicates the date of death.

For the transcription of Syriac, we have not marked the spirantization of consonants in certain positions, nor the long vowels. *Memra* in the singular and *memre* in the plural mark the pronunciation of ancient Syriac as preserved in East Syriac; in West Syriac, the same word is pronounced *memro* in the singular and *mimre* in the plural. We have decided to treat the difference according to context since the *a/o* and *e/i* variation occurs in a number of other words.

The authors and editor thank the Syriac Orthodox Patriarchate, the Syriac Catholic Patriarchate, Kaslik University in Lebanon, the Directorate of Antiquities and Museums in Syria, Hill Museum and

Manuscript Library (HMML), the Dominican center for manuscripts in Mosul, and the archaeological missions of Bayzan, Failaka, Kilwa, Mor Gabriel, and Nisibis for their generous authorization for the use of their pictures.

The
Syriac World

The Aramaic World at the Beginning of the First Millennium

Origins

A Culture of Encounter and Contact

S yriac is a dialect of Aramaic, a Semitic language that is most notably related to Hebrew and Arabic but which is more precisely
part of the Northwest Semitic language group. The culture that
is known as "Syriac" is the heir to a millennium of Aramaic
culture and history. The fact that the Syriac language can be known
as *suryāyā* (the adjectival form of "Syrian" in the old sense), *arāmāyā*
(formed from "Aramean"), or *urhāyā* (formed from the Aramaic name
of Edessa, Urhay) shows the complexity of identity and self-definition
within this culture.

Aramaic Origins

The first known mention of the Arameans dates from 1111 BC and is
found in the annals of the Assyrian king Tiglath-Pileser I. The record
mentions a campaign led in that year by the Assyrian army against the
"Ahlamu-Arameans," in the region between the Ḥabur and the Euphrates in the northeast of modern-day Syria, as well as the region beyond
the river in the Syrian plain north of Palmyra, known as Jabal Bishri.
These Arameans are descendants of the Amorites who lived in Syria in
the second millennium BC, rather than being new arrivals as had long
been thought. The records of the Assyrian kings mention several towns

but no fortifications or sieges. This suggests that at the end of the second millennium, the Aramaic population was living in a tribal society and leading the kind of semi-nomadic life that had become widespread in the area since the end of the Bronze Age empires around 1200 BC.

THE ARAMAIC KINGDOMS

At the beginning of the first millennium, Aramaic tribes organized themselves into small kingdoms along the arc of the Fertile Crescent, from the southwest of Syria (the kingdom of Damascus), to the northeast in the region of the Ḥabur. They developed towns, an architectural and artistic style that already showed a culture of intermixture and contact, and notably a strong Neo-Hittite influence.

INSCRIPTION OF ZAKKUR

The stele that Zakkur, king of Ḥamath and Luʾaš, has set up for Ilu-Wēr [his god]. I am Zakkur, king of Ḥamath and Luʾaš. I was an oppressed man, but Baal Shamain [delivered] me and stood by me, and Baal Shamain made me king in Hazrak. Now Bar-Hadad, the son of Hazael, king of Aram, united against me se[ven]teen kings. Bar-Hadad and his army, Bar-Gūš and his army . . . they were with their armies. And all these kings set up a bulwark against Hazrak and they erected a wall higher than the wall of Hazrak and they dug a moat deeper than its moat. But I lifted up my hands to Baal Shamain and Baal Shamain answered me. And Baal Shamain spoke to me through seers and through messengers. And Baal Shamain said to me: "Do not fear, for I made you king, and I shall stand with you, and I shall deliver you from all these kings who have raised a bulwark against you."

INSCRIPTION OF TELL FEKHERIYE

The figure of Hadad-yisʿi, which he placed before Hadad of Sikkān, water controller of heaven and earth, who brings down prosperity, and provides pasture and watering place for all the lands, and provides water-supply and jugs to all the gods his

Inscription of Zakkur: a basalt stele found at Afis, not far from Aleppo in Syria. Dated to the end of the 9th century BC. Musée du Louvre, Paris, France. © RMN-Grand Palais / Art Resource, NY.

brothers, water controller of all the rivers, who makes all the lands luxuriant, the merciful god to whom praying is sweet, who dwells in Sikkān, the great lord, the lord of Hadad-yis'i, king of Gozān, son of Sasnūrī, king of Gozān, for enlivening his soul, and for lengthening his days, and for multiplying his years, and for safeguarding his house, and for safeguarding his offspring, and for safeguarding his people, and for removing illness from him, and that his prayer may be heard, and that the utterance of his mouth may be acceptable, he set [it] up and gave to him.

The oldest Aramaic inscriptions date to the 9th century BC. The script is a linear alphabet often described as Phoenician, but which was common to all West Semitic peoples at this time. These are royal

inscriptions, either commemorative or dedicatory, which can be identified chronologically by their connection with the history of Israel or
Assyria; for example, the inscription of the king of Ḥamath and Lu'ash,
Zakkur, mentions the war waged against him by the king of Damascus, Bar Hadad, who is also referenced in the book of Kings under the
Hebrew name of Ben Hadad in the context of his siege of the Israelite
capital of Samaria (2 Kgs. 6:24). In the inscription, Zakkur calls on the
aid of his god, Baal Shamin, who speaks to him by the mediation of seers
and prophets. The pressure of these first Assyrian campaigns caused the
Arameans to gather themselves together into kingdoms and principalities, but these kingdoms were progressively subdued and then annexed
during the 9th and 8th centuries BC. However, their rulers were sometimes left on the throne as Assyrian governors, as shown, for example, in
the inscription on the statue of Hadad-yis'i discovered at Tell Fekheriye.
By 720 BC, all of Syria had been integrated into the Assyrian Empire.

THE SPREAD OF THE ARAMAIC LANGUAGE

If the political history of the Arameans more or less stops there after
only a brief existence, the same cannot be said for Aramaic cultural history; the Assyrian conquest, far from breaking Aramaic culture, was undoubtedly the driving force that caused it to spread. The usual practice
of the Assyrians during their conquests was to deport important figures
from the local population. This was partly meant to prevent resistance
after the conquest by breaking local solidarity but was also a way to
bring specialized labor to the capital or other places in need of development. The book of Kings in the Bible, for example, mentions how the
Assyrians deported the inhabitants of the kingdom of Samaria into their
empire. As a result, this practice spread the Aramaic-speaking population across the Near East. Arameans found a place in the administration of the Assyrian Empire at all levels, including the very highest ones.
The empire became bilingual, speaking both Assyrian and Aramaic, and
employed two scripts (using both the logo-syllabic cuneiform writing
system and a linear alphabetic script).

By the 7th century BC, Aramaic was already the lingua franca of
the people of the Near East, as shown by the instance where Hezekiah,

Tablet inscribed in Aramaic from around 570 BC. It
is dated to the reign of Nebuchadnezzar (r. ca. 605–
562 BC). © Musée du Louvre, Dist. RMN-Grand Palais /
Raphaël Chipault / Art Resource, NY.

the king of Judah, wanted to conduct negotiations in Aramaic with the
commander leading the Assyrian army that besieged Jerusalem (2 Kgs.
18:26). At the same time, Mesopotamian culture increasingly became
part of Syria.

This mixed culture produced the oldest text in Aramaic literature,
The Story and Wisdom of Aḥiqar, the story of an Assyrian notable of
Aramaic origins, a minister at the court of the Assyrian kings Sennacherib and Esarhaddon. Aḥiqar was betrayed by his nephew Nadin, dis-
missed by the king, and finally rehabilitated, following a literary motif
that was already well known in the ancient world. Preserved in a papyrus from the 5th century BC found in Elephantine in Egypt, this text
consists of two independent parts, assembled later and written in two
slightly different dialects. The first part consists of wisdom proverbs in
a classical Aramaic dialect, doubtless a remnant of traditional Aramaic
culture, while the second is the story itself, in an Aramaic style full of
Assyrian influences. The reach of *The Story and Wisdom of Aḥiqar* was
considerable. It was integrated into Jewish culture (there is a reference
to it in the biblical book of Tobit) and, most likely through the Jewish

community of Edessa, entered Aramaic Christian culture. There are five extant Syriac versions, forming the basis of an Armenian version (itself the foundation of later Georgian and Old Turkic versions) as well as Arabic versions, which would be the root of an Ethiopic adaptation. Versions of the story in modern Syriac depend on both Classical Syriac and Arabic. The story of Aḥiqar also passed into European culture, where it was adapted in the first century in Greek as the life of the fable-writer Aesop and then translated into French by La Fontaine in the 17th century.

THE STORY OF AḤIQAR, ACCORDING TO THE ARAMAIC VERSION

The account of the words of the one named Aḥiqar, a wise and expert scribe who taught the son of his sister after he had prayed to god and had said, "May I have a son?"

The beginning of his words: I am Aḥiqar, and I dwelt in the Gate of the Palace, in the house of the seal [bearer] of Sennacherib, king of Assyria. And I said, "I have no children to give my home or my words to." [Now] Sennacherib was king of Assyria. After Sennacherib, the king of Assyria, had died, I served the one named Esarhaddon, his son. And he was king in Assyria; he replaced Sennacherib, his father. [. . .] old . . . So I took my nephew. And I said, "He shall be my son. At my death he will bury me." And I taught him wisdom.

THE WISDOM OF AḤIQAR, ACCORDING TO THE ARAMAIC VERSION: FROM THE MAXIMS OF WISDOM

My son, do not damn the day until you see night. Do not let it come into your mind that in every place their eyes and their ears are near your mouth. Watch yourself; let it not be their prey. More than all watchfulness watch your mouth and over what you heard harden your heart. For a bird is a word and he who sends it forth is a person of no heart . . . Do not cover (= ignore) the word of a king; let it be healing for your heart. Soft is the speech of a king, yet it is sharper and mightier than a double-edged knife. See before you a hard thing: against the face of a king, do not stand. His rage is swifter than lightning. You, watch yourself. Let him not show it because of your sayings lest you die not in your days. See the good of a king. If something is commanded to you, it is a burning fire. Hurry, do it. Do not kindle it against you and do not cover your palms. Moreover, do the word of the king with heat/delight of the heart. How can wood contest with fire, flesh with knife, man with king?

After the Assyrian period, Aramaic continued to spread widely. The Persian conquest of the Near East (including the taking of Babylon by Cyrus in 539 BC) gave a new impetus to the spread and influence of Aramaic. From Egypt to Uzbekistan and from Anatolia to northern India, the administration of the Persian Empire was conducted not in Persian but in Aramaic: for instance, a recently published administrative archive of Aramaic documents recorded on leather and wooden rods recounts the administration of Bactria by the Persian satrap.

During this period, Aramaic became the language in which people wrote—the language of culture, different from the local dialects that they spoke, a phenomenon that remained one of the characteristics of the Syriac world much later.

Rod of wood inscribed in Aramaic, from Bactria, third year of Darius III, 333 BC. It acted as an accounting tool, with numbers being marked by its notches. Khalili Collection.

ARAMAIC AND GREEK

If the Near East was already in contact with Greek merchants and Greek culture very early on, the Greco-Macedonian conquest (333–331 BC) truly made it part of the Greek world. Greek gradually replaced Aramaic as the language of power, administration, and culture, and became the language spoken both by elites and by a large part of the population. The dialect of Greek from this period is known as *koine,* or the common language of the Hellenistic kingdoms. Aramaic barely appears in documents dating from the Hellenistic period, except in the Jewish world (for instance, certain passages of the Bible are written in Aramaic) or in the regions on the edge of the Hellenistic world, such as the Caucasus, Iran, and India. Around 300 BC, the emperor Ashoka, who founded the first empire in India and was a convert to Buddhism, wrote inscriptions in several languages, including Aramaic.

Only at the end of the Hellenistic period, during the weakening of the Seleucid Empire, would Aramaic become visible again and new inscriptions be written. Although it had always been spoken, it had been eclipsed by Greek as the official language for writing and public display. Now it reappeared in different small kingdoms on the edge of the Roman world—Nabatea, Osrhoene (Edessa), Ḥatra—and, in the most unusual case, in a city within Roman territory as well, Palmyra.

In the Jewish world, inscriptions on ossuaries show the emergence of a style of writing known as "Square Hebrew," deriving from Aramaic origins and still in use. Aramaic forms of the alphabet were used to engrave funerary inscriptions and votive offerings, along with other inscriptions relevant to political and local social life. On perishable material, such as papyrus or parchment, some contracts have been preserved. The written records from this period reveal forms of Aramaic that are very different from the unified language of the Achaemenid era, because there was no longer a government that could maintain a single written version of Aramaic or a political and administrative context that centralized the use of the language. As a result, Aramaic evolved, taking on different local and provincial characteristics in both written and spoken forms: for instance, the Nabatean dialect is markedly different from Palmyrene, from Edessan, from the Aramaic spoken in Ḥatra, or

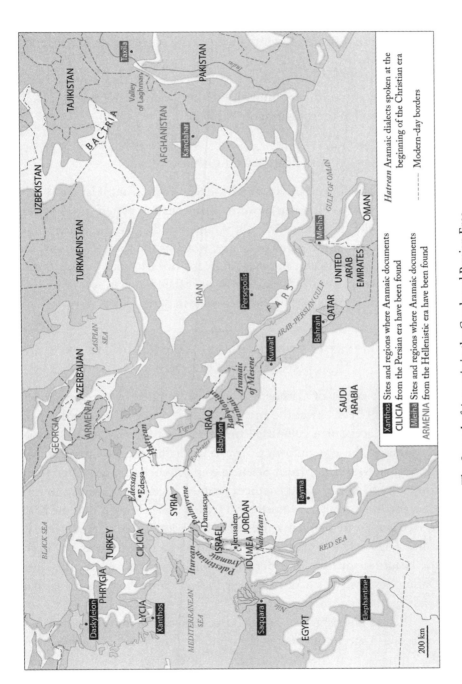

The Spread of Aramaic in the Greek and Persian Eras

Xanthos Sites and regions where Aramaic documents from the Persian era have been found
CILICIA

Mleiha Sites and regions where Aramaic documents from the Hellenistic era have been found
ARMENIA

Hatrean Aramaic dialects spoken at the beginning of the Christian era

------- Modern-day borders

the Jewish Aramaic of Babylon or Palestine. Not only are their grammatical forms different, but also their writing, since each one developed its own alphabet.

Among these local forms of Aramaic, the one that would be destined for an extraordinary future is Edessan Aramaic, the dialect spoken in Edessa and in the kingdom of Osrhoene.

Edessa and Osrhoene

We know very little of the ancient history of Edessa, but it is most likely the same place as the town of Adma mentioned in cuneiform Assyrian sources in the 7th century BC. The Aramaic and Syriac documents that mention it give it the name of Urhay, which is the root of the Turkish name of Urfa and later, in 1984, Şanlıurfa, or "Glorious Urfa," to celebrate the victory of the Turkish army over the French in 1920, who had occupied the area as part of their mandate in Syria.

GREEK FOUNDATION, ARAMAIC KINGDOM, AND ROMAN COLONY

Edessa, the center of Osrhoene, had been founded by the general Seleucus as a Greek city at the end of the 4th century BC (around 303 or 302) for Macedonian colonists from the army of Alexander the Great. In doing so, he was following a model that flourished across the Alexandrian Near East, from Seleucia and Antioch (named after their founders) to Apamea and Laodicea (named after their spouses). In this case, the Macedonian colonists who settled there thought that the land looked similar to their native Edessa in Macedonia; hence, the town was called Edessa. It was also known by the nickname Callirhoe, or "from the beautiful source," in order to celebrate its water source, the river Daisan/Scyrtos, which ran through the city and filled the pools that made up its water reserves.

Edessa flourished because of its location on the route that ran from Syria—and specifically one of the capitals of the kingdom, Antioch on the Orontes, near the Mediterranean—to the Tigris valley, where another capital stood, Seleucia on the Tigris. It is also connected to Birecik,

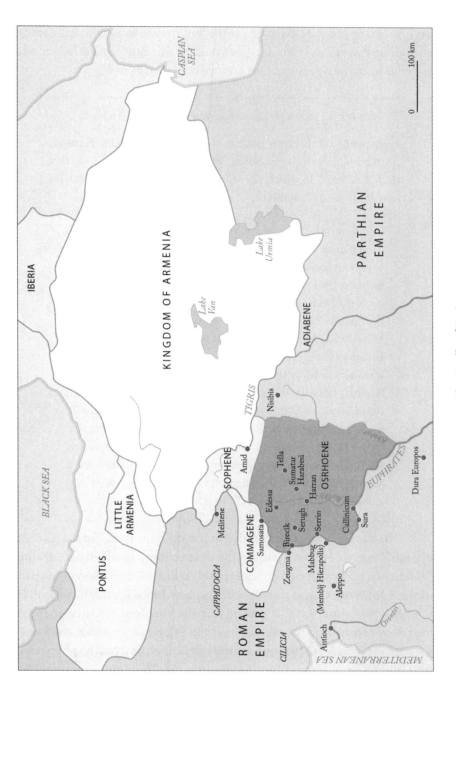

The Cradle of Syriac

an important point of passage on the Euphrates, as well as to a route going northward to Armenia. As a result, it was not just a strategic site to build a city but an important commercial stop as well.

THE CHRONICLE OF MICHAEL THE GREAT

After the Flood that took place in the days of Noah, King Nimrod, from among the sons of Canaan, built Urhoy and called it Ur, that is Quriat "city" in which the Chaldeans dwelled. Jacob of Edessa said about its destruction:

> Concerning its destruction, we did not find who caused it, it is thought that it was destroyed during the time of Sennacherib who marched up against Jerusalem, and it remained desolate until the time of Alexander the Builder. Those who marched up with him from Macedonia rebuilt it and named it Edessa, that is the Beautiful One, after the name of their city in Macedonia, and for this reason, the Macedonian name was added to it. And on this account, the computation of years was carried from the beginning of [the reign of] Seleucus Nicator, because he rebuilt it. After three hundred years, Abgar son of Ma'nu, who believed in Christ, reigned in it. And after Abgar and his sons, it became part of the dominion of the Roman emperors who were still pagans, worshiping idols; it remained under their power for three hundred years. After King Constantine reigned, Christianity increased in it and great churches were built in it.

The Parthian Empire, founded in the 3rd century BC on the Iranian plateau, largely developed during the next century, gradually absorbing Seleucid territory through conquest until it included all the regions east of the Euphrates. Consequently, Edessa passed into Parthian control. It is within the bounds of this empire that the kingdom of Osrhoene first took shape sometime between 135 and 130 BC, beginning as a small vassal state led by rulers who are variously described as dynasts, phylarchs, or toparchs until around the 3rd century AD. Their succession can be traced both by their coinage and by the historical sources. They held linguistically Arab names; a number of them are called Abgar, a name that would become famous in the Christian tradition, but they also include Waʾel, Maʿnu, and others.

The arrival of Rome in the area, beginning with the campaigns of Pompey, made Osrhoene the object of clashes between the Romans and the Parthians, because the kingdom was situated in a strategic zone, vulnerable to attack from both sides. The kings of Edessa, while always staying within the Parthian sphere, tried their best to navigate between the two empires and sometimes suffered serious consequences as a result. During the campaign of Trajan, Abgar VII, who first submitted and then revolted against Rome, was deposed in 118 and replaced by a king chosen by Rome. Four years later, another Abgarid regained power. Other, similar crises punctuated the 2nd century. In 166, following the campaigns of Lucius Verus in Mesopotamia, Edessa moved temporarily to the Roman side. In 193 the governor of Syria, Pescennius Niger, revolted against the Roman emperor Septimius Severus (r. 193–211) and was supported by the kingdoms of Osrhoene and Adiabene. Edessa came under siege and was captured by the troops of Severus, as commemorated in the triumphal arch in the Roman Forum. However, the king, Abgar VIII, managed to preserve the kingdom itself.

Edessa passed definitively into the Roman orbit at the beginning of the 3rd century. In 212–213 it became a Roman colony, even though its dynasty still played a role and despite a brief restoration of its kingship under Abgar X in 238–242. It stayed in the Eastern Roman Empire until its conquest by Arab-Islamic forces in 641, but only as a buffer province, vulnerable to Roman and Persian armies in each new war.

THE CITY AND ITS TERRITORIES

Without a written record, it is hard to know precisely what the urban landscape of Edessa looked like. The citadel of the city is still visible today, dominated by two Greek-style columns. The river that crosses the city, the Scyrtos (literally, "the bound river"), or Daisan as it is known in Aramaic, frequently rises above its bed, resulting in deadly floods, as recounted in Syriac chronicles of the city. It was partly diverted by the emperor Justinian in the 6th century. The Callirhoe spring is still at the base of the hill where the citadel was built. If one believes the *Teaching of Addai*, the archives were located in the center of the city, next to a large pagan temple.

EXCERPT FROM THE ANONYMOUS *CHRONICLE OF EDESSA* UP TO 540: THE FLOOD OF AD 202

In the year 513 in the reign of [Septimius] Severus, and the reign of king Abgar, son of king Maʿnu, in the month of the latter Teshri [November], the spring of water that comes forth from the great palace of King Abgar the Great became abundant; and it rose abundantly as had been its wont previously and it became full and overflowed on all sides. The royal courtyards and porticoes and rooms began to be filled with water. When our lord king Abgar saw this, he went up a safe place on the hill, above his palace where the workmen of the royal works reside and dwell . . . The river Daisan came before the usual time and month . . . the waters broke down the western wall of the city and entered into the city. They destroyed the great and beautiful palace of our lord king and removed everything that was found in their path—the charming and beautiful buildings of the city, everything that was near the river to the south and north. They caused damage moreover to the nave of the church of the Christians . . . Maryhab, the son of Shemesh, and Qayuma, the son of Magartat, the scribes of Edessa, recorded this incident and the decree of King Abgar in writing. Bardin and Bulid, the administrators of the archives of Edessa, received them and deposited them in these archives in their capacity of city officials.

According to the famous account of the flood that took place in Edessa in 202, which is copied in the anonymous Syriac chronicle of 540 and which seems to have been stored in the city archives, the shops of the artisans were built along the river on the roads to the gate, which were lit at night with lanterns. The royal palace and the aristocratic houses were located not far away, while the poorest (beggars, palace servants) were located on the hill. The palace of the king was known as the *apadana,* a Persian word that was also used for the palace of Darius at Persepolis. The names of certain quarters are mentioned in various chronicles of the city. A hippodrome and theater, indispensable parts of the ancient city, provided a venue for circus games and mime shows, respectively. A *tetrapylon* was located at the intersection of the two main avenues, and several doors in the walls gave access to the main roads.

Edessa was the capital of a kingdom, Osrhoene, whose borders are still unknown, but the distribution of inscriptions in Edessan Aramaic allows for some hypotheses. To the northwest, these inscriptions can be found up to the Euphrates, which for a long time marked the border between the Roman and Persian worlds. The two most ancient Edessan inscriptions put the western limits of Osrhoene on the Euphrates, and its southern limits in Serrin, in today's Syria, around AD 73, and Birecik, probably in AD 106. To the east, it stretched beyond the Balikh River, at least to Sumatar, where there are a good number of inscriptions, dedications, and epitaphs, but not up to the source of the Tigris, which was part of the territory of the city of Amida. To the south, it included Ḥarran and Tell Matin, also in Syria, where a small altar with an Edessan Aramaic inscription was found.

Edessan Culture: A Culture of Contact

Osrhoene was a cosmopolitan region. To the old Aramaic population of the region were added settlers from Greece, Macedonia, and Syria, along with their families. Merchants from Syria and Mesopotamia traveled there, carrying with them the ancient Assyro-Babylonian culture as well with the heritage of Parthian Persia. The area east of Edessa, around Sumatar Harabesi, was inhabited by semi-nomadic or only recently sedentarized Arabs. The Edessan inscriptions that are found in that region mention several notables who have the title ŠLYTʾ DʿRB, or "governor of the Arabs," which one also finds in the inscriptions of Ḥatra. Strabo describes Arab Scenites—literally, "those who live in tents"—in Upper Mesopotamia. It is perhaps to this group that the Edessan dynasts—who, as mentioned above, bore Arab names—belonged. This situation explains where Edessa drew the originality and richness of its cosmopolitan character. The use of Greek and Aramaic languages is closely entangled in this region, and the two languages can be found together in inscriptions and civic texts. But we should also note the Mesopotamian, Jewish, Arab, and Persian influences in Edessa. From the Parthian Empire, Persian words relating to administrative and civic culture entered into the Syriac lexicon, including the words for the royal palace, ambassador, architect, and crown prince.

BEGINNING OF THE TEXT ON THE PARCHMENT FOUND IN DURA-EUROPOS (AD 243)

In the year 6 of Autocrator Caesar Marcus Antonius Gordianus Eusebes Eutyches Sebastos, in the consulship of Annius Arrianus and of Cervonius Papus, in the month of Iyyar, the year five hundred and fifty-four in the former reckoning, and in the year thirty-one of the liberation of Antoniana Edessa the Glorious, Colonia, Metropolis Aurelia Alexandria . . . I, Marcia Aurelia Matarʿata daughter of Šamenbaraz son of Abgar, Edessene resident, I declare to Lucas Aurelius Tiro son of Barbaʿšamin, Ḥarranian, that I have received from him seven hundred denarii and I have sold Amatsin my female slave, purchased—she is aged twenty-eight years, more or less—from captivity . . .

HISTORY OF ABGAR AND JESUS (*TEACHING OF ADDAI*)

As is the custom in the kingdom of King Abgar and in all kingdoms, everything which is said before him is written and placed among the records. Labubna, the son of Senaq the son of Abshadar, the scribe of the king, therefore, wrote the things concerning the Apostle Addai from the beginning to the end, while Ḥanan, the faithful archivist of the king, set the hand of witness and placed it among the records of the royal books, where the statutes and ordinances are placed. The matters belonging to those who buy and sell are also kept there with care and concern.

Parchment from the Euphrates (240 BC). It describes the transfer of a debt corresponding to a prior loan that the debtor had not repaid. With this document, the new creditor who had purchased the debt is claiming his due. Below the text is the signature of two of the five witnesses (the other three signatures are on the back). The document is dated to the "consulate" of King Abgar of Edessa, the second year of his rule. Institut de Papyrologie de la Sorbonne, P.Euphr.Inv.19, *P Euphrate* 18. © Adam Bülow-Jacobsen.

ARCHIVAL PRACTICES

Most likely, the archival practices of the small kingdom of Osrhoene are the reason behind the development of the Edessan Aramaic alphabet. Administrative record-keeping had a prominent role in Edessan culture, influenced by older Aramaic and Mesopotamian practices that endured in the kingdom of Osrhoene and passed into the Syriac tradition. There were official scribes (*sephre*), which are mentioned in later commercial documents and literary texts. One famous parchment found in Dura Europos (P. Dura 28), dating to 243, contains a record of the sale of a slave by a woman from Edessa. It was written by one of the official Edessan scribes, under the supervision of the superintendent of the archives, where, according to the document, a copy would be deposited.

Besides a handful of documents from the Euphrates, the archives themselves were not preserved, but they are mentioned by the Greek historian Eusebius, the Armenian historian Movses Khorenats'i, and various Syriac texts. The Syriac Chronicle of 540, for instance, mentions that the royal edicts meant to prevent the flooding of the city were put into writing by a royal scribe and deposited in the archives. In the 3rd century, the archives were still functional. A quick, cursive form of chancellery writing was taught to official scribes, probably in schools specially designated for their training.

These archives had an influence beyond writing and archival practices. Some texts mention the archives to give an air of authenticity to certain fictional stories: the *Teaching of Addai* claims that the history of the conversion of Edessa was deposited there, and the writers of the *Acts* of the martyrs of the city claim that their sources were stored there as well. By claiming that the archives preserved records of these accounts—or had preserved them at one time—the writers bolstered the credibility of their stories.

CULTS AND WORSHIP IN EDESSA

Pre-Christian religion and cultic worship in Edessa also show its mixed culture. The Mesopotamian deities Bel, the supreme god, and Nabu, the god of writing, were probably at the top of the Edessan pantheon, which also included the god of the underworld, Nergal.

CULTS IN EDESSA (*TEACHING OF ADDAI*)

I see that this city is filled with paganism which is contrary to God. Who is this [man-] made idol Nebo which you worship, and Bel which you honor? Behold there are those among you who worship Bath Nical, like the inhabitants of Ḥaran your neighbors, and Taratha, like the inhabitants of Mabbug, and the Eagle, like the Arabs, and the sun and the moon, like the rest of the inhabitants of Haran who are like you.

Edessans also venerated the Syrian goddess Atargatis and the Aramean god Hadad, as well as the sun—under the name Shamash, which was common throughout the Semitic world—and the moon, under the name of the Mesopotamian god Sin, as well as under the name of the goddess Nikkal. Other gods included Azizos and Monimos, which we can recognize as the Arab divinities ʿAziz and Munʿim, or the planet Venus in the form of a morning and evening star, respectively. The expression "Lord of the gods" in these inscriptions generally refers to Baal Shamin, the "Master of Heaven" in the Aramaic pantheon, but, at least in one case, it refers to the Greek god Zeus.

One mosaic, known as the Marallahe, shows the adoption of Greek divinities but also the modes of thought that prevailed in the Roman world between Antioch and Alexandria in the 3rd century. It depicts five gods: the most important, enthroned on the right side of the mosaic, is Zeus, but the writing identifies him by the Aramaic title *mar allahe* (Lord of the gods). Next to him, the Greek name of his wife, Hera, is written in Aramaic letters, as is that of Prometheus and, most likely, Cosmos. Athena, although without a legend of her own, is easily recognizable to his left. Below him is a scene where Hermes puts a small winged soul into a body, just as a pair seems to emerge from the sleep of death, evoking themes from Neoplatonic philosophy. The Syriac letter of Mara Bar Serapion bears witness to the importance of Greek philosophical thought in Osrhoene; probably written between the 1st and

Edessan mosaic of Marallahe. © William A. Haseltine.

3rd century AD, it contains an exhortation from a father to a son to study Greek thought.

Judaism was also highly visible in Edessa, and the story of the *Teaching of Addai* shows the apostle staying at the house of a Jewish man named Tobit on his arrival in the city. Perhaps roughly 10 percent of the population of the city was Jewish at the beginning of the Christian era. Manichaeism, the religion created by Mani in the 3rd century AD in Mesopotamia, spread to Edessa as well and represented a rival to Christianity in its nascent forms. Various other groups, including the Quqites and the Bardaisanites, were excluded and labeled heretical by the growing consensus of official Christianity. When the Christians became the majority, they of course passed down only their own texts, but in the beginning Syriac was not only a Christian language in ancient Edessa but also the language of all these other religious groups, including the Jews (who contributed to the translation of the Old Testament version of the Peshiṭta, or Syriac Bible), polytheists (at least until the 9th century), and the Manichaeans, even if little remains of their writings.

ORNAMENTAL AND FUNERARY MOSAICS: A MIRROR OF EDESSAN SOCIETY

As in the rest of Syria, mosaics were known in Edessa as part of the flourishing of Roman culture, but they also captured local artistic trends. Rich Edessans decorated their homes with lavish mosaics using the style—and probably the same materials and artisans as well—that originally came from Antioch, famous for this kind of work. The most spectacular, already mentioned, is the Marallahe mosaic. Another is a series of panels that would have decorated a reception area. It is made up of scenes depicting episodes from Homer: we see Achilles and Patroclus, Priam and Hecuba, Briseis with a servant, and, further on, Troilos, although the writing on these Greek images is entirely in Edessan Aramaic. These scenes show the influence of Greek culture through its most emblematic work, *The Iliad,* as does the Syriac translation of the *Hypomnemata* of Ambrosios, which mentions the same figures. A mosaic from another cycle shows Andromeda. Discovered in 2007, the mosaics of the palace of Haleplibahçe, part of Şanlıurfa where a new mosaic museum has been constructed, show the taste of aristocratic Edessans from the 3rd or 4th century with a string of Greek mythological motifs, featuring the queens of the Amazons, Hippolytus, Antiope, Melanippe, and Penthesilea, hunting, as well as episodes from the life of Achilles. There is also an exotic twist: an image of a black man dragging a zebra by a bridle.

If these images give a glimpse into a common culture, the art of the mosaic also saw developments original to Edessa. Among the most typical monuments of Edessan culture are funerary mosaics, both figurative and written, which decorate the tombs of rich nobles belonging

Edessan mosaic representing Achilles and Patroclus. Courtesy of
the Bible Lands Museum Jerusalem, Israel.

to the 3rd century. It is a form typical of Edessa, whereas in Palmyra and
the Roman world of the East these inscriptions are always carved on
stone and not on mosaic. A number of these mosaics represent a family
group: the father and the founder of the tomb in the center, surrounded
by his wife and children, each of whom are identified by their name and
surname written in Edessan Aramaic by their heads. In certain cases, a
more detailed inscription, placed in the frame, mentions the foundation
of the tomb. The men generally wear a type of Parthian clothing, with
large pleated pants, long tunics embroidered with elaborate motifs, as
well as a beard and a Persian hat. The women wear a kind of robe close
to classical dress, attached to the shoulders by fibulae, and often a very
tall device covered by a veil. This kind of clothing was also worn by
notables in Palmyra, where one also finds figural reliefs on tombstones.
Other Edessans chose to decorate their tombstones not with a gallery of
familial portraits but with motifs of Greek mythology tied to symbolism
of death and life after death: two motifs representing Orpheus, the van-

quisher of the underworld, calming the animals with the sound of his lyre; another of the phoenix, the mythical bird that after death is born again from its ashes. In the absence of other evidence, it is impossible to say whether these suggestions of life after death come from pagans, Jews, or Christians. A very recent discovery of a funerary mosaic with a cross

Votive stele with two people in Parthian dress.
The accompanying inscription is in Greek. Photo by
Françoise Briquel Chatonnet.

but nonfigurative decorations shows that this last possibility should not be excluded.

The names of certain deceased persons are also mentioned on funerary steles in either Greek or Aramaic inscriptions: for instance, there is an inscription in Greek on a bas-relief featuring the deceased in Parthian clothing, showing the hybridity of this culture.

It was in this milieu of cultural interaction, bringing together multiple influences, that Aramaic, or Syriac, Christianity was born.

Between Memory and History
Syriac Christianity up to the 4th Century

Many accounts of Christianity gloss over the fact that the life of Jesus in Palestine makes Christianity an Asiatic religion, one that spread west through the Roman Empire but also east, beyond the borders of the Roman world. It is in the east, for instance, at Antioch, where the name "Christian" was used for the first time (Acts 11:26), and the eastern city of Edessa claimed to have been Christianized during the apostolic era, on the initiative of Christ himself. The legend of the evangelization of Edessa gave it a prestige above the usual stories about apostolic foundations and very quickly earned it a reputation as far away as Europe. In the Syriac churches, the memory of their Christian origins centers on oral and written traditions of the Christianization of Edessa, Mesopotamia, and India, which imagine Christianity coming to the region very early, sometimes even before the episode of sending the disciples that appears in the book of the Acts of the Apostles in the New Testament. In reality, this first Christianization happened when the Edessan kingdom oscillated between the Parthian and Roman Empires, during the Roman-Persian wars that marked the 3rd and 4th centuries AD.

The Apostolic Traditions

The Syriac legends about the evangelization of the East are centered on the apostle Thomas, both his own mission to India and those of two of his disciples, named Addai and Mari, who were chosen from among the seventy-two disciples who were sent out by Christ (Luke 10:1) and who were later sent beyond the Euphrates to spread the good news. Additionally, especially in the Church of the East, there is a parallel tradition that credits the magi from the story of Jesus's birth with the first Christianization of Persia.

ADDAI, THE LETTER, AND THE PORTRAIT OF JESUS

The most well known of the apostles of the East, Addai in Syriac, Thaddeus in Greek, is credited with evangelizing both the Syriac people and the Armenians. Traditions linked to Addai passed beyond the borders of Osrhoene and became part of the heritage of Christianity as a whole. The earliest version of the legend is said to have been translated from a Syriac version preserved in the archives of Edessa and served as the foundation for the story in the *Ecclesiastical History* written in Greek by Eusebius, the bishop of Caesarea in Palestine, at the end of the 4th century. It was also the foundation for a more developed apocryphal tale, the *Teaching of Addai*, or the *History of Jesus and King Abgar*, which was written in Syriac at the beginning of the 5th century.

MESSAGE OF JESUS TO ABGAR
(*TEACHING OF ADDAI*)

When Jesus received the letter in the house of the chief priest of the Jews, he said to Ḥanan the archivist: "Go and say to your lord who sent you to me: 'Blessed are you who though not having seen me have believed in me. For it is written concerning me that those who see me will not believe in me, but those who do not see me will believe in me. With regard to the fact that you have written to me that I should come to you, that for which I was sent here is now finished and I ascend to my Father who sent me. But when I have ascended to Him, I will send to you one of my disciples who will

heal and make your particular illness well and will turn all who are
with you to eternal life. As for your city, may it be blessed and may
no enemy ever again rule over it.'"

According to these stories, the messengers of the king of Edessa,
Abgar, traveling to Palestine, hear rumors of a magician who preaches
and performs miraculous cures. Upon their return to Edessa, they tell
King Abgar, who is afflicted with a mysterious sickness, about this man
who can perform healing miracles without medicines, some of which
they heard about and some of which they saw themselves. Abgar immediately sends a letter to Jesus through his secretary, Ḥanan, asking him
to come to Edessa in order to heal him and in return offering to share
his small kingdom and guaranteeing his protection from the Jews who
want to do him harm. Jesus, who is in Jerusalem on the eve of his passion when he receives the letter, declines Abgar's invitation but promises Abgar that he will send a disciple after his ascension into heaven to
heal him and convert both him and his kingdom. After the ascension,
the apostle Thomas sends Addai to Edessa. Addai takes up residence at
the house of a Jew named Tobit. Upon his arrival at the court, Abgar,
dazzled by the glory of Addai's face, prostrates himself at his feet. Addai lays his hands on Abgar, heals him, and preaches faith in Christ,
to which the king converts along with his entourage (the names of the
nobles of the court who convert are given). The king gives license to
Addai to preach, baptize, and build churches, both in Edessa and in all
of Osrhoene. Addai also organizes worship, creates the community of
the Sons and Daughters of the Covenant (see chapter 3), and, before
his death, secures the leadership of the church of Edessa by naming his
successor. The story of all these events was supposedly deposited in the
Edessan archives (see chapter 1).

Several elements that are part of the story of the Abgar legend were
developed in later versions, such as the protection that Jesus promises
to the city of Edessa against its enemies and the transformation of the
letter in the oldest version to a portrait of Jesus on a linen cloth, or as an
icon in later ones.

The main point that was kept in the Syriac tradition was Jesus's
promise, added in certain versions to his response to Abgar, that enemies

will not prevail against Edessa; this was particularly important to a community located on the frontier and prey to constant war. This protection, all the more powerful as it was supposedly given by Jesus himself, gave Edessa the nickname of "The Blessed City." This name reappears in episodes of war, especially during the sieges by the Persians. The answer of Jesus, which in some versions became a letter that was written by his own hand, and which was thus particularly holy, was declared apocryphal in the 5th century as part of the *Decretum Gelasianum*, which determined canonical and apocryphal books. Its words were nevertheless copied as far away as Eastern Europe and were used as a talisman to protect both individuals and cities, either in the form of amulets worn around the neck or as inscriptions or copies inserted into the niches of walls and above the gates of cities.

The story of the portrait of Jesus would appear only later, but it, too, became famous well beyond Mesopotamia. Neither Eusebius, who visited Edessa around 300, nor the pilgrim Egeria, who visited around 380, makes reference to an image of Jesus. Around 400, the *Teaching of Addai* mentions that Ḥanan, the scribe of the king, was also a painter and made a portrait of Jesus. Jacob of Serugh, in the 6th century, mentions that Daniel of Glosh, who lived at the beginning of the 5th century, went to Edessa to see the image. It is in the middle of the 6th century, however, that the story of the portrait takes on its importance, a little after the unsuccessful Persian siege of Edessa in 544. Evagrius the Scholastic, in his *Ecclesiastical History*, written in Greek, relates that the defenders of the city carried the image through the tunnels that had been dug to undermine the Persian siege equipment. According to some of these versions, the image was produced by Jesus himself, who had imparted the image of his face by rubbing it on a linen cloth. This story contributed to the tradition that developed in the 6th century of "acheiropoieta" icons, or icons made not by hands but instead by divine power. This story is the source of the legend of the *mandylion*, or square cloth, of Edessa. Stories of the image as a wooden icon and as a cloth both circulated. According to Syriac sources, in the early days of Islam in the 7th century, the rivalry between Syriac Orthodox Christians and Chalcedonians led the Syriac Orthodox to paint a copy of the image that was so similar to the original that they were able to substitute it and leave the Chalcedonians unaware. In this case, the image is an icon and not a piece of cloth.

The debates in Byzantium around iconoclasm only heightened the image's prestige, which spread beyond its local origins and became one of the most precious possessions of eastern Christianity in the 8th and 9th centuries. A cloth image of the Holy Face was acquired by the Byzantine emperor Romanus I Lekapenos from the Muslims who held Edessa, and was transferred to Constantinople in 944, to be placed in the Pharos chapel in the royal palace, next to the crown of thorns, the lance, and the tunic of Christ. This cloth was placed between two pieces of baked earth in order to protect it and produced another miraculous impression on the two tiles. One icon, held at Sinai and made in the 10th or 11th century, depicts a cloth, showing that the iconography that had become traditional by that point represented the image of the holy face on the cloth *mandylion* rather than a wooden icon.

The *mandylion* was pillaged in the sack of Constantinople in 1204 during the Fourth Crusade and disappeared. Speculations on its fate have identified it with icons in the West and even with the Shroud of Turin and the cloth of Veronica, which became popular in the Western tradition.

A similar relic appeared in Rome in 1208, and Pope Innocent III established a procession and liturgical celebration in its honor. Eighty years later, Rabban Ṣauma, the Ilkhanid ambassador to the West (see chapter 5), claimed to have seen in St. Peter's in Rome "the piece of pure linen on which our Savior imprinted his holy face and sent to King Abgar in Edessa." From a painting to an image of the holy face on a piece of linen, the story evolved and spread through all of ancient Christendom, making the image one of its most precious relics, even if lost.

MARI

Sent by Addai from Edessa, Mari carried out his work in the East. In fact, his *Acts*, the text of which dates only to the 6th century, presents itself as the continuation of the story of Addai, part of which it retells in the beginning. The *Acts of Mar Mari* is among the first texts to mention the image of Jesus on a *sindon*, or linen cloth. The journey of Mari

Representation of the *mandylion* of Edessa, icon on wood, 9th century. The image of Jesus, miraculously imprinted on a linen cloth, is being handed to Abgar. By permission of Saint Catherine's Monastery, Sinai, *Egypt*.

extended along the length of the Tigris valley, where he founded communities and erected churches and monasteries from Nisibis to the
Arab-Persian Gulf and Elam. The text attributes to him the symbolic
number of 365 churches and monasteries to the north of the capital,
Seleucia-Ctesiphon. The story also attributes to Mari the foundation of
the church of Kokhe, near Ctesiphon, thus creating an apostolic foundation legend for the patriarchal see of the Church of the East, even
though the church was actually built in the 5th century. The *Acts* was
perhaps written in the monastery of Deir d-Qunni, where Mari would
die, a monastery that would become famous in the Islamic period.

ACTS OF MAR MARI

While the blessed one was traveling in the land of Erbil, working
on conversion, our Lord appeared to him one night in a dream,
saying: "Send your disciple Ṭūmīs to the land of Dasen, so that he
might go and turn its people away from their error." For their land
and their religions were very obscene: some worshiped trees and
others worshiped stones and sources of water, to such an extent
that they used to make their sons and daughters pass through fire,
as the citizens of Athōr and Erbil used to do. Then Mār Mārī placed
his hand on Ṭūmīs his disciple and sent him to the lands of Dasen
and Zawzan, as far as Outer Armenia and the regions of Media . . .

  When the blessed Mār Mārī entered the village of Brūgiā, he
converted a man—the king's chief of the Magians—who was
governing there. Because the chief of the Magians heard that the
king and all his nobles had converted, he too accepted the faith
and was baptized, along with the whole city. Then he passed to
Ra'amsīs and Wāziq, which he converted through the opening
of the eyes of two blind people—notable people who were there.
There he built churches after the names of Peter, Paul, and Addai
the apostles.

THOMAS

The mission of the apostle Thomas, traditionally said to have taken place
in AD 52, represents the height of apostolic preaching. It is narrated in

the *Acts of Thomas*, a text that belongs to the beginning of the 3rd century and that is among our oldest extant Syriac texts. Two older Syriac texts, *The Hymn of the Soul* and *The Hymn of the Pearl*, are woven into the text of the *Acts*. They represent two of the oldest witnesses to Syriac poetry, formed from Gnostic, Iranian, and Semitic influences but reused as part of the story of the apostle who evangelized India. The narrative combines these older elements with liturgical passages in which one can recognize very early forms of the sacraments of Christian initiation (baptism and the Eucharist). Certain parts have a deeply encratic tone, advocating a radical asceticism and the complete renunciation of all sexual life for all Christians.

The story itself begins with the division of missionary zones among the apostles in Jerusalem. India is assigned to Judas Thomas, presented here as the twin (Didymus in Greek) of Jesus. At first he refuses out of fear but then accepts his mission following a vision of the Lord. Sold by Jesus to an Indian merchant, he sails to the kingdom of the king Gondophares, from whom he asks money supposedly to build a palace but in reality to give to the poor, reasoning that the palace is in heaven, the place where the righteous will dwell in the beyond. After having performed a number of miracles, Thomas is martyred by the king Mazdai. His relics, gathered together by his disciples, are brought back west to Edessa.

These *Acts* provide the earliest connection between Thomas and the Christians of India who define themselves even today as "Christians of St. Thomas" (see chapter 5). But the India of the *Acts of Thomas* is very abstract and lacking in the geographical details that one finds in the *Teaching of Addai* or the *Acts of Mar Mari*, which attribute apostolic origins to actual places.

HYMN OF THE PEARL
(FROM THE ACTS OF THOMAS)

The hymn of the apostle Judas Thomas
When he was in the country of the Indians
When I was a little child,
and dwelling in my kingdom,

in my father's house, and was content with the wealth and the
luxuries of my nourishers,
from the East, our home,
my parents equipped me [and] sent me forth;
and of the wealth of our treasury
they took abundantly, [and] tied up for me a load
large and [yet] light, which I myself could carry,
gold of Beth-Ellaya,
and silver of Gazak the great,
and rubies of India,
and agates from Beth-Kashan,
and they furnished me with the adamant,
which can crush iron.
And they took off from me the glittering robe,
which in their affection they made for me,
and the purple toga,
which was measured [and] woven to my stature.
And they made a compact with me,
and wrote it in my heart, that it might not be forgotten:
"If thou goest down into Egypt,
and bringest the one pearl,
which is in the midst of the sea
around the loud-breathing serpent,
thou shalt put on thy glittering robe
and thy toga, with which [thou art] contented,
and with thy brother, who is next to us in authority,
thou shalt be heir in our kingdom."

ANOTHER EXCERPT FROM THE *ACTS OF THOMAS*

And when Judas had entered into the realm of India with the
merchant Habban, Habban went to salute Gundaphar, the king of
India, and he told him of the artificer whom he had brought for
him. And the king was very glad, and ordered Judas to come into
his presence. And the king says to him: "What art do you know to
practice?" Judas says to him: "I am a carpenter, the servant of a
carpenter and architect . . ." The king says to him: "Will you build

me a palace?" Judas says to him: "I will build it and finish it, for
I have come to work at building and carpentry . . ." And he was
sending silver and gold from time to time. But Judas was going
about in the villages and cities, and was ministering to the poor, and
was making the afflicted comfortable . . . And when the king came
to the city, he was asking every one of his friends about the palace
which Judas had built for him; but they say to him: "There is no
palace built, nor has he done anything else, but he was going about
the cities and villages, and giving to the poor, and teaching them
the new God and also healing the sick, and driving out demons,
and doing many things; and we think that he is a sorcerer; but his
compassion and his healing, which was done without recompense,
and his ascetism, and his piety, make [us] think of him either that
he is a magus, or an Apostle of the new God; for he fasts much and
prays much, and eats bread and salt and drinks water, and wears
one garment, and takes nothing from any man for himself; and
whatever he has he gives to others."

THE MAGI

The Gospels speak of the "magi who came from the East" (Matt. 2:1).
The East Syrian tradition latched onto this story to prove the absolute
preeminence of Iranian Christianity over all other communities, claiming that the visit of the magi shows that it was members of the Parthian
Empire who were the first worshipers of Christ, thirty years before he
even called the first apostles. These twelve wise men—according to
the number given in the Syriac tradition—are the forerunners of the
apostles and are considered the true apostles in the East. Their story
became extremely widespread, even in the Far East, as shown by their
inclusion on the Xi'an stele in China and on a Sogdian fragment in the
Turfan oasis.

Many aspects of this story reflect Iranian beliefs: the wise men are
Parthian priests, and the "Mountain of Victory" where the Syriac tradition places them is identified with a location in Sistan where the *Sao-
shyant*, or Zoroastrian savior, is supposed to come. Like the child Mithra,
they find Christ in a cave, not in a manger, and each wise man sees him

as a different age, as though he were Zurvan (the high Zoroastrian god of time). For the Church of the East, this story establishes the wise men as central to the economy of salvation, even though they were considered to be marginal and (after the 5th century) heretical by the Christians of the Roman Empire. The Syriac Orthodox *Chronicle of Zuqnin*, in the 8th century, reconciled the apostolic tradition and the story of the magi by showing the wise men coming to be baptized by Thomas.

THE LETTER OF PATRIARCH TIMOTHY I (CA. LATE 7TH OR 8TH CENTURY)

Concerning our throne of the East, which all evidence shows to be the first source of life, I want to speak of salvation, because it is equally just to reserve to our throne both the first rank and primacy, while as regards the four others, from whom the entire world drinks the spiritual drink, it is correct to place them on a lower level and to consider them as having a secondary place. And if it is because of the apostle Peter that some people reserve to Rome the first rank and the primacy, how much more should it befit Seleucia-Ctesiphon with regard to the Lord of Peter? And if it is right that the first rank and dignity should belong to those who were the first to confess Christ and believed in him, then it belongs to us Easterners, who confessed Christ and believed in him first of all. We have given an example explaining our faith in the twelve messengers who were guided by the star, by the gifts which they offered him: gold for the King of all the kings and to the Lord of all the lords, incense to the one who is God and above all things, and myrrh, the symbol of the suffering of his humanity for everyone.

The Initial Spread of Christianity in the Roman World

The material evidence for Christianity in the first centuries creates a blurry picture. It is only with the peace of the 4th century, when the emperor Constantine (ca. 272–337) legalized Christianity by the Edict of Milan of 313, that the contours of what is known as the Great Church took form. The local communities, led by their bishops, developed institutional ties with each other. Time and space were progressively Christianized, churches and martyria constructed, with their halls, porticoes, baptistries, and, for the most important, hostels and hospices.

The oldest witness of the eastward spread of Christianity is the funerary inscription of Abercius, found in Phrygia and dated to before 216. Written in the first person under the name of the deceased, it describes his travels and hints at the spread of Christianity eastward: "I saw Nisibis as I was going beyond the Euphrates. Everywhere I went, I met brothers." The oldest witness of a Christian presence of the community in Edessa, however, comes from the philosopher Bardaisan of Edessa (154–212).

BARDAISAN OF EDESSA

Dubbed by Ephrem as "The Philosopher of the Arameans," Bardaisan (literally Bar-Daisan, or Son of Daisan, the river that flows through Edessa) demonstrates in his writings the same melding of the Parthian-Arab and Greek cultures described above in the discussion of material remains from Edessa. He was part of the aristocratic circles in Edessa and frequented the court of Abgar IX of Edessa, where he also became famous as an archer in the Parthian style and was educated in Greek, astronomy, and Mesopotamian astrology. The figure of Bardaisan is presented by later authors, whether Mani himself (d. 276) or Ephrem (d. 373) in his *Hymns against Heresies*, as a rebel and an arch-heretic. He is still better known through these negative depictions rather than his own work.

The only complete writing of Bardaisan that survives, and one of the oldest extant Syriac texts, is his *Dialogue on Fate*, better known as *The Book of the Laws of Countries*, written like a Greek philosophical dialogue between Bardaisan and his disciples Avida and Philip, the latter of whom is the editor of the dialogue. The main theme is about human free will and God's omnipotence. The text is especially valuable because of its ethnographic aspect and the descriptions it gives of the customs distinct to each region, including those of the Indian Brahmins. It also confirms the spread of Christianity to the Caspian Sea on the one hand and Gaul on the other in the second half of the 2nd century. On the

Family funerary mosaic of a notable Edessan named Abgar
(2nd–3rd century AD). The clothing style is Parthian, while
the inscription is in Edessan Aramaic.

basis of what we can reconstruct afterward from later sources, Bardaisan
explains the origins of evil by creating an elaborate cosmogony and on-
tology in which the material world is presented as coeternal with God.

BARDAISAN

Then I said to him: "Oh Father Bardaisan, of this you have
convinced us and we know that it is true. Yet you are also aware,
that the Chaldeans maintain that the earth is divided into seven
parts named climates, and that one of the Seven rules over each
of these parts, and that in each of these regions the will of his
government rules and is called law?"

He replied to me: "In the first place you must know, my son
Philippus, that the Chaldeans have invented this doctrine to bolster
up their fallacy. Even if the earth is divided into seven parts, yet
in each of these parts many laws are found that differ from one

another. [. . .] You surely remember I told you that in the one climate of the Hindus there are people who do not eat the flesh of animals and other who eat human flesh. Then I have told you of the Persians and the Magians, who not only marry their daughters and sisters in the climate of Persia, but in every place they came to, they have kept the law of their fathers. [. . .] All the Jews that have received the law of Moses, circumcise their male children on the eighth day, without waiting for the coming of stars and without regard to the local law. And the star that rules the climate they are in, has no compulsive power over them. But whether they live in Edom or in Arabia, in Greece or in Persia, in the North or in the South, they keep to the law laid upon them by their fathers. And clearly they do not do this because of their horoscope."

Following either an accident or chance, darkness penetrated this world and the resulting chaos required God to send "the power of the original Word," which was responsible for creation and remained to uphold it. Bardaisan's work should be read in the context of the spread of Valentinian Gnosticism and Marcionism, the most vibrant and active religious movements in Mesopotamia. Marcion (d. ca. 160) separated the God of the Old Testament, whom he claimed created the material world, from the God revealed by Jesus, and as a result cut the Old Testament entirely from his teachings. Bardaisan was the first to compose works against the Marcionites, which have not been preserved.

THE *ODES OF SOLOMON*

Tentatively dated between the 1st and 3rd centuries, the collection of the *Odes of Solomon* is one of the oldest and most extraordinary Syriac texts. These forty-two Christian poems, deeply imbued with Gnosticism, were discovered at the beginning of the 20th century in two Syriac manuscripts and contain passages of great imaginative power that still touch modern readers. The *Odes* have been translated many times, but translations struggle to do justice to the Semitic voice, inspired by the Bible, as expressed in the originals. The *Odes* show the literary vitality of these first Christian environments.

ODES OF SOLOMON 11, "PARADISE"

My heart was pruned, and its blossom appeared,
grace sprouted in my heart,
so that it produced fruits for the Lord.

For the Most High has circumcised me by his Holy Spirit;
He disclosed my inside before his face,
and filled me with his affection.

His circumcision became my salvation,
and I made progress on the way, in his peace,
on the way of truth.

From the beginning and to the end
I have received his knowledge.

I was secure on a solid rock,
where He had prepared a place for me.

Speaking water reached my lips
streaming from the generous source of the Lord.

I drank and got drunk,
by the living water that never dies.

My drunkenness did not render me ignorant;
I rather put all vanity aside,

And turned to the Most High, my God,
to be enriched by his generosity.

I renounced all foolishness, that had been thrown on earth,
I took off the dress of foolishness and threw it from me.

The Lord made me new by clothing me with his dress
and made me his own through his light [. . .]

ABGAR: A CONVERSION BETWEEN MEMORY AND HISTORY

The conversion of King Abgar of Edessa supposedly belongs to these first centuries. The story is inextricably linked to the tradition of the evangelization of Edessa by the apostle Addai in the 1st century, and the discussion has often turned on who is the Abgar who converted, but this conversion in itself is not a solid historical fact. Considered to be a saint in the Armenian Church, which produced icons that treat the king as an Armenian himself, the first Christian Abgar remains evasive. The *Teaching of Addai* identifies him with Abgar V Ukkama, "The Black" (r. 4 BC–AD 7, then AD 13–50), because he lived contemporaneously with Jesus. Historians have thought that the correct Abgar is Abgar VIII, or Abgar the Great (r. 177–212), a contemporary of Bardaisan, in the period when Christianity is first attested in Edessa. This period was then retrojected into the era of Abgar the Black. Even so, nothing shows that this Abgar was Christian either. It is thus uncertain whether a king Abgar converted to Christianity, especially since much of the Syriac tradition holds that Constantine was the first Christian king. The stories

Bronze coin of Abgar VIII. Bibliothèque
nationale de France.

intend to suggest that Edessa was converted through its ruling dynasty and its aristocracy. The only solid evidence is that Christianity existed in Edessa during the beginning of the 3rd century and thus during the time of Abgar VIII and Bardaisan, and was officially tolerated. Only a blurred memory of the origins of Edessan Christianity is reflected in these apocryphal texts, in order to establish a direct link between Jesus and the aristocratic society of Edessa, but the story of how this Christianization actually happened largely remains clouded.

THE CONTEXT OF CHRISTIANIZATION

The sanctuary or nave of a Christian church in Edessa is mentioned in the record of the flood in 201/202 (see chapter 1), a reference that was drawn from the archives and preserved in an anonymous Edessan chronicle in Syriac dating from 540. Most likely, however, the mention of this first space for worship was added to the chronicle later: the word "church" would be anachronistic for this time, and the archaeological record shows no building in Edessa that was used specifically for worship at that time. It is certain in any case that the mention of several churches built by Addai and Mari in the stories about the evangelization of Edessa are retrojections dating to the period when the legend reached its final form (3rd or 4th century), at which point it was no longer possible to imagine the Christian world without a network of churches.

Christianization took place in a multireligious world, marked by Mesopotamian and pagan Roman cults and temples (see chapter 1), along with a strong Jewish presence. Around AD 150, the Jews of Edessa wrote on their tombstones in an Edessan dialect with Jewish Aramaic letters and were also most likely those who translated the Bible into the local Aramaic dialect, whether Edessan or Syriac. Christians from a pagan background would not have known enough Hebrew to be able to complete such a work, which implies that either Jews themselves or converts to Christianity from Judaism were the ones who did the translation. It is impossible to say without further evidence whether this Jewish environment had already produced a partial translation into

Edessan Aramaic, in square letters, for their own use. The choice of Edessan Aramaic demonstrates a piece of local identity, though doubtless also religious if it were really the Christian context that produced this scripture. The oldest Syriac manuscripts of the Bible, dating to the 5th century, are all Christian, and it is impossible to trace their earlier evolution.

Next to the Greek translation known as the Septuagint, the Syriac version represents the only ancient tradition of the Old Testament taken directly from Hebrew versions similar to the Masoretic texts (the fixing of the *massorah*, or canonical Hebrew reading, dates to the 8th century AD). The Syriac version is known as the Peshiṭta, or "simple," and holds great interest for the ancient Jewish and Christian exegetical traditions. This Jewish tradition, which was not yet under the control of the rabbis until the 4th century AD, transmitted a number of original interpretations into Syriac. For instance, in the Peshiṭta, the landing place of Noah's Ark is Mount Qardu in Iraq, where other Jewish targums place it as well, rather than Mount Ararat as is common in other Christian traditions.

Edessan Christianity of the second half of the 2nd century defined itself against heretical movements, whether Gnostics like the Valentinians, or the Marcionites. If the Peshiṭta was translated by Christians, it is possible that they needed a version of the Old Testament because of Marcionite activity around Edessa. The oldest Syriac version of the New Testament is the *Diatessaron*, or the *Harmony of the Four Gospels*, which is now thought to have been composed directly in Syriac. It is the work of Tatian (ca. AD 170), a Mesopotamian or "(As)syrian," who stayed in Rome at the same time as Justin Martyr. In producing the *Diatessaron*, which erased the contradictions between the Gospels in favor of a single narrative, Tatian was wrestling with the problem posed by Marcion, who proposed his own canon of Scripture (based on the Gospel of Luke and severely edited letters of Paul). Although used by the early Syriac churches, the *Diatessaron* was eventually condemned by the bishop Rabbula of Edessa (ca. 411–435). Because of this, it disappeared and is no longer attested apart from references in the Syriac fathers, particularly the *Commentary on the Diatessaron* produced by St. Ephrem, which still exists in Syriac and an Armenian version.

Commentary on Tatian's *Diatessaron*, or *The Harmony of the Four Gospels*, by Ephrem. Manuscript in *esṭrangela* script. CBL Syc 709.1 f.38r © The Trustees of the Chester Beatty Library, Dublin.

The Spread of Christianity in the Persian Empire
THE FIRST DEVELOPMENTS

We know little about how the Persian Empire was first Christianized. The later histories of Karka d-Beth Slok (modern-day Kirkuk in Iraq) and Arbela (modern-day Erbil), composed in the 6th century, as well as the Syro-Arabic Chronicle of Seert, dated to the 11th century, are our main sources for this early period. The mention of travelers from Parthia, Media, and Elam (modern-day Khuzestan) at Pentecost in Acts 2:9 suggests that there was a Jewish community in Persia that formed the first core of converts. Judaism was widespread in Mesopotamia: ever since the deportation of the Jewish community to Babylon by Nebuchadnezzar in 587 BC, there had been a strong Jewish community on the banks of the Tigris. As far away as Adiabene, a region in northeastern Iraq between the Great and Lesser Zab Rivers where the goddess Ishtar was worshiped, Flavius Josephus mentions the conversion of the royal family to Judaism around 40 BC, one member of which, Helen, was buried in Jerusalem. It was among these flourishing Jewish communities that the first conversions to Christianity took place.

The Book of the Laws of Countries, written in the 2nd century by Bardaisan, mentions Christians already among the Gelae and the Kushans in Bactria (north of modern-day Afghanistan), in Parthia, in Media, at Kashan, and in Fars. If the Syriac history of Arbela can be believed, the first bishop of Arbela was appointed in AD 100. Christians were also able to take refuge in the Parthian Empire during episodes of Roman persecution. The spread of the gospel took place along commercial routes, and early missionaries were often merchants, as attested in the Acts of Thomas, which shows the apostle sold as a slave by a merchant.

A major change took place in the region with the rise of the Sasanian dynasty in Iran after the revolt of Ardashir I (r. 224–240) against the Arsacids. The end of Parthian power and the foundation of Sasanian power in 224 also had repercussions on Roman-Persian relations. The new empire defined itself as "Eranshahr," also known as "the land of the Iranians" or "the empire of the Iranians," encompassing Ērān and Anerān (non-Iran). It consisted of a religio-political system where the Shahanshah, the king of kings, also had a religious function, while members of the warrior and administrative class also served as Zoroastrian (also known as Mazdean) priests, known as mobeds. A dualist religion, Zoroastrianism set the good creation of the god Ohrmazd, also known as Ahura Mazda, who was the head of the Mazdean pantheon, which also included Mithra and Verethragna, against the chaos introduced by the evil spirit Ahriman. Consequently, political and religious networks were intertwined, with the kings supported by Parthian and Sasanian nobility both militarily and religiously.

During the 3rd and 4th centuries, Syriac Christians predominantly lived in the borderlands between the Roman and Persian Empires, especially Mesopotamia, Syria, Cilicia, Armenia, and Cappadocia. These territories were constantly shifting between the two powers, especially in the many campaigns that the Persian kings launched against the Roman Empire. The first Sasanian sovereign, Ardashir, threatened Mesopotamia and Syria and tried to control trade with India via the Persian Gulf and eastern Arabia. In 235–236 he took Nisibis and Carrhae/Ḥarran, along with Ḥatra in 240, an important caravan stop on the road to Nisibis. Consequently, Romans resumed hostilities during the time of his successor, Shapur I (r. 239–270).

DEPORTATIONS AND CHRISTIANIZATION

The campaigns of Shapur I in the 3rd century inadvertently gave Christianity real momentum in the Persian world. After ascending the throne in 239, Shapur expanded his dominions to the east, taking Bactria, part of the Kushan Empire, before returning to fight the Romans. After a series of victories against the emperor Gordian and a very advantageous treaty signed with Gordian's successor, Philip the Arab (r. 244–249), he resumed the war against the emperor Valerian (r. 253–260). In 260 he took Valerian prisoner and detained him until his death, immortalizing his triumph on a series of bas-reliefs. He took thirty-seven cities in Cappadocia, Cilicia, and Syria, including Antioch, deporting an important part of the population and resettling them in his empire, following a custom that had been practiced since the time of the Assyrian Empire. Craftsmen of all types (masons, specialists in silk fabric, stoneworkers, mosaic artisans) were particularly sought out in order to build new cities in various regions of the empire. Among these deportees were Greek and Aramaic-speaking Christians, including priests and bishops, who then formed the core of communities in the Persian Empire alongside native Aramaic- and Middle Persian-speaking groups. Although highly diverse in both language and origin—Jewish, Zoroastrian, pagan, or Christianized for several generations—both local and resettled communities managed to coexist. Multiple liturgies, sometimes in two churches in the same place, are attested in the 5th century, and the acts of the first known council, the Council of Mar Isaac in 410, still have to insist that there should not be more than one bishop in the same city.

RELIGION IN PERSIAN SOCIETY

The growing influence of the head priest of Zoroastrianism, Kirdir, resulted in the political repression of all non-Zoroastrian religions by Bahram I (r. 271–274) and Bahram II (r. 274–291). Kirdir's inscriptions have left an indelible testimony of the diversity in the Sasanian Empire. It mentions a number of different religions that were persecuted by the state and shows that the Sasanians did not perceive Christianity to be a united faith, since it is listed twice under different names. Despite these

Bas-relief of the triumph of the king of kings Shapur I over the emperor Valerian at Bishapur, Iran. Photo by Muriel Debié.

sporadic persecutions, Christianity grew rapidly in the Persian Empire, both coexisting and competing with other religions. Although Zoroastrians did not try to win converts, both Manichaeans and Christians did, with considerable success.

KIRDIR'S INSCRIPTION

Bahram, king of kings, son of Bahram, who in the empire [is] generous and righteous and kind and beneficent and altruistic, established himself in the kingdom, for love of Ohrmezd and the gods and [for] his own soul he made for me in the empire a higher position and honor, and gave me the position and honor of the magnates . . . And he made me Mobed and judge of the whole empire. And he made me director and authority over the fire of Anahid-ardashir and Anahid the Lady [in] Stakhr. And he named me "Kerdir, soul-saver of Bahram, Mobed of Ohrmezd." And from province to province, place to place, throughout the empire the rites of Ohrmezd and the gods became more important and the Mazdayasnian religion and Magians were greatly honored in the empire and great satisfaction befell the gods and water and fire and beneficent creatures, and great blows and torment befell Ahreman and the demons, and the heresy of Ahreman and the demons departed and was routed from the empire. And Jews and Buddhists and Hindus and Nazarenes and Christians and Baptists and Manichaeans were smitten in the empire, and idols were destroyed and the abodes of the demons disrupted and made into thrones and seats of the gods.

Mani (ca. 216–276) grew up in a Jewish-Christian baptizing sect known as the Elkasaites. As a young man, he encountered his "twin," who gave him revelations from God, and thereafter he presented himself as "The Apostle of Light," the Paraclete incarnate. He made many converts in Mesopotamia, thanks in part to the protection of Shapur I, but under the influence of the high priest Kirdir, he was arrested and put to death during the reign of Bahram I in 276. His religion, Manichaeism, took many elements from Gnostic cosmology, Zoroastrianism, Buddhism, Judaism, and Christianity. The Manichaeans were divided into two categories of believers, the elect and the auditors, and the religion sought to be universal; to spread his message, Mani painted pictures and wrote in Aramaic and Pahlavi. Afterward, missionaries brought his teachings westward—Manichaeans can be found in Edessa in the 3rd century, for example, while Manichaean writings have been discovered in Egypt and in North Africa and St. Augustine was Manichaean for a time. It also spread to the East, where it survived in China until the 17th century. A number of anti-Manichaean polemical texts were written in Syriac.

Although the Roman emperor Carus (r. 282–283) was able to take Seleucia-Ctesiphon during the time of Bahram II, the Romans did not make any permanent territorial gains. In 288 a treaty was signed between Diocletian and Bahram. The Church of the East continued to grow in Persian territory, basing its ecclesiastical networks on Persian administrative structure. In Syriac histories in the 3rd century, twenty bishoprics are listed. In 297 the Roman emperor Diocletian issued an anti-Manichaean edict against those who were seen as following a Persian religion, as war had resumed between the Roman Empire and the Persian king of kings, Narseh. The Diocletian reforms allowed for Roman victories to counterbalance those won by Shapur I earlier. He then secured the border with a string of forts built along the *Strata Diocletiana*, the route between Damascus and Sura, via Palmyra, which was also used for commerce in the region. At this time Christians were persecuted in the Roman Empire, while in the Persian world, Hormizd II (r. 303–309) was their protector.

The Peace of the Church in the 4th Century

Beginning in the 4th century, the sources on the history of the church are more abundant and allow us to see the formation of what is called the Great Church, which increasingly defined itself over against those whom it declared to be heretics. The reign of Constantine the Great (r. 306–337), during which the Edict of Milan legalized Christianity in the Roman Empire, had repercussions on both sides of the eastern frontier and marked the end of persecutions in the Roman Empire. Henceforth, the church enjoyed imperial protection and its councils were placed under the patronage of the emperor.

THE BIRTH OF CHRISTIAN ARCHITECTURE

In the east, just as in the Mediterranean, the peace enjoyed by the church allowed for the visibility of Christian life and the construction of Christian buildings. The oldest churches recovered by archaeology are in Syria. Besides the "Christian house" in Dura Europos, which is an ordinary residential building adapted for worship, there are also churches in the limestone massif in northern Syria. Syriac inscriptions inside show that they were frequented by Aramaic-speaking people, though their structures were no different from those of Greek speakers.

In the Syriac world, churches follow a "basilica" style, with one nave for the simplest and three for the most important. The sanctuary is situated on the east side of the church, raised above the level of the nave. It could be integrated into the main structure of the building or appear as a protruding apse. On either side of the sanctuary, there are two small chambers. One of these is dedicated to the cult of relics (*bet qadishe*), often furnished with a reliquary, while the other functions as a sacristy, which opens into the sanctuary. They open to the west side, either in front of the main nave or one of the side naves, or to an outer gallery that is next to the nave. On the south side, the outer gallery is adapted to prayer in open air, especially in places where the weather is hot, and is called the house of prayer (*bet ṣlota*). Churches sometimes open to the west, but most to the southern side, via two doors. Because men would have stood in front, near the sanctuary, and women behind, the door closer to the east is known as "the men's door," and the other "the women's door."

CAVE OF TREASURES

Noah's entrance into the ark took place on a Friday in the blessed month of Iyyar, on the seventeenth, a Friday. In the morning the wild animals and cattle entered into the lower deck, at noon the birds and all reptiles entered into the middle deck, and at sunset Noah and all his sons entered the eastern side of the ark, while his wife and his sons' wives (entered) the ark's western side. Adam's body was put down in the middle of the ark, for all the mysteries of the Church are foreshadowed in it. Inside church, women stay on the western side and men on the eastern side so that men cannot see the women's faces, nor do the women see the faces of the men. Thus also in the ark the women were on the western side and the men on the eastern side. Adam's body, however, was put in the middle like the Bema, and just as there is silence between men and women in church so there was peace inside the ark between animals, birds, and reptiles.

The most distinctive characteristics include a raised platform in the center of the nave, known as the *bema*, which is used for the liturgy of the word and could accommodate the whole ensemble of clergy who carry out the liturgy: priest, deacons, subdeacons, and lectors. It is connected to the sanctuary by a narrow passage, sometimes closed, known

Remains of a church, Bayzan in Iraq, with *bema* and *shqaqona*.
Mission archéologique de Bazyan (Kurdistan, Iraq).

as the *shqaqona,* by which the celebrants proceed toward the choir, where they display the Eucharist for the second part of the liturgy, the consecration, in a moment charged with symbolism. In Tur ʿAbdin during the Middle Ages, monastic churches also featured wide naves where monks could line up on either side in front of the sanctuary.

Churches could take many forms, from the simplest village churches to the elaborate churches commissioned by the emperor, such as the monastery of Mor Gabriel or the cathedral of Edessa, built by the emperor Anastasius (491–518) and decorated with the most precious materials. Others were decorated with frescoes, like Mar Musa, or sculptures. In foreign lands, especially those that were in missionary territory, they could take still other forms. William of Rubruck and Mar Yahballaha (see page 135) both mention a church tent at the court of the great khan, set up very close to the tent where he lived.

SYRIAC *SOGITHA* CELEBRATING THE CATHEDRAL CHURCH OF EDESSA

For it truly is a wonder that its smallness is like the wide world, not in size but in type; like the sea, waters surround it.

Behold! Its ceiling is stretched out like the sky and without columns [it is] arched and simple, and it is also decorated with golden mosaic, as the firmament [is] with shining stars.

And its lofty dome-behold, it resembles the highest heaven, and like a helmet it is firmly placed on its lower [part].

The splendor of its broad arches—they portray the four ends of the earth. They resemble also by the variety of their colors the glorious rainbow.

Other arches surround it like crags jutting out from a mountain, upon, by and through which its entire ceiling is fastened on the vaults.

Its marble resembles an image not [made] by hands, and its walls are suitably overlaid [with marble]. And from its brightness, polished and white, light gathers in it like the sun [. . .]

It is surrounded by magnificent courts with two porticoes composed of columns, which portray the tribes of Israelites who surrounded the [temporal] Tabernacle.

On every side it has the same façade; the form of the three of them is one, Just as the form of the holy Trinity is one [. . .]

The ambo is placed in the middle of [the church] on the model of the Upper Room at Zion, And under it are eleven columns, like the eleven apostles that were hidden.

The column that is behind the ambo portrays Golgotha in its form, And fastened above it is the cross of light, like Our Lord between the thieves [. . .]

Exalted are the mysteries of this temple in which heaven and earth Symbolize the most exalted Trinity and our Savior's Dispensation.

Mosaic from the church in the Mor Gabriel monastery.
Photo by Saima Altunkaya.

THE FIRST ECUMENICAL COUNCILS

The Council of Nicaea in 325 affirmed, against the doubts raised by the Alexandrian priest Arius, that the Son was fully God, existing from all eternity and consubstantial with the Father. Building on this definition, the Council of Constantinople, convened in 381 at the initiative of the Roman emperor Theodosius, proclaimed the full divinity of the Holy Spirit. Although Arianism would stay alive for some time after—for example, among certain Germanic tribes—these councils were generally accepted. The "Symbol of the Faith" defined by these two councils, or the Niceno-Constantinopolitan Creed, is still recited by all Christians today. One representative from the East, John the Persian, was present in Nicaea, showing the integration of the Church of Persia into the universal or ecumenical church. Legend has it that Jacob of Nisibis and St. Ephrem, two of the best-known saints of the Syriac churches, also assisted at the council.

Two especially notable Syriac writers lived during the official establishment of the church in the 4th century—Aphrahat, known as "The Persian Sage," and St. Ephrem, known as "The Syrian."

APHRAHAT

Aphrahat's twenty-three "Demonstrations" were composed in the Persian Empire during two periods. The first group, which dates to 337, discusses ascetic topics, especially the Sons and Daughters of the Covenant and solitaries. The second concerns Judaism and separates Christian practice from Jewish customs. This latter group, which is anti-Jewish in tone, was written in 344, when the persecution by the king of kings, Shapur I, had begun. At this time, Judaism and Christianity were not entirely separated yet, and certain Christians had taken refuge in the synagogues and received help from the Jews. Composed in an acrostic, where the first letter of each demonstration follows the order of the alphabet, it is the first important Syriac work and is rendered in a highly literary prose. It demonstrates the ascetic bent of the Church of Persia and its slow separation from Judaism, its biblical and exegetical traditions, and the relations between the church and the Sasanian state.

EPHREM

Ephrem (d. 373) is the most famous poet and theologian in the Syriac tradition. Proclaimed a doctor of the universal church in 1920 by the Roman Catholic Church, he is a theologian whose profundity and subtlety are expressed in poetic form through unique, highly creative imagery rather than through analytical reasoning. Recognizing that nature and the Scriptures are the two means by which humans can bridge the gulf that separates them from God, he employs symbolism and typology to express the infiniteness and ineffability of the divine. His work opens the path to a social and ecological vision far ahead of its time, based on the idea of interconnection and interdependence of humans with each other, but also with animals and nature. Containing great imaginary and literary richness, in a form often deep yet concise which partly echoes modern poetry, his poems were translated very early into Greek, Armenian, Ethiopic, Georgian, and Arabic, along with a considerable number of modern languages. Many of his *madrashe*, around four hundred of which have survived, have been integrated into the Syriac liturgy, as well as other liturgical traditions, and are still chanted both in the original and in translation. These hymns have their melodies noted and are arranged into collections: on the Nativity, the Crucifixion, the Resurrection, the fast, faith, virginity, the unleavened bread, the church, and Paradise.

Ephrem was originally from Nisibis, but it was only during his exile in Edessa after the transfer of Nisibis to the Sasanians after the defeat of the emperor Julian in 363 that he pursued his career as a deacon and a poet. His *madrashe* outline a theological history of the people who lived on the frontiers in the 4th century, whether in his descriptions of the city of Nisibis and its inhabitants, the repeated sieges it endured at the hands of the Persians, the earthquake at Nicomedia, or his polemics against Emperor Julian.

Later, he played a role in the defense of the church and the outline of orthodox theology with his writings against the heretics Bardaisan, Marcion, and Mani. He also composed *memre* in a seven-syllable meter, a style known thereafter as "the meter of St. Ephrem," most famously *On Faith*, *On the Adulterous Woman*, and *On Jonah and the Ninevites*.

A number of other works are attributed to him, though many of them seem to be pseudonymous.

EPHREM, *HYMNS ON PARADISE* 5.2

In his book Moses described
The creation of the natural world,
So that both the natural world and his book
Might testify to the Creator:
The natural world, through humanity's use of it,
The book, through his reading of it.

EPHREM, *LETTER TO HYPATIUS*

For just as in the case of the limbs of the body, their individual needs are fulfilled by one another, so too the inhabitants of the world fill in the common need from the common excess. We should rejoice in this need on the part of us all, for out of it is born harmony for us all: for in that people need one another, those in high position stoop to the lowly and are not ashamed, and the insignificant reach out to the powerful and are not afraid. Even in the case of animals, seeing that we have a need for them, we take care of them. Clearly our need for everything binds us with a love for everything.

EPHREM, *PASCHAL HYMN* 9

1. In the flowering month
What joyous sounds
The tambourine of Myriam made
In the presence of the People!

Refrain: Praise to the Firstborn!
By His Crucifixion
He makes the nations to turn
Towards the One who sends Him

2. The roar of the sea
Against the Egyptians!
The jubilation of drums
For the sons of Jacob!

[. . .]

6. The women of the Hebrews
Carried, that April,
Their children in broad daylight
On the shore of the sea

7. The nightmare fled far
From the little children
Who saw the shipwreck
Of their wicked wreckers

8. The children hid themselves
Deep within their bedchambers
As Moses did
In his own infancy

9. In that April ventured out
New buds, which had been imprisoned
They went out of their chambers
Also these newly born

10. In that feast
Children and flowers
Rejoiced together
In their gentle Lord

11. The corselet of lilies
Bore beautiful buds
And the bosom of women
Carried their children

12. In Egypt, the serfs
Were afraid to cry
They acted very lowly
And spoke in a low voice

13. In that babbling April
Which gave songs to the world
Even the little children
Chattered without fear.

Many of the legends about St. Ephrem were composed in Greek
and try to fit him into a Greek model, presenting him as a monk rather
than a deacon in order to give more legitimacy to his work. He is also
presented as meeting Basil the Great, one of the most famous Greek fathers, seeking to learn about Greek Christian culture. The Greek stories
about him depict him as a rigid ascetic, often scolding women, but to
the contrary, a *mimro* by Jacob of Serugh dedicated to him depicts him
as moderate and recalls his literary contributions to the Daughters of
the Covenant (*bnāt qyāmē*), whom he believed should be able to sing
praises to God just like men.

THE FIRST ECCLESIASTICAL DIVIDES:
THE BIRTH OF THE CHURCH IN PERSIA

If ecclesiastical history depicts the 4th century in favorable terms, the
political situation was chaotic, marked by a number of aggressive campaigns launched by Shapur II (r. 309–379) against the Roman Empire.
Latin, Greek, and Syriac historical texts all document these wars. Upon
the death of Constantine in 337, Shapur took Armenia; he besieged Nisibis three times in 338, 346, and 350 during the episcopate of Jacob of
Nisibis, memories of which appear in Syriac literature. The Roman emperor Julian (r. 361–363) temporarily reversed these successes and led an
army into Persia, but died on the field of battle. After his death, Nisibis
was ceded to the Persians and its Christian population dispersed in Roman lands. The final campaign of Shapur, in 371, resulted in the division
of Armenia between the two empires.

The only extant representation of Ephrem as a deacon. Icon on wood, 10th century. By permission of Saint Catherine's Monastery, Sinai, Egypt.

THE PERSIAN MARTYRS

Now, the blessed Mārōn, the bishop of Karka, through the love of God that was found in him, he built a monastery in that place in which 531 the victorious ones were crowned, and he created for them an annual commemoration [day] in the fervent heat of his faith. He and Mar Bābōi the Catholicos assembled a synod of the bishops of Bet Garmai [and] also of Adiabene, and they wrote and sealed and agreed in a firm contract that there would be a commemoration for these saints [for] three days a year, that is, on the Friday, and on the Saturday, and on the Sunday of the sixth week after the Fast of the Apostles. Because the metropolitan of Adiabene was also crowned there, and the bishop of Bet Nuhadrâ, and the bishop of Maʿaltâ, and those other victorious ones who were crowned with them in that great company, so then, it was written down and placed in the archives of the church of the metropolitan.

During these wars, religion became a matter of intense interest to the state, and the persecution of Christians in the Persian Empire coincided with conflict with Rome. A letter that, according to tradition, would have been sent by Constantine to Shapur II, in which he demanded that he stop persecuting Christians and named himself as their protector, put the Christians in Persia in a delicate position. Because they were considered the religious subjects of the Roman emperor, they were objects of suspicion in the eyes of the Persian state. Later, the Persian emperor would assume the same role as the Byzantine emperor, protecting church councils and the Church of the East, who prayed for him and the empire of which they were a part, but at this time, the martyr stories written in Syriac attest to massive persecutions launched by Shapur II and constitute an irreplaceable source for Sasanian history.

The famous Syriac doctor Marutha of Maipherqat / Martyropolis (d. ca. 420) won the favor of the Persian emperor Yazdegerd I (r. 399–420), after successfully treating him twice after being sent as an ambassador by the Roman emperor Arcadius. He adopted a role as a defender of the Christians and convinced Yazdegerd to convene a council of the Church of the East in 410. He also brought back the relics of Persian martyrs in the West as well as the *Acts* that told the stories of their martyrdoms.

During this council, the Church of the East adopted the canons of the Council of Nicaea, in full communion with the church in the Roman Empire, as well as the same calendar of liturgical feasts. But it also mentioned for the first time the preeminence of the bishop of Seleucia-Ctesiphon, the capital of the Sasanian Empire, as having authority over all other bishops in the empire. The Synod of Dadisho, in 424, asserted even more strongly that the Church of the East was independent from the church of the Roman Empire. It highlighted that the bishop of Seleucia-Ctesiphon, later called the catholicos, was the head of the Church of the East, holding the same title as Peter held over the apostles: there was no authority greater than him, and the church of the Roman Empire had no power to interfere in his decisions. It would not be accurate to describe this as a "separation," especially not a theological one; rather, it was an affirmation of ecclesiastical independence that made the Apostolic Church of the East—as it styled itself—an autocephalous church, which already existed in reality as a result of geopolitical circumstances that had separated it from the western part of the Christian world.

T • H • R • E • E

The Solitaries
Monastic Networks and the
Retreat from the World

A sceticism is an essential element of Syriac Christianity, and
it has left its mark on religious practice, literature, and ecclesiastical and social organization both in teaching and in
written culture. The stories of solitaries who chose a life of
poverty and chastity, both men and women, reflect a variety of ascetic
practices, some of which are indigenous to the Syro-Mesopotamian
world and others of which developed in Egypt or Palestine. These approaches to the ascetic life evolved over time and took on regional differences, but they are especially associated with monasticism beginning
in the 5th century and spread via a powerful and missionary monastic
network. It was mostly in the monasteries where people learned to read
and write, and mostly from among the monks that bishops and patriarchs were chosen—since, unlike priests, they had to be celibate—and
consequently, it was mostly through monasteries that Syriac culture,
both religious and profane, was written down and passed down to the
present. Heirs of the martyrs, ascetics were the new athletes of the Christian life in the 5th century after the end of the Roman persecutions,
when the struggle shifted from state persecutors (except in the Persian
Empire, until its fall in the 7th century) to the ultimate enemy, Satan,
in a spiritual combat. As simple passers-through in earthly life, they described themselves as "strangers" to the world, just as the Hebrews were

strangers in a foreign land during their exile in Babylon (see Ps. 137:4 in the Old Testament and Heb. 11:13 in the New). This motif of being strangers appears frequently in Syriac ascetic literature: just as Christ did not belong to the world, neither did ascetics.

The First Forms of Christian Asceticism in Syro-Mesopotamia

Syro-Mesopotamia had its own forms of asceticism, sometimes extreme, which are impossible to understand without situating them within a form of Christianity that was highly influenced by encratic tendencies (condemnation of marriage, abstention from meat and wine, absolute poverty). Encratic tendencies are visible in the beginnings of local versions of Christianity in the Jewish-Christian communities of Mesopotamia, supported by some of the Beatitudes, such as those in the Gospel of Luke (6:20), which mentions the poor and starving in the actual sense, not in the symbolic sense of the term ("in spirit") that the other Gospels use. These encratic tendencies also manifest themselves in the work of Tatian the (As)syrian, in the 2nd century, who foregrounded the importance of a strict vegetarian diet in his *Diatessaron*, which became very popular in the Syriac churches in the early centuries. In this version, John the Baptist does not eat locusts in the desert, but rather milk and honey, the two foods given to the newly baptized in the early church as a prefiguration of the future life in Paradise. Tatian condemned marriage and procreation, just like another text produced in the area, the pseudo-Clementine *On Virginity*, which is extant only in Syriac. The apocryphal *Acts of Thomas*, one of the earliest surviving Christian texts, which belongs to the 3rd century, also echoes ascetic tendencies in Syriac Christianity, presenting everything related to the body as corruptible and an obstacle to the journey of the soul toward incorruptibility. Thomas even dissuades the daughter of the king of India, Gondophares, from marrying, preaching celibacy instead.

The weight given to celibacy in this world, as an anticipation of the angelic life where men and women would no longer marry, because they were no longer subject to death (Luke 20:36), is a distinctive feature of Christianity in these regions. Syriac literature attests that, until the

3rd century or the very beginning of the 4th, celibacy was a condition for being baptized. The choice of sexual continence included two categories, the "virgins," or men and women who never married, and the *qadishe*, indicating those who renounced the marriages that they had in order to practice continence. The term consists of the Semitic root *qdš* which has the primary meaning of "separation," and signifies those who are not affected by the world in which they find themselves and are by extension continent.

APHRAHAT ABOUT THE SONS AND DAUGHTERS OF THE COVENANT

Pay attention to what I am writing to you concerning what is appropriate for single ones, the covenanters ([who are] virgins), and holy ones. In the first place, the man upon whom the yoke is laid ought to have a firm faith [. . .] He should be diligent in fasting and prayer, intense in his love for Christ, and humble and moderate and reasonable. Let his speech be peaceful and pleasant, and let his mind be clear toward everyone. Let him weigh his words carefully, and set a fence against harmful words around his mouth, and may foolish laughter be far from him. He should not love the adornment of clothing, nor let his hair grow long in order to decorate it, nor should he anoint it with aromatic oils. He should not recline at banquets, nor is it appropriate for him to wear fancy clothing. He should not boldly drink too much wine, and a proud mind should be far from him. It is not appropriate for him to look at fancy clothing, or to wear stylish cloaks. He should get rid of a deceitful tongue, put away envy and strife, and cast away lying lips.

This concept explains the existence of "Sons and Daughters of the Covenant," or *qyāmā*, in Mesopotamia. The term, which is difficult to fully decipher, has one of two interpretations: either it refers to the fact that they decided to respect their pact or vow taken in baptism for celibacy, or perhaps it makes reference to the resurrection (a meaning carried by the root that forms the word *qyāmā*) and thus to the angelic life led after the resurrection. Whichever one it is, the Sons and Daughters of the Covenant practiced a completely original form of asceticism.

Canons from the 5th century describe their appearance: a different form of dress than laypeople (perhaps black like monks or nuns), a belt (which signified a departure from the world, as belts were worn by travelers), and a tonsure in the form of a crown for those "dedicated" to the service of the church. The story of Simeon the Mountaineer, told by John of Ephesus in the 6th century, shows that, in order to fully participate in ministry, consecrated boys and girls were set apart in childhood, were tonsured (the sign of consecration), and received a basic education from the priest in the "schools" of the village, in which they learned to read and write and studied the Psalms and the Scriptures. They also learned to chant the *madrashe* (poems) in prayer seven times a day and in liturgies on Sunday and feast days. They seem to have increasingly assumed a diaconal role among both villagers and city dwellers, caring for the poor and sick, as well as teaching, all in service of the church and fully integrated in the lay community.

Ascetics are mentioned in the works of Aphrahat the Persian Sage and Ephrem as living both alone and in small groups. The term used for them in both cases is generally *ihidaye*, or solitaries. Besides a number of poems on ascetic matters, Ephrem dedicated two poetic cycles to the Mesopotamian solitaries Julian Saba and Abraham Qidunaya.

Syriac asceticism looks very different from the kind of cenobitic monasticism (from *coenobion*, "community" in Greek) popular in Egypt. The ascetics who appear in the works of Ephrem live in mountains and deserts, far from civilization, eating plants and using them for clothing (when they have clothing), letting their hair and nails grow wild. Living in harmony with nature and wild beasts, their asceticism is in some ways a retrospective eschatology, anticipating a return to the situation of Adam and Eve before the Fall. The extreme ascetic practices described by Theodoret of Cyr in his *History of the Monks in Syria*, composed in Greek in the middle of the 5th century, are understood to be a triumph over the body, marking both penitence after the Fall and a return to Paradise. Consequently, the "grazers," who live on wild plants, let their hair grow, and wander around naked, are either struck by divine folly or else close to the state of innocence. The sometimes morbid creativity of their mortifications described by Theodoret varies from person to person: wearing iron chains and sleeping on rocks seem to have been among the most popular, but there were also those who wore heavy weights around their necks, or who isolated themselves in trees, known as "dendrites," in wells or cisterns, in cages or towers, or standing on top of a column, practiced by "stylites." These mortifications were a means of mourning one's own sins as well as those of humanity and sharing in the suffering endured by Christ.

In Syria and Mesopotamia, asceticism was a matter of individual exploits, which sets it apart from Egypt and Palestine, where cenobitic monasticism was the norm. The well-known figure of Simeon Stylites the Elder, who lived at the beginning of the 5th century, is emblematic of these extreme ascetics. He is known to us under slightly different forms in Syriac and Greek, and his *Life* was translated into Coptic as well. Simeon was driven from the monastery of Teleda because his companions and superior judged his ascetic practices to be too extreme—for instance, he wrapped himself in a cord that infected his flesh, and he fasted constantly—and instead pursued his experience in solitude, living in a pit or cistern (or a swamp in the Coptic version of his *Life*).

THEODORET OF CYRRHUS, *LIFE OF SYMEON* (*HISTORY OF THE MONKS OF SYRIA/HISTORIA RELIGIOSA* 26.12)

As the visitors came in increasing numbers and they all tried to touch him and gain some blessing from those skin garments, he found it annoying and tedious and therefore devised the standing on a column. First he had one hewn of six cubits, then one of twelve, after that one of twenty-six, for he longs to soar to heaven and leave this earthly sojourn.

His holiness then being recognized, Simeon returned to the monastery, only then to separate himself from the community and become an anchorite, and later a stylite, at Telanissos/Telneshe (not far from Aleppo). He spent his life on three columns—five according to the *Life*—which were raised higher and higher as his asceticism progressed, and where he made himself like an offering so that his prayers would rise to God more easily. He remained on the last column until his death

Plaque representing Simeon Stylites on his tower, with the ladder used
to resupply it and the demon below in the form of a serpent. Musée du
Louvre, Paris, France. © RMN-Grand Palais / Art Resource, NY.

in 459, at the age of sixty. Two places are associated with his life: Antioch, where his body was transported and buried in the cathedral, and
Qaʿlat Semʿan, where his column became the center of the monastery
and a place of pilgrimage. Blessed with supernatural powers, Simeon
performed miracles, healed the sick, and taught from on top of his col-

umn. He also intervened for the poor and oppressed, participated in the life of the church, and protected the area from wild animals, epidemics, and natural catastrophes, restoring the primordial order. Separated from the world and a stranger to it, he was nevertheless not completely isolated, as he continued to be a member of the church and a beacon to outsiders—in particular, the Arab tribesmen who camped around his column and pressed forward eagerly to see this phenomenon.

INSCRIPTION OF NABGHA

In the year 718 (= AD 406–407), [. . .] this martyrion was adorned with mosaics, which is in St John's. In the days of Father Superior Mar Barnaba the work was started in that martyrion, and in the days of Father Superior Mares this work was completed. Lord, in the kingdom, remember the deacons Theodotus and Cosma, and the mosaicist Noah, and John, who all undertook the charge for Our Lord and have adorned this house with mosaics so that whoever readeth shall pray for them.

BOOK OF STEPS

The diligent among us merely give alms from their possessions; this is a proper thing to do—in order to get saved thereby—for worldly people. But we really should leave everything, enter in the lowliness of our Lord and into his self-emptying. These things belong to the major commandments; we shall show in more detail what they consist of. Yet as it is, we are living by the minor commandments only, the "vegetables" and the "milk," and not by the major ones, the true "solid food." . . . Therefore, we do not know how to distinguish the major commandments from the minor ones, nor the higher ministry from the lower ministry. And we do not understand what the significance is of the "food of the sick," which consists of "vegetables," or of the "milk of the children."

The example of Simeon shows the concurrence of two forms of asceticism starting in the 4th century, that of heroic individualism and that of communal monasticism. The Sons and Daughters of the

Mosaic uncovered at Nabgha (north of Aleppo). A geographic pattern to the west, succeeded by a panel with trees and animals in the east. The inscription is located on both sides of the steps going up to the sanctuary. Direction Générale des Antiquités et des musées de Syrie.

Covenant continued to play an important role in Syriac religious life, as shown by Aphrahat's Demonstration 6, which he dedicated to them in 337. The *Book of Steps* (written somewhere between the middle of the 4th century and ca. 430), produced in northeastern Iraq, is a work from this pre-monastic period which consists of thirty *memre* about the spiritual life and the pursuit of perfection by means of increasing degrees of asceticism that lead to the heavenly city of Christ. Beginning in the 4th century and especially from the 5th century, a combination of cenobitic monasticism and the solitary life in cells—or tents in southern Mesopotamia—spread west as well as east. Even so, cenobitic monasticism in the East never meant a confined life as in the cloisters in the West: Syriac monasteries are convents in the literal sense.

West Syrian Monasticism

Edessa was an important monastic center with cells and monasteries both in the town and its surroundings. If this setting is particularly famous, it is because it contributed to the spread of written Christian culture. Whether the main influence was Jewish books, known to those who translated the Old Testament version of the Peshitta, or Greek books that circulated in the region, a calligraphic tradition of writing developed in these monasteries. The copyists were no longer scribes working in the administration and archives on documents dealing with practical matters, but monks putting Christian culture into writing, foremost of which were the Old and New Testaments. As shown by ancient colophons (the signatures of copyists at the end of manuscripts), they were trained in Edessa. In Edessan monasteries, they learned the beautiful and difficult *estrangela* script, which required an apprenticeship to learn the shape of the calamus, the angle, and the formation of the letters in several characteristics, as well as the organization of the leaves of parchment, which were then assembled into codices, and that of the writing surface in order to ensure that the page was well laid out, in two or three columns for the oldest manuscripts. In the 6th century, the monk Marutha of Tagrit came from the Sasanian Empire to learn Edessan calligraphy, spreading it eastward. Of course, the fact that every monk knew how to read did not mean that every monk was a copyist.

Gospel manuscript on parchment copied on two columns in a beautiful old *estrangela* hand. Bibliothèque nationale de France.

THE LIFE OF MARUTA OF TAGRIT

As our father wanted to imitate these saints by reading and by the love of divine knowledge and in every kind of perfection, he went to the country of the Romans and arrived at the holy monastery of Mar Zaki, near Callinicum, and remained there ten years in order

to read the books of the orthodox doctors, especially Gregory the
Great Theologian [a Greek Father: that is, Gregory of Nazianzus],
interpreted and explained by Theodore, doctor and superior in the
monastery of Mar Zaki.

He returned from there to the cells which were near Edessa,
the blessed city. He lived a pure life there and kept company with
a monk who was a copyist. He learned the art of writing from him
and wrote in perfection, as the writings which he left after him attest.

Monasteries occupied a special place in the Syriac Orthodox
Church: their patriarchs were forbidden from staying in Antioch, their
nominal see, because they were considered to be non-orthodox and il-
legitimate in the Byzantine Church on account of their opposition to
the Council of Chalcedon. As a result, between 518 and the Arab conquest (see chapter 6), Miaphysites usually lived in the great monasteries in Mesopotamia and Syria. The leadership of the Syriac Orthodox
Church became itinerant in 518, during the time of the Emperor Justin II, when the Miaphysite patriarch Severus of Antioch was exiled.
Beginning in Egypt, at the monastery of Enaton, nine miles from Alexandria, the non-Chalcedonian exiles took up residence in a number
of local monasteries, creating a network of Miaphysites from Egypt to
Syria that would last until the end of the Middle Ages. Of the sixteen
patriarchs who would succeed Severus up to the year 800, twelve were
connected to the three great monasteries of Qenneshre ("Eagle's Nest")
on the Euphrates, Gubba Baroyo ("The Outer Cistern") west of the Euphrates, and Speculos ("The Watchtower") not far from Theodosiopo-
lis/Resh'aina. The great monasteries of Tur 'Abdin in the southeast of
modern-day Turkey—literally "The Mountain of the Servants," a name
that originally referred to pagan cults but later took on a new meaning
because of the many monasteries that were built there—and, briefly in
the 10th century, those around Melitene (Malatya), when it was reconquered by the Byzantines, became the seats of the patriarchs and their
courts. Monasteries also became objects of power struggles between the
Christian denominations: the monastery of Qa'lat Se'man, which was
originally of the party of Severus of Antioch (that is, Miaphysite), passed
into the hands of the Chalcedonians most likely in the 10th century.

Sculpted decorations on the façade of Mor Gabriel monastery.

Among the oldest monasteries, and still active today, is the monastery of Qarṭmin in Tur ʿAbdin, founded by Samuel and Simeon in 350 and made an imperial foundation in 397. Because it was situated not far from the frontier zone, the prayers of its monks were believed to serve as protection against Sasanian raids. It is under the name of Mor Gabriel, after Gabriel of Bet Qusṭan, a holy abbot from the 7th century, that the monastery became known and is still known today.

Monasticism in the Church of the East

It was in the 6th century that an important monastic reform took place in the Church of the East under the impetus of Abraham of Kashkar (ca. 508–588). Originally from the south of modern-day Iraq, he studied at the School of Nisibis and made a pilgrimage to Egypt on the trail of Antony, the most famous solitary, and Pachomius, the founder of Egyptian monasticism. Upon his return, he founded the Great Monastery on Mount Izla near Nisibis, where he issued a series of canons in 571. The monastery included a *coenobium* where monks led a communal life (a meal with readings, offices, work duties), but after three years of probation, they could obtain permission to lead a solitary life in a cell separate from the monastery. Abraham introduced a specific kind of tonsure in order to distinguish monks of the Church of the East from their West Syrian counterparts, who were becoming more and more numerous in the Sasanian Empire.

THE LIFE OF ABRAHAM OF KASHKAR

Now as God of old brought out the blessed Abraham from Ur of the Chaldees, and made him, by faith, the father of a multitude of nations, so also He spread abroad and made to increase this holy habit of the solitary life in all the country of the East, by the hand of this spiritual man, worthy of Abraham in name, and country, and deed, whom He established to be the father of the army of virgins and men of abstinence. [. . .] The everlasting fore-knowledge of Him . . . set him apart aforetime, that at his hands, and by his means, the holy fathers who were to become the founders of famous monasteries of the lands of the Persians, and Assyrians, and Babylonians, might become disciples. [. . .] He invented this distinguishing mark of ours, and commanded that the disciples of this holy habit of life should have their heads shaved like a crown; now before the days and time of his coming, the mark of the true Christians could not be distinguished from the tonsure of the Sêwaryânê [followers of Severus].

His many disciples in their turn founded monasteries in Persia and Mesopotamia, giving a new energy to monasticism in the Sasanian Empire despite the strong disapproval of monasticism by Zoroastrians. His successors, Dadisho and Babai, finished his canons.

During the 6th century, the historical memory of monasticism in the Church of the East underplayed its Syro-Mesopotamian roots in favor of the Egyptian model. This change is partly due to the numerous Lives dedicated to Mar Awgin (Eugene) and the many disciples—eighteen to seventy, depending on the version—that he was supposed to have had at the end of the 4th and the beginning of the 5th century. Awgin and his followers supposedly dotted Mesopotamia with monasteries based on the Pachomian model from Egypt, but the oldest mention of these monasteries dates to the 7th century, which suggests that the history was rewritten in retrospect. Around the same time, in the second half of the 7th century, the Egyptian spiritual literature of the *apothegmata*, or short proverbs of the fathers, was translated from Greek into Syriac by the monk Henan'isho along with the *Lausiac History* of Palladius of Helenopolis. They were then combined with the *Paradise of the Fathers*, which were in turn partially integrated into monastic anthologies read by ascetics both east and west. Trained at the School of Nisibis, Henan'isho made a pilgrimage to Egypt and then settled at the monastery of Beth 'Abe in modern-day Iraq, where he composed a lexicographical work meant to explain difficulties in patristic texts as well as a work on homography. He also collaborated in revising the *Ḥudra*, the book of the liturgical year for the Church of the East.

Babai the Great (551–628) was the most notable theologian of the Church of the East during the 7th century. After having studied theology and medicine at Nisibis, he became an archimandrite at the Great Monastery at Izla. He wrote no fewer than eighty-six works. His book *On Union* and the profession of faith of 612, which he wrote for an encounter between the Syriac Orthodox and members of the Church of the East at the court of the Persian emperor, established the formula henceforth adopted by the Church of the East in which Christ is "one person (*prosopon*) in two natures (*kyane*) and two *qnome* (a term whose precise interpretation is debated between churches)." He also wrote commentaries on the works of Evagrius Ponticus and Mark the Deacon.

Babai also composed a number of Lives of Persian saints, among them the noble Christina of Karka d-Bet Slok, which is extant only in fragments, and Mihramgushnasp/George, which is the only one that is intact.

Beth 'Abe (ca. 100 km northeast of Mosul), founded in 595/596 by a disciple of Abraham of Kashkar, is another of the great monasteries where a number of the bishops and catholicoi of the Church of the East completed their formation.

We must learn and recount that many shepherds have been chosen for all parts of the world from this holy monastery, who, through their splendid triumphs, have appeared in their generations like unto lamps set upon the candlestick of the Church, [and we must learn and recount that the monastery] hath been named by the ancients the "house of the priesthood," and the "father of the pillars of the holy Church" by reason of the men who have in all generations gone forth [from it], and who have become shepherds set over the flocks of Christ. And they did not only accept established and princely thrones, which were [situated] in flourishing towns and civilized countries, but also [those of] the countries which were destitute of all knowledge of Divine things and holy doctrine, and which abounded in sorcery and idolatry and all corrupt and abominable practices.

Around the middle of the 7th century, it numbered no fewer than three hundred monks and had been richly endowed with buildings, liturgical instruments, and manuscripts by a catholicos who had been a monk. Thomas of Marga was a monk there before becoming the secretary to the catholicos Abraham (r. 837–850), one of his fellow monks at the monastery and later bishop of Marga. Around 850 he composed a monastic history called *The Book of Governors*, which relies on a number of hagiographic texts that have been lost today. It is a key source of information on the history of monasticism as well as scholastic and monastic networks in the Church of the East more broadly. He describes the monastery as "the father of the pillars of the holy Church," on account of the many missionaries who received their training there and who were sent "to all parts of the world."

The monastery of Rabban Shapur, near Shushtar in Iran, is another of the great eastern monasteries, which seems to have existed in the monastic environment of Bet Qaṭraye west of the Persian Gulf (see

chapter 5). The monastic schools of Bet Qaṭraye produced some of the
most famous writers on the topics of asceticism and mysticism, some of
which is similar to Islamic mysticism.

The best known of these authors is Isaac of Nineveh, who was
born toward the end of the 7th century and lived in Bet Qaṭraye for a
time. His work was a success in monastic circles far beyond the Syriac
world. The first part of his writings was translated into Greek in the
monastery of Saint Sabas in Palestine and had a considerable influence
on Greek and Slavic monasticism. The second and third parts were partially translated into Arabic. John the Solitary and Evagrius Ponticus are
two of the authors most frequently cited by Isaac.

Aḥob (the end of the 6th century?), Dadisho (the end of the
7th century), and Abraham bar Lipeh (7th century) all bear the name
"Qaṭraya," which marks them as monks of Bet Qaṭraye, and no less
than eight Gabriels are associated with the region (corresponding no
doubt to four persons and their homonyms, including Gabriel bar Lipeh, known as Qaṭraya; Gabriel Arya, "the Lion," also known as Gabriel
Qaṭraya; and Gabriel Qaṭraya). Their biblical, patristic, and liturgical
commentaries and their ascetic works show a familiarity with the Greek
fathers who had been translated into Syriac (Basil and Evagrius Ponticus
in particular), earlier Syriac authors such as Narsai, but also the *Organon* of Aristotle and popular philosophical texts. Their horizons were
open to the Byzantine world as well as aligned with Sinai. Their works
were read well beyond the Persian Gulf: the commentary of Dadisho
Qaṭraya on the *Paradise of the Fathers*, already mentioned, was translated into Sogdian, Ethiopic, and Arabic, which shows its influence in
monastic circles in both East and West beginning in the 7th century.
This environment was productive despite the political changes in the
Near East in the 7th century, such as the Sasanian domination of the
region and the Arab Muslim conquest that followed.

Activities and Economy in the Monasteries

Although places of prayer first and foremost, monasteries were open
to travelers and pilgrims. The most important had hospices for the
poor and sick. On desert routes, the monasteries founded by Mar

Aḥudemmeh and Marutha of Tagrit in the 6th century, or Sergiopolis, where both the Roman and Persian emperors came to St. Sergius, were oases for travelers and helped convert the Arab tribes of the desert. They were also places that had a strong influence on pulling visitors to this or that denomination. The liturgy played a role in affirming denominational identity and in attempts to pull converts from one church to another.

SIMEON OF THE OLIVES

He also began to buy up with the gold farms and numerous villages, donating them to the Abbey of Qartmin. Thus, the Abbey of Qartmin acquired possessions such as are not to be found elsewhere in the world. [. . .] First of all, Mar Simeon bought the agricultural land of the monastery of the Column, where he was enclosed, as well as its fields, water [rights], springs, and entire property. He planted it with numerous olives, using the water of its springs, some 12,000 olive stocks. He brought the plants from a great distance, from faraway regions, and he planted the olives with great care and much labor. [. . .] Then he appointed agricultural laborers and ploughmen to work and fully take care of the plantations. After five years the olives began to bear fruit. Thus, they had numerous olives which were very productive, and from them lighting was provided for the whole Abbey and for the churches throughout the whole region of Tur ʿAbdin.

Monasteries could function thanks to gifts of money and land, receiving donations of valuables and manuscripts. They were also centers of economic activity, employing people to cultivate their property and in some cases keeping slaves bound to the land. Monks participated in this agricultural work as well. The *Life* of Mor Simeon of the Olives in Tur ʿAbdin in the 7th century shows that his surname came from the fact that he planted thousands of olive trees. Olive oil was crucial for light, food, and medicine, and the surplus could bring a substantial income, and orchards of fruit trees, walnut trees in northern Mesopotamia, or palm trees in the Persian Gulf played the same role. Besides agricultural plots, monasteries also owned herds, inns and places of lodging, and mills, all of which generated revenue that they could then use to pay taxes to the powers that governed the region. They received both private donations and imperial favors from the Byzantine and Persian emperors alike. After the Arab Muslim conquest, they were appreciated by the first caliphs as well, and early Muslim literature celebrates them as places to relax in enchanting gardens and read poetry and drink wine. Monasteries earned a place in the Muslim imagination after the first caliphs began to use them as places to rest while traveling.

EXCERPT FROM AL-SHABUSHTI'S *BOOK OF MONASTERIES (KITAB AL-DIYARAT)*

The Monastery of Samālū

This monastery is located east of Baghdad, at Bāb aš-Šamāsiyya, by the shore of the river al-Mahdī. This monastery has watermills and is surrounded by orchards, trees, and palms. The place is pleasant and the architecture is beautiful, and it is peopled by passers-by as well as monks.

Easter at Baghdad is particularly stunning in this monastery, because of all the Christians as well as the Muslims who wish to celebrate and amuse themselves by strolling there. This monastery is one of the best-known parks in Baghdad, and a well-known place of festivities.

The great monasteries attracted huge crowds, which came to collect objects of benediction (sacred dust of relics—*ḥnana* in Syriac—and holy oil) as well as to pray. A system of trade developed as monasteries began to sell holy oil, food, and objects of daily use. Fairs, which drew people, sometimes from far away, were organized around feast days.

Monasteries and Knowledge

Although monasteries traditionally follow an educational model of master and disciple, the monks, who should in theory have been able to read and write and know all the psalms by heart (each day they recited a section of the Psalter), received a basic education in schools in city and village before entering the monastery. The reading of the Scriptures was an individual practice, tied to meditation in the solitude of a cell, as well as communal practice, in periods dedicated to instruction or mealtimes, and of course part of the liturgy as well. A third of each day was supposed to be set aside for the reading and the offices. The books read in monasteries are those essential for understanding the Scriptures, especially the Gospels: biblical and patristic commentaries, hagiographies, and ascetic and mystical literature. Monks who were both readers

Stylite's tower, monastery of Mor Lozoor, Tur ʿAbdin.
Photo by Françoise Briquel Chatonnet.

and writers are also the subject of such literature. To write the *Lives* of the holy founders of the monasteries was considered a pious act. The *Lives* were read before the congregation on the day commemorating the saint or on the anniversary of the monastery's foundation. Besides being written in prose, they were sometimes also abbreviated and rewritten in verse.

Certain stylites were both copyists and writers as well: John the Stylite of Litarb (or Litarib), in the 7th century, wrote a grammar and chronicle that have since been lost, and around 775 Joshua the Stylite probably wrote the *Zuqnin Chronicle*, which takes its name from a nearby monastery, while Sergius the Stylite wrote a dialogue with a Jew. Because of these writings, we should picture stylitism as often being temporary or a phase of retreat from the world in a narrow tower rather than as sitting on top of a column, as shown by Simeon of the Olives, who managed a monastery from his tower and sometimes left to handle his affairs. Women also participated in this form of asceticism.

There were also monks who were trained in medicine, studying both philosophy and science. The monastery of Qenneshre, founded by John bar Aphtonia on the banks of the Euphrates, shows the place of Hellenism in the monastic world and distinguished itself in the 7th century by its translations and commentaries on astronomical, mathematical, medical, and philosophical texts, especially those of Aristotle, alongside the usual works of grammar, the Bible, and patristic literature. A number of the best-known writers in the Syriac world were monks first before becoming bishops: Athanasius of Balad, Severus Sebokht, Jacob of Edessa, George of the Arabs. The "translation movement" in Baghdad in the 9th century, where a number of Greek texts were translated into Arabic (and then reintroduced to the Western world centuries later), is incomprehensible without taking into account the constant work of Syriac monks on the Greek intellectual heritage.

The Survival of Monastic Libraries

Wearing their black hoods embroidered with white crosses, Syriac monks are always easily recognizable. A few great monasteries still remain active today, and some of them are places where manuscripts

remain preserved, such as Deir al-Za'faran (the monastery of Saf-
ran), dedicated to Mor Hananyo, which held around three hundred
manuscripts at the beginning of the 20th century, and the monastery
of Our Lady of the Seeds in Alqosh. But there are also two Egyptian
monasteries that played a key role in the preservation of Syriac manuscripts. St. Catherine of Sinai, a Greek monastery with a multilingual
community, was a longtime shelter of Chalcedonian Syriac monks. The
Monastery of the Syrians, originally Syriac Orthodox but now Coptic, Deir al-Suryan, in the Nitrean Desert, also played a major role in
the preservation of Syriac culture. We are indebted to a copyist, Moses
of Nisibis, who later became the superior of the monastery and traveled to Baghdad in order to appeal to the caliph against the new taxes
that were being levied. While there around 931/932, he assembled and
then transported around two hundred manuscripts from all across
Mesopotamia. Preserved thanks to the dry Egyptian climate and the
isolated location of the monastery, they represent an essential collection of Syriac Orthodox—and, to a much lesser extent, East Syrian—
manuscripts. The holdings of these two monasteries, which are scattered today across European libraries (particularly the British Library
in London and the Vatican Library, but also the Bibliothèque nationale
in France and the Ambrosian Library in Milan), still contain Syriac
manuscripts and in two cases during the 20th century resulted in new
discoveries in closed rooms.

In Syria, in Iraq, in Lebanon, many patriarchal libraries and monasteries remain, their thick walls partially sheltering them from the ef-
fects of war. Since the beginning of the 2000s, scans have begun to be
made to ensure that copies of the manuscripts survive, especially as carried out by the Hill Museum and Manuscript Library in Collegeville,
Minnesota, in the United States, which now numbers 13,500 Syriac and
garshuni manuscripts in its digital collection (see pages 87 and 223) from
Lebanon, Syria, Turkey, Iraq, and India—which are now made freely
available online at www.hmml.org. Conservation measures are still in-
sufficient, however, and the manuscripts themselves are not moved to
safe areas. The preservation of this written culture is endangered more
than ever by the tumults of the end of the 20th century and the beginning of the 21st.

COLOPHON

In the year 1395 of the Greeks (AD 1083/1084), in the terrible time that came to the region of Syria and the land of the Romans by the hands of the Persians, which is to say the Turks, the latter ravaged and devastated these places and many of the Syrian monks from there came to establish themselves in our monastery here, the Monastery of the Syrians, in the desert of Scete.

There were there among those monks—who numbered around seventy—a young man, who was very modest, loved virtue, was brilliant in his intelligence, applied himself hard to reading, and was very well learned in the teaching of the Church. A little later after moving into this monastery, he looked and saw many books with broken bindings, pages falling out, and many of the leaves scattered, and heaps were piled up throughout the whole monastery, in cells, in closets, and in corners of the church, and they were piled up at the feet of many people . . .

But right away he showed great diligence and gathered all the pages and leaves which had been scattered in his cell. And using the notes which he found in the books, he put each one in its place and bound them together as they had been previously. And he restored all the old books which had fallen to pieces and which the sewing and the thread had been deteriorated and degraded. And he worked with manual labor and he bought thread, parchment, and glue. And in three years he restored all the books. During the night he worked for his needs and during the day he worked in gluing and binding the books.

F • O • U • R

God as Teacher
A Culture of Knowledge

Both writing and writing culture are highly valued in the Syriac tradition, which not only inherited the Aramaic tradition of inscriptions but also gave birth to a rich body of literature, especially between the 2nd and the 14th century. According to a number of Syriac writers, Syriac was the language of Paradise, which God spoke with Adam and Eve before the Fall. The apostle Addai claimed that at the Last Judgment, at the end of time, everyone would have their deeds written on their bodies, and that everyone—male and female, great and small—would know how to read their deeds themselves, without needing the help of anyone else, because they would have received the illumination of the Christian faith. This vivid image of everyone finally being able to read shows how prevalent illiteracy was in late antique society and consequently the importance that Syriac Christianity attached to writing.

TEACHING OF ADDAI

For the whole of that for which our Lord came into the world was that he might teach and show us that at the consummation of created things there will be a resurrection for all people. At that time their manner of life will be represented in their own persons and their bodies will become parchment skins for the books of justice. There will be no one there who cannot read, because in that day everyone will read the writings of his own book. He will hold a reckoning of his deeds in the fingers of his hands. Moreover, the unlearned will know the new writing of the new language. No one will say to his companion: "read this for me," because teaching and instruction will rule over all people.

The Development of Syriac Writing

Edessan Aramaic, part of an ancient Aramaic literary culture that existed well before the arrival of Christianity, was used in pagan times for inscriptions on mosaics and funerary stones as well as in the administration of the Oshroenian state. In this respect, it differed from other forms of writing in the region, such as Coptic, Armenian, and Slavonic, which were created only upon Christianization in order to write the lives of the saints. In this period, a cursive alphabet in which certain letters already took a *serṭo* form was used for legal and administrative writing

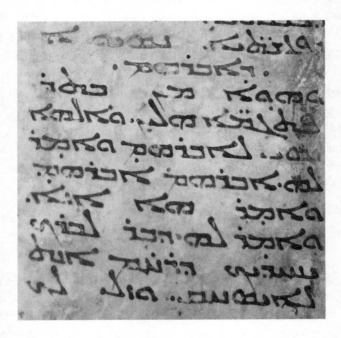

Examples of old *esṭrangela* writing.

Consecration ritual for patriarchs, metropolitans, and bishops in
the Syriac Orthodox Church, written in *serto* script.

(cf. Euphrates parchment, page 16), alongside a more formal writing
used for display on stone. Writing on mosaic uses an intermediary form.

The translations of the Bible in Edessa in the 2nd century and the
first Christian literary texts like *The Odes of Solomon* and *The Hymn
of the Pearl* contributed to the diffusion of the Edessan dialect of Aramaic as a religious and cultural language, and a formal literary hand,
estrangela, stemmed from the existing formal script, developed for these
new genres of literature. We do not know anything about the development of this writing up to the 5th century, but our oldest extant manuscript, from 411, shows a skillfully rendered script, the result of scribal
practices that had already been formalized and passed down in Christian environments, likely monastic ones (see chapter 3). *Estrangela* was
the common script used for manuscripts before other, more distinctive
forms of writing gradually appeared.

However, colophons (the final notes written by copyists) during
this period bear witness to a less formal script, most likely the script
used in common practice. Starting from the 8th century, the western

churches (Syriac Orthodox, Maronite, and Melkite) adopted this common script, under the name of *serto* (*serto peshitto*, or "simple line"), for
writing books and formal documents as well. A notation system using
small Greek vowels written above and below the main letters to indicate
pronunciation was developed, but its use was always sporadic.

In the Persian Empire, Syriac arrived with Christianization, although there were other forms of Aramaic with a slightly different
alphabet that were used locally. Another regional form of writing developed from the *estrangela* used in ancient manuscripts, usually described as eastern, Nestorian, or (in older publications) Chaldean. In

Manuscript page from the Ḥudra, the book
of hours of the Church of the East. Ms des
Dominicains de Mossoul DFM 13, f. 62r.

this system, vowels are denoted by dots. The difference between western and eastern scripts corresponds partly to the difference in phonology between western and eastern forms of Syriac, and partly to different local and ecclesiastical traditions.

In Melkite settings, and particularly in the Melkite monasteries on the Black Mountain near Antioch and in Sinai, another distinctive form of writing developed in the 9th century. It is close to Christian Palestinian writing, used by Chalcedonian Christians in Palestine whose dialect was similar to Judeo-Aramaic, but which used an alphabet very close to Syriac from the 6th century onward.

In Central Asia, the Syriac alphabet was adapted to Sogdian, an eastern Iranian language attested in the 4th century, which was used to write Buddhist, Manichaean, and Christian scriptures, as well as letters, administrative documents, and monetary inscriptions. In India, Syro-Malabar writing, isolated from the evolution that took place in the Near and Middle East, underwent its own development into a specific regional form beginning in the 16th century that emphasized East Syrian characters.

The Syriac script, together with Nabatean Aramaic, was one of the foundations of what would develop into the modern Arabic alphabet, which first emerged in an Arab Christian context around AD 500. Some early pre-Islamic Arabic forms of writing have been attested in inscriptions recently uncovered in Saudi Arabia, but the one attested in Syria is officially recognized as the first.

When Arabic became the vernacular and cultural language of West Syrian Christians at the beginning of the 9th century, the phenomenon of *garshuni* also appeared, in which Arabic was written in Syriac letters. *Garshuni* was a way of adapting to the spread of Arabic, which was often associated with Islam, by using Syriac letters to affirm a Christian visual identity. Thousands of *garshuni* manuscripts from the 9th century onward, especially Syriac Orthodox and Maronite, remain to be studied. Sogdian manuscripts written in Syriac letters have also been found, as well as Armenian, Kurdish, Turkish, and Malayalam exemplars in Syriac writing.

Centers of Syriac Culture in the Pre-Islamic Period

Manuscript Culture

Manuscripts were produced in monasteries and sometimes churches, almost exclusively by men. Colophons in Syriac manuscripts (where copyists wax more loquacious than their Greek and Latin counterparts) usually mention the date and place where the manuscript was copied and provide information of varying length about contemporary local or historical events (such as wars, epidemics, and natural disasters) as well as about the copyist himself, his family, or his community. The names of the current patriarch and the abbot of the monastery are often mentioned, as the copyists were often deacons, priests, bishops, or even patriarchs. Such sources are of course valuable for historians.

The act of copying biblical or hagiographical texts was considered a spiritual activity in and of itself. The practice of copying by hand continued well after the advent of the printing press, especially in the Church of the East: in the Ottoman period, manuscript copying in monasteries declined significantly, to the benefit of families of copyists active in the Mosul region. Printing presses in the Near East and in Europe developed different kinds of Syriac fonts, and in the 20th century Syriac writing leaped into the computerized era with the development of digital fonts (thanks in particular to Beth Mardutho).

Copyists wrote on leaves of parchment (specially treated animal skin), though beginning in the 9th century parchment was progressively replaced by paper. These leaves were then assembled into codices, which were sewn together and bound. Syriac bindings, though very similar to Byzantine exemplars, nevertheless have their own distinctive characteristics. Time-consuming to copy and expensive to produce, manuscripts were not widely distributed for private use. Apart from ascetics who kept some books in their cells, it was primarily in the libraries of monasteries, schools, and churches where books were read, copied, and preserved up to the present.

For authors, producing new texts or making translations required networks to prepare and copy manuscripts. Manuscripts circulated between churches of different theological confessions, and copyists sometimes modified the attribution of the author to make the text acceptable to one side or another. Liturgical or dogmatic texts were passed down in

The four evangelists are represented as copyist monks.
Bibliothèque nationale de France.

the same tradition. The production and possession of manuscripts was an instrument of ecclesial power, involving the highest church officials (bishops, patriarchs, and abbots of the most powerful monasteries), until the 20th and 21st centuries, in the copying, production, and transmission of knowledge in Syriac (as well as Arabic and Western languages).

The library of the bishop Mare in Amida was brought back to Alexandria in the 6th century by his sisters after his death in exile; in the 7th century, Jacob of Edessa died on the road while traveling in search of books for his library; the catholicos of the Church of the East at the beginning of the 9th century, Timothy I, was always on the lookout for Greek manuscripts and frequently asked for copies from his correspondents. Rare and precious, books were purchased or offered in donation to churches and monasteries, such as a Gospel book copied in gold and silver ink by the patriarch Michael the Great for his monastery of Mor Barṣaumo.

Example of Syriac binding: wooden boards covered with leather, with an embossed cover decorated with metal flowers arranged in the shape of a cross. Bibliothèque patriarcale de Charfet (Lebanon).

Letter 33 to Sergius, Metropolitan of Elam

With this [letter] I implore you to take care to search Mar Mattai
and to see what the best edition of Dionysius [Pseudo-Dionysius
the Areopagite] is: if it is that of Athanasius or Phocas. Make a
copy of it if there is a copyist, and if there is not, send it to me by an
intermediary, a faithful man, and I will send it back quickly.

Letter 37, to the Same

Send the copy of Dionysius in the edition of Athanasius or
Phocas, and in a month I will copy it and send it back. Ask it for
yourself, in order to read it, so that no one will know that you are
going to send it, and I will copy it quickly and will return it. And
I will send it with a man in whom you have confidence, so that
nobody has any doubt about the matter.

A World of Schools

Catechetical "schools" for spreading Christian doctrine existed alongside the philosophical schools of the ancient world in Athens, Alexandria, and Antioch or the schools of law in Beirut. The Christian
"schools" in Alexandria and Antioch distinguished themselves by their
respective exegetical approaches. Antioch, which could claim Greek-
speaking fathers of the church like Eusebius of Emesa, Diodore of Tarsus, and Theodore of Mopsuestia, and Syriac fathers like Ephrem and
Narsai, was without a doubt the one that exerted the greatest influence over Syriac authors. Meanwhile, Alexandria was also a significant
place of study for both West and East Syrians until the conquest of the
city by the Arabs in the 7th century, boasting an extensive Greek library of books on philosophy, medicine, geography, mathematics, and
astronomy.

EPHREM, *HYMNS ON PARADISE* 6.1

The keys of doctrine which unlock all Scripture
Have opened up before my eyes the book of creation,
The treasure house of the Ark, the crown of the Law.
It is Scripture in its narrative which, above all its companions,
Has perceived the Creator and transmitted his works;
Beholding all His handiwork it has made manifest
The objects of His Craftmanship

A key element to the theology that emerged from the school of Antioch was the belief that God is the teacher of mankind, and that the world was a school in which people were taught and shaped. Both humans and angels were rational beings, capable of receiving instruction, and God revealed himself to them by his actions as Creator and Sustainer. The idea of divine *paideia* ("education" in Greek) is at the heart of this conception and the root of its exegetical methods, conveying that God spoke to mankind in the Scriptures as one would speak to a child who was still learning. The resources of philology and interpretation taught in the schools by grammarians and rhetors were directed toward this exegetical work. Schools as we understand them today thus occupied an essential place in this tradition, and in particular in the Church of the East, according to an idea in which the history of mankind and the world was conceived as a succession of earthly schools (from God at the moment of creation to the patriarchs of the Old Testament, Jesus and the apostles in the New Testament, the church fathers, and so on).

THE NETWORK OF SCHOOLS

Different levels of schools existed in the Syriac world, with elementary schools attached to churches in cities and villages, where grammarians taught reading, grammar, and the correct vocalization of words, essential in a Semitic language that did not mark vowels. Creating the correct pronunciation for the text was the base of teaching, both written and oral.

More advanced schools existed in Edessa and throughout the Sasanian Empire. We do not know the exact content of the curriculum of these schools, but the Greek *paideia* was maintained in Syriac schools as a precursor to theology. Severus bar Shakko (13th century), who was trained by the famous mathematician, astronomer, and Arab philosopher Kamal al-Din Musa ibn Yunus, penned the *Book of Dialogues*, which was dedicated to secular knowledge and shows the division of knowledge in his time as being very similar to that of the ancient and late antique world: grammar, logic, rhetoric, and poetry; various forms of philosophy (ethics, physics, and physiology); mathematics, metaphysics, and theology. Greek rhetoric was also included. Homer, already a classic, was still read despite having pagan content in his work, as Anthony of Tagrit (Syriac Orthodox, 9th century?) noted in his treatise on rhetoric. Meanwhile, Gregory of Nazianzus, also known as Gregory the Theologian (Greek, 4th century), represented the literary model par excellence. Philosophy, especially logic, according to the first books of the *Organon* by Aristotle and with the *Isagoge* of Porphry of Tyr, which were read by Neoplatonists, became part of the highest levels of education, just below theology proper, which was considered the queen of the disciplines.

BARHADBESHABBA ʿARBAYA, *CAUSE OF THE FOUNDATION OF SCHOOLS*

Let us come then to this [school] of ours, and let us see how he led it and in what way he dealt with it, and with what letters he composed names, so it could be read and be instructed. Now at the same time that he made Adam and Eve, he caused to be made before them in the order of the letters the wild and domestic animals, and he whispered in him [i.e., Adam] secretly so that he might read openly. Adam read in this first tablet the names for all the domestic animals and for all the wild animals of the field and all the birds in the heavens. Everything Adam called them, [each] living soul, that was their name. Because he repeated these unwritten letters well in the composition of exact names, [God] then introduced his school to the Garden of Eden and there he taught him the laws and judgements. After [God] first wrote the short psalm about the tree, beautiful to look at, so that he might read it and know by it the distinction between good and evil.

THE BOOK OF CHASTITY BY ISHO'DNAH OF BAṢRA

Notice 139: Saint Mar Isho'yahb, who left his country in order to go found a monastery in the mountain of Bet Nuhadra. When he was young, he went to the school of Tamanon, and he studied books there. He left the schools and went to find Mar Isho'zka in the land of Adiabene. He was a reader in the monastery of Mar Isha Sliba-Zka. After some time, Mar Zka sent him to Mar Babai of Nisibis, and he received the holy habit on Mount Izla. After the death of his master, he went to the mountain of Bet Nuhadra with three other brothers, and he founded a famous monastery in that place. Some brothers gathered near him. Later, the blessed Mar Isaac, bishop of Bet Nuhadra, implored him not to abandon his monastery. He let himself be persuaded by the bishop. After an illustrious life, he went to Our Lord at the age of fifty-six years old, and he was placed in the *martyrion* of the monastery that he had created.

REGULATIONS OF THE SCHOOL OF NISIBIS

4th canon of Narsai: The brothers who are in the school are not allowed to go over to the country of the Romans without precept and order of the brothers and that of the rabbaita of the school, neither for the cause of the instruction, nor because of a pretense of prayer, also not in order to buy or to sell.

5th canon: No one of the brothers shall practice business of craft. But if it is necessary to buy and to sell [then] from the month Āb until Tešrī qadīm outside of Nisibis, in other countries. In Nisibis, however, except the workers, they are not allowed to practice business.

8th canon of Narsai: The brothers, however, who [already] are in the rank of 'eskūlāiē are not allowed to cease from writing, reading and interpretation of the school and the "recitation of the choirs" without an urgent affair.

16th canon of Ḥenana: The brothers who are in the school, so long as they are in the school, shall not eat in the taverns and restaurants, they shall also not arrange picnics and drinking parties

in the gardens and parks, but shall endure all in their cells as is
becoming for the purpose and the manner of their qeiāmā.

The most famous school in Edessa was called "The School of the
Persians." It is mentioned in the acts of the Second Council of Ephesus
in 449, together with the Schools of the Armenians and Syrians. Most
likely, its name is due to the place of origin of its members. The scholars who translated the works of Diodorus of Tarsus and Theodore of
Mopsuestia into Syriac were associated with the School of the Persians
and taught Antiochian theology. It was closed in 489 precisely because
of its theological commitments, which were problematic in a time of
Christological controversy. Around that time, its director, Narsai (see
chapter 2), and those who followed him fled to Nisibis and rejoined the
Persian Empire. Considered to be a hotbed for heresy in the West, it was
by contrast seen as the core foundation of the School of Nisibis in the
East, though whether there was actual continuity between the School of
the Persians and the School of Nisibis is not clear.

The School of Nisibis trained most of the dignitaries of the
Church of the East and sent its best students to teach and create
schools in their turn. The canons of the school, created by Narsai in
496 and expanded by others in 602, have survived to the present, as
well as the opening discussion of an academic session, unique for the
period that preceded the creation of universities in the West during
the Middle Ages. The exegetical tradition of the Church of the East,
founded by Theodore of Mopsuestia, was the main subject, but medicine was also taught there, associated with a hospital supported by rev-
enues from nearby baths. The students lived as though they were at the
monastery, and future doctors were the only ones who frequented the
town. Doubtless following this first model, other schools are known to
have existed in the Sasanian Empire—such as the school of Seleucia-
Ctesiphon and the medical school of Beth Lapaṭ/Gondeshapur, which
became famous in the 8th and 9th centuries—as well as hospitals in
Edessa and the Persian Empire, from the 5th century until the time of
the Mongols. *The History of the Founders of Monasteries and Schools*,
also called *The Book of Chastity*, written by Isho'dnaḥ of Basra around
850, centered on this original scholastic tradition of monasteries and

urban schools of the Church of the East where the two coincided (see chapter 3).

KALILAH AND DIMNAH

It is related that Dabdahram, king of India, said to Nadrab the philosopher, the wise man, and chief of the wise men: "Show me the similitude of two men, companions or friends, between whom a false or astute cunning individual has produced dissension, so that they have turned from mutual love and harmony to hatred and enmity."

Nadrab the philosopher answered: "[. . .] Now in [a certain region] was a certain lion, who was king of the animals therein and was named Pingalaka; and there were with him many animals of every kind. Now this lion was exceedingly haughty in spirit, and whatever he wished to do, he did independently, without employing the advice of anyone. Notwithstanding, his knowledge was not very perfect. [. . .] Now in his camp, that is at the royal gate, there were two jackals, who were brothers, and named, the one Kalīlah, and the other Dimnah. They were crafty, and trained too in learning and wisdom."

Greek medicine was introduced into Persia during the time of King Shapur by prisoners of war who were brought from the Eastern Roman Empire; physicians from the Roman Empire played the role of negotiators and intermediaries, like the famous Marutha of Maypher-qat (d. ca. 420). From the time of Khosrow I Anushirvan (r. 531–579), the "philosopher king" who was interested in the theoretical knowledge and techniques of the Roman Empire, both Greek and West and East Syriac physicians became influential. It was during this time that an eastern physician, Burzoe or Burzoy, translated the Indian *Pananchan-tra*, known as *Kalila wa Dimnah* or *The Fables of Bidpai*, from Sanskrit into Pahlavi, and copied several Indian books, demonstrating the connections with India during that period. A man named Bud, a *periodeutes* or traveling priest, later translated it into Syriac. The phenomenon went on at the courts of the caliphs and Mongols, where further translations from the original Indian and Iranian languages were made.

THE MASSORAH

As Syriac slowly ceased to be a widely spoken language, compilations of material, both West and East Syrian, were made in the 8th and 9th centuries in order to provide philological and grammatical metrics to standardize Syriac pronunciation and orthography, using biblical and patristic texts and relying on the heritage of works by Jacob of Edessa. This work was called the Massorah, from the Hebrew word meaning "tradition," and coincided with the period when Jewish scholars fixed the pronunciation and orthography of the Hebrew Bible. By creating lexicographical and orthographical works, the massoretes contributed to consolidating and preserving the classical language with which Syriac became so closely associated.

Questions of Genre and Culture

The Syriac world had a special place for women, which was especially unusual in antiquity. In ordinary churches, deaconesses were in charge of visiting and caring for sick women, and the wives of priests played an important role for women in the community, receiving a special ordination to do so. In the 4th century, the bishop Rabbula founded a special hospital for women in Edessa. The Daughters of the Covenant, by virtue of their role in the church and the duties of their office, received a basic education of the same quality as the boys who were educated in the schools attached to churches.

ODES OF SOLOMON 19, "CUP"

A cup of milk was brought to me,
And I drank it, in the sweetness of the Lord's kindness

The Son is the cup;
And the Father is He who was milked;
And the Holy Spirit is She who milked Him.

Because His breasts [of the Father] were full,
And it was undesirable that His milk should be ineffectually released,

The Holy Spirit opened Her bosom,
And mixed the milk of the two breasts of the Father.

And She gave the mixture to the generation, without their knowing.
And those who have received are in the perfection of the right hand.

The womb of the Virgin took [it],
And she received conception and gave birth. [. . .]

She brought forth like a strong man with desire,
And she bore according to the manifestation
And acquired with great power.
And she loved with redemption,
And guarded with kindness,
And declared with grandeur.

Syriac theology underscores the importance of women with imagery linking the feminine to God. As in old Greek and Latin literature, God is portrayed as breastfeeding the faithful; the *Odes of Solomon*
shows, in images that seem strange after centuries of masculine interpretation of the sacred texts, Christ drawing milk from the breasts of the
Father in order to nurse his flock. Because "Spirit" is a feminine word
in Syriac, as it is in Hebrew and all Semitic languages, the Holy Spirit
is associated with feminine activities. Syriac authors also gave a voice to
female characters that otherwise remain silent in the Bible. For example,
the subjects of various poems include Sarah, Tamar, the Sinful Woman
opposing Satan, and the Virgin rocking the infant Jesus or arguing with
Joseph about the conception of Jesus, reimagining these women as pro-
tagonists and fully developed persons.

Some Pearls of the Crown of Letters

It is impossible to do justice in such a brief space to the richness of
Syriac literature, but here we will throw light on some of these "pearls."
Syriac literature flourished in a range of multireligious and multilingual
contexts and struggled under the sway of hostile political powers. It was

frequently inspired by the border conflicts and the frequency of war or siege, recurring in Syriac texts from Aphrahat and Ephrem in the 4th century to the Neo-Aramaic poems of the 17th century.

Pearls constituted a central symbol in Syriac theological poetry. The role of merchants on the routes from Ethiopia and Arabia to the Caucasus on the one hand, and from the Mediterranean to the Far East on the other hand, explain the importance of the pearl in Syriac literature. A jewel for kings and the stuff of dreams, unparalleled in their brightness, perfection, and mysterious origin, the pearls from the Arab-Persian Gulf also became a Christian symbol.

Pearls were thought to be produced when lightning struck the oyster in the sea, and thus symbolized Christ, the perfect pearl, the fire in the womb of the Virgin Mary. The pearl also represented beauty and the hidden meanings of Scripture. This symbolic interpretation in theological expression is characteristic of the entire Syriac tradition.

Theological discussions during councils and controversies both internal and external to Christianity also played a driving role in this literature. Poems were written not only for the beauty of the liturgy but as catechetical means and as defenses of orthodoxy, such as the *madrashe* of Ephrem during the 4th century, which were directed against Manichaeans or against groups of heretical Christians, such as the Bardaisanites. The *memre* of Narsai (Church of the East) and Jacob of Serugh (Syriac Orthodox) in the 5th and 6th centuries were mirror images but produced for rival churches. The liturgical reforms of the Church of the East, its texts and its chants, were intended to reach the faithful through the senses as its competition with the Syriac Orthodox Church and early Islam escalated. Theology was preached, chanted, painted, and prayed by the faithful as well as ecclesiastical elites and was not solely the province of theologians. The councils and religious controversies are rightly understood as periods of dispute and confrontation, but also reflection, dialogue, questioning, and deepening understanding, which spurred the editing of new texts, new translations, and the composition of collections of excerpts from biblical and patristic writers, which functioned as dogmatic or spiritual authorities in a given tradition.

The phenomenon of translation developed in the context of the relationship of Syriac with the dominant culture, Greek and later Arabic, first as appropriation and subsequently also as transformation: the translator transformed the text and was himself transformed by the process as much as what he was translating. Translation should thus be understood as a dynamic process and not as a simple exercise of putting one passage into another language, especially since the translators were themselves the authors and practitioners of the scientific or philosophical texts that they translated. Translation was also an opportunity to reflect on and innovate language, as seen in the writing that developed from this movement (the introduction of Greek vowels in the west, a vowel-point system in the east), as well as in grammar and lexicography.

JACOB OF SERUGH, *ON THE PEARL*

The Books of the Son are like an ocean where the pearl is hidden; the commentator, like a diver, dives there to retrieve it. Intelligence is like a diver diving into the Scriptures to retrieve the pearl and show it to the merchants in order to appraise it. Intelligence dives into the Bible and takes the divine pearl. The tongue presents it to the listeners by speaking; therefore, hang the daughter of light on your ears as an ornament.

EPHREM, *HYMN ON RESURRECTION*

1. Your law has been my vehicle,
Revealing to me something of Paradise

Your Cross has been to me the key,
Which opened up Paradise

From the Garden of Delights did I gather
And carry back with me from Paradise

Roses and other eloquent blooms
Which are there scattered about for Your feast

Amid songs [as they flutter down] on Humanity
Blessed is He who both gave and received the crown! [. . .]

6. Who has ever beheld blossoms
Gathered from the Scriptures, as though it were from the hills?

With them have chaste women
Filled the spacious bosom of the mind

The sound of songs, like a servant, has scattered
Blossoms all over the crowds:

These flowers are sacred, catch them with your senses,

Just as our Lord [caught] Mary's unguent.
Blessed is he who is garlanded with his handmaids!

EPHREM, *MADRASHA* ON MARY AND EVE

Illuminate with Your teaching the voice of the speaker
And the ear of the hearer; like the pupils of the eye
Let the ears be illuminated, for the voice provides the rays of light

---

THE BIBLE

The Syriac tradition is central to the study of the Bible, because it preserves several ancient versions of the books of the Bible that Christians call the Old and New Testaments. Several translations were made in response to philological and exegetical needs as well as dialogue "with the Greeks." Apart from the Greek translation of the Old Testament known as the Septuagint, Syriac offers the only ancient translation of the Old Testament made directly from Hebrew before the Masoretic texts (that is, before the fixation of the *massorah* or the canonical Hebrew reading established in the 8th century). This version, the Peshitta or "simple" version, was most likely made by Jews or converted Jews in northern Mesopotamia around AD 150 and is of great interest for ancient Jewish and Christian exegetical practices.

Other translations, this time made from the Septuagint rather than directly from Hebrew, were made for exegetical and polemical purposes: at the beginning of the 6th century, a partial translation

(Genesis, Exodus, and parts of Isaiah at least) was commissioned for the bishop Polycarp by Philoxenus, bishop of Mabbug/Hierapolis. This translation, known as the Philoxenian version, produced in 507/508, was used for the purposes of revision and disappeared thereafter. The version that replaced it, the Syro-Hexapla, was produced by Paul, bishop of Tella, and made at the Enaton, near Alexandria, around 616/617 (the period when the Sasanian Empire occupied nearly all of the Near East). This highly literal version is important because it relies on a lost version of the Greek text based on the fifth (that of the Septuagint) of the six columns of the *Hexaples* (the four Greek translations of the Jewish Bible listed parallel to the Hebrew, in Hebrew characters and Greek transliteration by Origen). The edition marks adjustments and changes to the text in the margins and makes references to the Greek translations by Aquila, Symmachus, and Theodotion (the other columns of the *Hexaples*). In the 7th century, Jacob of Edessa revised certain translations of the Old Testament as well. Although these versions played an important role in the exegetical and theological reflection of the Syriac Orthodox Church, it is the Peshiṭta that remained the version used for liturgy everywhere.

The oldest Syriac version of the New Testament (though whether it was composed in Greek and then translated into Syriac or actually composed in Syriac is still debated) is the *Diatessaron,* or *Harmony of the Four Gospels,* composed by Tatian (ca. 170), a Mesopotamian writer who traveled to Rome along with Justin Martyr. Condemned by Rabbula, the bishop of Edessa (r. 411–435), this version disappeared and is attested only indirectly by the writings of the Syriac fathers. Instead, an "Old Syriac" version of separate Gospels was produced circa 200 and attested in a number of manuscripts. A new translation, which made use of these earlier versions, was produced at the end of the 4th century and the beginning of the 5th: the Peshiṭta of the New Testament, promoted by Bishop Rabbula of Edessa to replace the *Diatessaron.* The revised version commissioned by Philoxenus of Mabbug in 507/508, mentioned above, was meant to render Greek theological phrases more precisely into Syriac. This version disappeared in favor of a subsequent edition, known as the Ḥarqlean version, because it was made by Thomas, the Syriac Orthodox bishop of Ḥarqel (Heraclium), around 615/616 at the

Rabbula Gospels, the Ascension (6th century).
Courtesy of Wikimedia Commons.

monastery of the Enaton, near Alexandria. It shares several characteristics with the Syro-Hexapla, which was produced at the same time and at the same place, particularly a very literal rendering of the Greek, translated word for word with all its morphological specificities.

The Bible also made space for parabiblical literature, often called "apocryphal." Besides narratives of the acts of various apostles, which were already mentioned (see chapter 2), there were retellings of the biblical history between Adam and Christ, known as the *Cave of Treasures.*

EXEGETICAL COMMENTARIES

Biblical commentaries occupy a special place in Syriac, as in other Christian traditions. The exegetical tradition of Antioch, which insists on a literal interpretation of Scripture, aimed to illuminate the meaning of the biblical text with a set of tools provided by the scholastic tradition developed in schools by philologists and grammarians. Physical or spiritual, this exegesis relies on a typological interpretation and commentary on the mystery and symbols hidden in the Old Testament but revealed in the New.

CAVE OF TREASURES

Because Adam was priest, king and prophet, God brought him into Paradise in order to minister in Eden like a priest of the holy Church as testifies the blessed Moses concerning him: "that he may tend it," that is, for God through priestly ministry in glory, "and keep it," that is, the commandment which had been entrusted to him by God's mercy. Then God planted this tree of life in the middle of paradise. It is a true word heralding our salvation that this tree of life in the middle of paradise signifies our savior's cross, and this is the one which has been fastened in the middle of the earth.

JACOB OF SERUGH, ON BIBLICAL EXEGESIS

Moses, if your text is not commented upon, it creates doubt in the soul of the reader. If we are not capable of commenting, it

seems contradictory . . . If the exegesis does not raise the veil of
your subject, your word remains hidden under allegories without
being able to be seen. If the examinations do not dive into the sea
of your story, we cannot retrieve the pearl of your Book. Your word
is imprisoned if the commentator is not able to free it; how could
it come out? A page of your Book lies exposed in front of me, I tire
myself out in order to be able to comment on your text and show
its beauty. I ask of your Book to show me its true word: Moses,
your Book will not leave my hands until it reveals its secrets to
its listeners.

LITURGY

Syriac liturgy is characterized by its great variety, centered on two
branches: East Syrian, practiced today by the Assyrian Church of the
East, the Ancient Church of the East, and the Chaldean Catholic Church;
and the three West Syrian varieties—the Syriac Orthodox Church,
the Maronite Church, and, originally, the *Rum* (Byzantine) Orthodox
Church of the Patriarchate of Antioch, which abandoned Syriac (used
concurrently with Greek and especially Arabic as its liturgical language)
only in the 17th century. To varying extents, Latinization was imposed
on churches that joined with Rome.

The variety in each liturgical tradition can be explained by the fact
that manuscripts (or photocopies of manuscripts) are still used today
for the major liturgical books that contain the chants of the entire yearly
cycle, with each manuscript being unique. Special books containing
choral hymns, crossing different poetic-liturgical genres, are of an as-
tonishing richness.

Syriac preserves the most ancient Christian anaphora (eucharistic prayer), called the Anaphora of Addai and Mari. More than sixty
anaphoras are known from the manuscripts.

HAGIOGRAPHY

Biographical writing, inherited from Greek antiquity, is one of the characteristics of Christian literature which comprises a memory that is at

once both local and universal. It is no different in Syriac, where a very rich literature of *Acts* and *Lives*, in prose and verse, retold the stories of lives real and imagined, translated from Greek, written in Syriac and translated into Middle Persian, Arabic, or Sogdian, and transcending both ecclesiastical and linguistic borders.

The *Acts* that celebrate Christian martyrs represent the most fundamental level of ecclesiastical memory. The *Acts* of "Western" martyrs, particularly those from Edessa during the time of the Roman persecutions, were written in Syriac. The story of the Martyrs of Najran in southern Arabia in the 6th century, who were oppressed by a Jewish king who took power in Yemen, opens a window into Syriac Christianity in Arabia. The numerous *Acts* of Christians who were martyred during the Sasanian period, between the 3rd and the 7th century, are an irreplaceable source for Sasanian history and culture as well as the history of Christianity in Persia. The *Lives* of ascetic heroes (such as Simeon Stylites the Elder and Julien Saba, the man of God from Edessa), of female saints (such as Febronia and Euphemia), the founders of monasteries (Gabriel of Qarṭmin; Awgen, a legendary figure in Mesopotamian monasticism, and his seventy-two disciples; Abraham of Kashkar, the reformer of Persian monasticism), of authors and theologians, both positive (Ephrem, Nestorius in the East Syrian tradition, Severus of Antioch, Bar Hebraeus) and negative (Nestorius in the West Syrian tradition, Maximus the Confessor in Greek Orthodoxy), contribute to the retelling of the history of the churches.

HISTORY

Many ecclesiastical histories and chronicles were written in Syriac to tell both secular and church history. Retelling the history of the world since creation in universal chronicles, the West Syrian tradition (both Chalcedonian and Miaphysite) reprised the chronicle and ecclesiastical history models of Eusebius of Caesarea, Socrates, Sozomen, and Theodoret. Beginning with the history (no longer extant) of Dionysius of Tel Maḥre (d. 845), the secular history of the empire and the religious history of the Miaphysites were presented in separate columns or separate works so as to do justice to the history of Syriac Christians, who did not have a state of their own. Similar works were composed: the great Chronicle of 1234, the history of the patriarch Michael the Syrian (the Great) in the 13th century, and the Syriac and Arabic chronicles of Bar Hebraeus (Bar ʿEbroyo). On the East Syrian side, the ecclesiastical history model was the basis for the historiographical tradition. The history of Christianity in Persia and Central Asia, beyond the frontiers of the Roman Empire, is told through the stories of schools and monasteries—the *Ecclesiastical History* of Barḥadbshabba of Beth ʿArbaye in the 6th century; the history of the School of Nisibis, also in the 6th century; *The History of the Founders of Schools and Monasteries* by Ishoʿdnaḥ of Basra around 850; and *The Book of Governors* by Thomas of Marga, around 850—before they were followed by the advent of Syro-Arabic histories such as the Chronicle of Seert.

PHILOSOPHY

The first commentaries and translations of philosophical works from Greek into Syriac were made in the 6th century. Sergios of Reshʿaina (d. 536, Syriac Orthodox) is one of the major figures for the study of philosophy and medicine in Syriac. He studied in Alexandria and became the *archiatros*, or the chief physician, of Reshʿaina. He traveled to Rome as an envoy to Pope Agapetus and died on the return journey in Constantinople. He translated the medical works of Galen, astronomical texts, the theological body of works of Dionysius the Areopagite, and philosophical treaties (including a pseudo-Aristotelian treatise on the universe). He wrote treatises on the spiritual life, on the *Categories* of Aristotle, and on the purpose of Aristotelian works. Another major figure, Paul the Persian (ca. 6th century, East Syrian) dedicated a treatise on logic based on Aristotelian logic to Khosrow Anushirvan. It was originally written in Middle Persian and translated by the great scholar of the monastery of Qenneshre in the Byzantine Empire, Severus Sebokht (d. 666/667), which shows the circulation of knowledge beyond political and linguistic borders. He also commented on the *Interpretation* of Aristotle, and his works were known to the philosophers al-Farabi (toward the end of the 10th century) and Miskawayh (early 11th century). In the 7th century, the activity of translation and commentary was centered around Qenneshre.

SERGIUS OF RESH ʿAINA

Without [the books of logic], the meaning of the books of medicine is incomprehensible. [. . .] There is essentially no way or path to any of the sciences, in the capabilities of man, except by dint of learning logic.

THE SCIENCES

Science did not have the same connotations in the premodern period as it does today and did not follow the same definitions. Scholars were also theologians and men of letters, and the division between science and humanities did not exist. Scholars were also frequently practitioners, doctors, and astronomers themselves, as well as translators of texts on those topics. Like its counterpart in Greek, the *Hexamaeron,* Jacob of Edessa's commentary on the six days of creation in Genesis was an opportunity to explore contemporary knowledge on physics, geography, astronomy, and natural sciences. In dialogue with the Indian and Iranian world, eastern cosmography, astronomy, astrology, mathematics, and medicine were combined with knowledge drawn from Greek and biblical material, the Bible being read as both a book of history and a book of science.

Severus Sebokht, who wrote a mathematical treatise on the astrolabe, is the first to mention Indian numbers from his monastery of Qenneshre. Theophilus of Edessa, an astrologer at the court of the caliph al-Mahdi at the beginning of the 8th century, was also a historian and a translator from Greek into Syriac. The family of Bokhtishoʿ was known for its doctors for seven generations, first in the court of the Sasanian kings and later the Arab caliphs; in 9th-century Baghdad, medicine was primarily in the hands of East Syrian Christians. The most famous of these ʿAbbasid-era physicians was Ḥunayn b. Isḥāq (ca. 808–873), an Arab Christian of al-Ḥīra/Ḥirta south of Baghdad and a member of the Church of the East. Ḥunayn is especially well known for his works of translation from Greek into Syriac, from Greek into Arabic, and from Syriac into Arabic of medical as well as philosophical, mathematical, and astrological texts. Bar Hebraeus/Bar ʿEbroyo, himself a doctor and

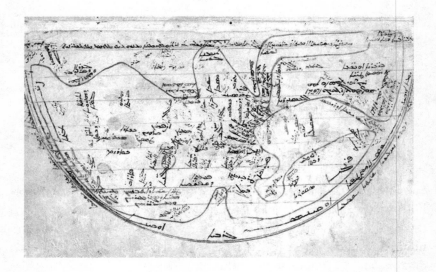

Map of the world (15th century), represented in seven climates
with the names of the seas (Pontic Sea, Adriatic Sea, Red Sea, etc.),
key regions (Scythia, France, Arab Andalusia, the Maghreb, Egypt,
India, etc.), cities (Constantinople, Rome, Antalya, Tarsus, Tripolia,
Caesarea, Alexandria, etc.), and islands.

a *maphrian* (the second-highest rank in the Syriac Orthodox Church
after the patriarch), integrated Arab, Persian, and Mongol science, as
practiced by Jews, Christians, Muslims, and "Sabeans," into his writings.

LAW

Not having a state of their own, Syriac Christians were subject to the law
of Roman and Sasanian societies and later the Arab caliphates. Canon
law, governing the churches, gives a glimpse of religious and magical
practices, weddings, and inheritance. In the Sasanian Empire, the fact
that Simeon of Rev Ardashir composed his lawbook in the 6th century
in Middle Persian and only later translated it into Syriac demonstrates
how rooted Syriac-speaking communities were in their vernacular contexts, both academic and official. The collections of conciliar decrees
(such as the *Synodicon Orientale* of the Church of the East), correspon-
dences where such discussions were also held, and the chronologies of

sacred history that are associated with them are the major sources for the history of the churches and their communities.

Magical practices (amulets, bowls, charms) are part of a religious and medical anthropology in which the use of relic dust, incubation practices, prayers, and exorcisms in the same way as remedies constitutes the counterpart of the written knowledge transmitted in the texts.

ARTS AND LETTERS

The Church of the East was for a long time considered aniconic, which is to say opposed to the use of images in worship. In reality, this was not the case: the Syriac tradition distinguished itself from Greek Christianity by placing very little importance on the cult of icons, but this is different from refusing to use images altogether. It is characteristic, however, that there are no "Syriac" images of the "Image" par excellence, the *mandylion* or icon of Christ, such as one finds in the Greek or Armenian traditions. The originality of the Syriac tradition is shown by the fact that the images are found first in texts, especially in theological poetry and liturgy, which influenced artists in their iconographic choices.

The pages of manuscripts, like the walls of churches, bear witness to a Christian art with its own peculiarities, but somewhat similar to those of other traditions, both Christian and non-Christian: the art of the late antique period found in manuscripts of the 6th century, the Islamic art of the 12th and 13th centuries, and Greek and Latin art. From the 6th century onward and after the condemnation of the Syriac churches as heretical, however, the imperial court and great nobles no longer sponsored Syriac artists. Noble families and high ecclesiastical dignitaries were the only financial sponsors in the Syriac world.

The image of the cross is omnipresent in Syriac, far more so than in Greek manuscripts, and innumerable examples of a decorated cross on a pedestal adorn manuscripts and textiles. The decorated cross includes the triumphal cross and never the crucifix with the crucified one, as in the Latin church. Covers and decorated headpieces in frontispieces, signatures in lavish codices, and tables of readings or columns of decorated Gospel canons are frequent. Representations of the patriarchs of the Old Testament, the twelve prophets, the evangelists, and especially episodes of the New Testament bear witness to different artistic styles between the 6th and the 20th century (with the introduction of blue as the dominant color in the 20th century, for instance, although red had prevailed to that point), along with the persistence of different motifs.

From the *Odes of Solomon* in the 2nd century to the late flourishing of eastern liturgical poetry in the 13th, Syriac poetry continued to evolve. If the structure of Mesopotamian debate literature remained, with titles like *The Wheat and the Gold* and *The Complaint of the Months*, others like *The Cup, the Pitcher, and the Jug* by the East Syrian poet Khamis bar Qardaḥe (fl. end of the 13th century) show new themes, inspired by Arab-Persian poetry, about the pleasures of wine, love, and bygone time. Starting in the 14th century, Neo-Aramaic texts began to replace Syriac, but *kthobonoyo*, or Classical Syriac (literally "book Syriac"), continues to dominate the ecclesiastical and literary realm, with translations of *Le Petit Prince* by Antoine Saint-Exupery or *Paul et Virginie* by Bernardin de Saint-Pierre, for example.

F • I • V • E

Missionary Communities
Syriac Christianity in Asia

S yriac churches, especially the Church of the East, were strongly evangelistic and carried the gospel beyond the Mediterranean world in an expansion unparalleled in either antiquity or the Middle Ages. This effort is all the more remarkable as these churches were not supported by a state that could sponsor or sustain their mission. Syriac missionaries did not arrive as part of an army or invading power, but rather in merchant caravans and among refugees.

The Syriac churches were thus in contact with all kinds of peoples, languages, and cultures. Bound together by the same religion, Syriac churches included not only those who spoke various vernacular forms of Aramaic but also those who spoke Persian, Arabic, Sogdian, Uighur, Turkic, and myriad languages from Central Asia, China, and India. As a result, Syriac could not be identified with a single people, ethnicity, or state, as was the case with Copts and Armenians. Instead, Syriac culture was truly international.

Bordered to the west by the Greek Christian world and to the north by the Armenians, the Syriac missions mainly focused on the south and the east.

Toward Armenia

The expansion of Christianity toward the north resulted in Syriac influence on southern Armenia, which was evangelized by Syriac ascetics
and holy men. The first missionary efforts are attributed to the apostle
Addai, known by the name T'addeos in Armenia, who was martyred
by the Armenian king Sanatruq. In the Armenian version, he was not
directly associated with Edessa, but according to the *Buzandaran,* a
5th-century Armenian history, Edessa was considered to have been
founded by Armenian kings, and Abgar himself to be Armenian. The
bishop Jacob of Nisibis, known as "the Persian Sage" in the Armenian
tradition, would go in search of Noah's ark on Mount Ararat and would
be associated with the son of Gregory the Illuminator, the missionary
who converted Armenia. Just as Greek influence predominated in the
west of Armenia, Syriac was dominant in the south. It would be a Syriac
bishop who would make the first attempt at creating Armenian letters,
although it would be an Armenian, Mesrop Mashtots, who would in-
vent both the Armenian and Georgian alphabets. Mashtots would send
his disciples to the Greek world and to Edessa to make translations of
indispensable ecclesiastical works. Several important translations from
Syriac into Armenian were made in the 5th century, including Greek
works like the *Ecclesiastical History* of Eusebius of Caesarea and the
Hexaemeron of Basil, which were translated partially from Greek and
largely from Syriac. Additionally, a substantial amount of ecclesiastical
vocabulary in Armenian was borrowed directly from Syriac. A School
of the Armenians is mentioned in Edessa alongside the famous School
of the Persians, and the controversial Miaphysite movement of Julian of
Halicarnassus was very active in Armenia, creating multiple early links
to West Syrian culture.

   Armenians were present in Amida and in Edessa from at least the
5th century, but it was in the medieval period when their presence grew.
The taking of Edessa from the Seljuks by King T'oros of Armenia in
1095 marked the beginning of a strong Armenian community in the city.
The chronicle of Michael the Syrian was translated into Armenian, and
the chronicler Matthew of Edessa (d. 1144) wrote a local chronicle in
Armenian during the time of the Crusades. In fact, the communities of

Amida, Melitene, and Edessa became more Armenian than Syriac from the Middle Ages onward.

Toward the South

ARABIA FELIX

Around 524, a Jewish king from Ḥimyar in southeast Arabia (Yemen and southeastern Saudi Arabia) massacred the Ethiopian garrison that was occupying the country in the name of the king of Axum and demanded that all the Christians in his kingdom convert to Judaism. He besieged and captured a great city in the north, Najran, and slaughtered the priests, the consecrated religious ("Sons and Daughters of the Covenant"), and prominent members of the Christian community who refused to convert to Judaism. This episode was very quickly recorded as a martyrdom and had an enormous impact in the eastern Christian world. Carried in a letter by the Miaphysite bishop Simeon of Beth Arsham (see chapter 6) on his way to monasteries in northern Syria, it became the subject of hagiographies in Syriac and then in Greek, Arabic, Ethiopic, and Armenian.

The hagiography situates the conflict in Arabia Felix (Fortunate Arabia) in the context of the geopolitical rivalry between the Persian and Roman Empires, as well as the southern Arabian kingdoms and Ethiopia, for the economic and religious control of the peninsula and the commerce on the Red Sea. This episode is also of interest to modern scholars because it attests the existence of Christianity in southern Arabia, which has otherwise left very few traces, with the exception of column capitals adorned with crosses from the cathedral of Sanaʿa (modern-day Yemen), which were reused for the construction of the great mosque. Arabic inscriptions in Arabic writing have very recently been found in the south of Saudi Arabia, of which the earliest, dating to 470, also bears witness to the presence of Christianity. New texts and inscriptions also contribute to a clearer picture of Judaism in the region.

These texts show two routes by which Christianity came to the region. The first is in the province of al-Ḥīra, in the south of Mesopotamia, where Christianity had been solidly established by the Church of

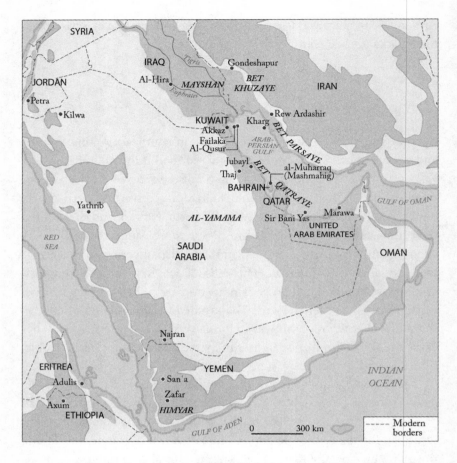

Areas of Syriac Influence in the South: Arabia, the Arab-Persian Gulf,
Ethiopia (5th–8th centuries)

Persia, which controlled the trans-Arabian commerce that crossed
from Mesopotamia to Arabia Felix: Christianity would have most likely
come to Najran by a merchant returning from al-Ḥīra. This tradition
connects part of the Christian community of Najran to the Church
of the East and the patriarchate of Seleucia-Ctesiphon. The texts also
indicate direct links to northern Syria. In one of the early episodes of
the persecution, the persecuting king killed a leading priest who had
been trained in the monastic life in Tella, to the east of Edessa. He also
dug up the remains of the first bishop of the city, who had been conse-

crated and sent by Philoxenus of Mabbug (see chapter 6). This suggests a community that adhered to a Miaphysite, non-Chalcedonian faith, of which Philoxenus was a champion, and a link between Arabia and Mabbug, Edessa, and Callinicum, all of which were leading centers of Miaphysitism. Other documents show that Arabia sometimes served as a refuge for persecuted Miaphysites, especially partisans of the most extreme sects, known as Julianists or "Phantasiasts" (see chapter 6). Their way of understanding the question of the divinity and humanity of Jesus at the moment of his crucifixion potentially had an influence on how the subject appears in the Qur'an, which suggests that Jesus only appeared to be crucified. Thus, in the 5th century, the two principal Syriac churches each had a foothold in southern Arabia, which was one of the few places where they lived in harmony.

LETTER OF SIMEON OF BETH ARSHAM
ON THE MARTYRS OF NAJRÂN

And when they had done this to them and had made sure that all their leaders had been bound, they immediately sent [to Najrân] the Jews and the pagans who [thus] captured the Christians of the city [and asked them] to show them the bones of the martyrs. And they gathered together all the bones of the martyrs and those of Mâr Paulos, the bishop, who had been consecrated the first bishop of Najrân by the holy mar Aksenâya, who is called Philoxenos— the bishop of Mabbug; for this Paulos had won the crown of martyrdom by stoning—as had Stephanos, the first martyr—at the hands of Jews from Tiberias, in the city of [Zafâr], the Royal City [of the Himyarites]. But now they burnt also his bones with fire together with Paulos, [the other] bishop, who was consecrated the second (bishop) of the city of Najrân by the very same Aksenâyâ, the bishop of Mabbug.

And the Jews thus brought all their [bones] together into the church and heaped them in the center of the church; and they brought in the presbyters, the deacons, the subdeacons, the readers, the sons of the covenant and the daughters of the covenant, and the laity, both men and women, some of whose names we intend to write at the end of our letter; and they filled the whole church from one side to the other, [with the Christians] all of whom came to about two thousand, as those who came from Najrân have said. And they brought wood and surrounded the church from the outside and threw fire into it and burnt it together with all that was found in it.

ETHIOPIA

The ties between the Syriac world and the Ethiopic church are complex and murky. Ethiopic traditions indicate two layers of evangelization, the first bringing two young boys, Frumentius and Edesius, originally from Tyr, who were the first to bring the good news to the country in the 4th century. A century later, nine (the number varies, but nine became the one accepted by tradition) "holy Syrians" arrived as part of a mission. If the first story is true, it is difficult to say what the reality underlying the second story might be. However, the link between Roman or Byzantine Syria does not necessarily imply a Syriac influence. In fact, the Ethiopian Church was placed under the authority of the patriarchate of Alexandria, to which it remained attached until 1959. Hence, it was primarily Greek, Coptic, and Copto-Arabic literature that influenced Ge'ez.

But there are traces of early contacts and remnants of influence of Syriac culture on Ethiopic Christianity. The first Ge'ez Bible was translated from Greek but bears the marks of Syriac influences, as does the architecture of the first church at Adoulis or Axum. Texts from Ephrem and Jacob of Serugh and liturgical prayers were translated into Ge'ez and introduced into the liturgy. The ancient name of Lalibela, Roha, is also related to the Syriac name for Edessa, Urhay, sharing the same root consonants.

The Sea Route

BETH QAṬRAYE

To the southwest, the Church of Persia spread throughout the Persian Gulf and along its shores. This maritime route to the Orient, a place of trade for millennia, had gained importance during the Hellenistic period and even more during the Roman. This arrangement made a

Cross from Kharg, Iran. Musée du Louvre, Paris, France.
© RMN-Grand Palais / Art Resource, NY.

fortune for Palmyra, which controlled the transfer by caravan between
the Mediterranean Sea and the Euphrates, where merchants would re-
sume their journey to India by ship via the Gulf. The presence of Christian merchants in this trade that flourished between the Persian Gulf
and the Indian Ocean is possible as early as the 1st century, as told in the
legend of the apostle Thomas, though only in the 5th century do definite
traces of verifiable Christian communities in India appear.

On the east coast of the Gulf, under Persian rule, in the provinces
of Mesene (Mayshan in Syriac), at the mouth of the Tigris and the Euphrates, Susiana (Beth Khuzaye), and Fars or Perside (Beth Parsaye), the
communities that would have been evangelized by Mari existed from a
very early date.

Christian communities would develop on the western shore of the Gulf as well, in the region called Beth Qaṭraye in Syriac. This area covered much more territory than the modern country of Qatar, which has inherited its name, and applied to virtually the entire western side of the Arabian Peninsula and the islands that neighbored it.

Our knowledge of the Christian communities in these regions is based on two kinds of documents: Syriac literature on the one hand, which includes the canons of various councils of the Church of the East mentioning which bishops were present and their dioceses as well as the seats elevated to the metropolitanate, local monastic chronicles, and the letters of the catholicos Ishoʿyahb, who had to resolve a crisis that emerged in the 6th century when the local hierarchy of the Gulf wanted to free itself from his leadership; and archaeology on the other hand, which has revealed religious buildings, churches, and monasteries.

THE LIFE OF MAR YONAN, 7TH OR 8TH CENTURY

Something came out of the sea that resembled a large house, but it was a crab. It seized us in the hands and raised the two of us upon it. Then it entered the sea and brought us to a certain island where Aba Philon met us . . . [Rabban Philon] sat with us upon the crab until it brought us to his cave . . . The crab stood in its place without moving until Rabban Philon commanded it, "Go to your feeding ground." [. . .]

Our monastery has had much assistance from him. For because of him Nuʿaym the believer gave us a ship and purchased it, and we sold it for one thousand and three hundred dinars. And with these we purchased land and date palms for the monastery. We also provided for the restoration of our church with the rest of them.

The above-mentioned acts of the synod, which was held at Seleucia-Ctesiphon in 410, are signed by a list of nearly forty bishops, of whom the last is a man named Elias, the bishop of Mashmahig, a locale identified as the modern-day al-Muharraq, an island in the Bahrain archipelago. The signatory bishop replaced a prior bishop who had been deposed during the same synod, which shows that the bishopric's existence predated the synod and that the community was structured enough to have a bishop from at least the end of the 4th century. There is also the question of other island bishops, most likely from the same region, who were absent but who should have countersigned the acts. Five episcopal seats are known from Beth Qaṭraye and the region of Oman. The dioceses of the Gulf depended, as in India, on the metropolitan of Beth Parsaye/Fars, whose seat was at Rev Ardashir and which was created between 415 and 420.

The last substantial mentions of the communities of Beth Qaṭraye in written sources appear in the 7th century, but it is unknown when or how they disappeared. However, their disappearance in literary sources is probably not due to the prohibition of non-Muslims on the Arabian peninsula by Muhammad or ʿUmar as stated in the Islamic tradition, since a bishopric is mentioned at Sanaʿa in the 9th century and Christians appear to have been present at Soqotra in the 13th century.

In fact, the period when Islam appeared was counterintuitively a time of flourishing for the Christian communities of Beth Qaṭraye: in the first half of the 7th century, Rabban Bar Sahde, originally a merchant from Beth Qaṭraye who traded with India, founded a monastery near al-Ḥīra. And monastic writers from Beth Qaṭraye, most notably Isaac of Nineveh, left their mark on Syriac literature and thought (see chapter 3).

Archaeological traces recovered from this Christian presence in the Gulf have multiplied over the past half century. Near the eastern shore, the island site of Kharg (Iran) was excavated in the years 1959–1960 to prepare for the installation of an oil terminal. It was a stopping point for merchant ships on their way to India, most likely in the early centuries of the Common Era, and the remnants of an East Syrian monastery were uncovered.

It is on the western shore of the Persian Gulf that the discoveries have been the most numerous, however; in Kuwait, on the island of Failaka, the site of al-Qusur yielded the remnants of two churches, one of which was huge, with a narthex and three naves, of which the middle circled a choir section and the two lateral ones had small sections in the form of a cross. A liturgical space on the outside of the church and along the side of the wall could be a *beth ṣlota*, or "house of prayer," allowing certain liturgies to take place outside the church during the hot season. The interpretation of the site as a monastery seems self-evident. In Kuwait, an ancient islet now connected to the mainland, Akkaz, also hosts the remnants of a church. Other traces of a Christian community have also been uncovered at Jubayl and Thaj, eighty kilometers to the south, both on the coast of Saudi Arabia. The remains of a monastery surrounding a church were excavated on the islet of Sir Bani Yas and at Marawa in the emirate of Abu Dhabi. At al-Qusur as well as Akkaz and Sir Bani Yas, stucco panels adorned with crosses in a typically East Syrian style, set in a frame, show the artistic unity that Gulf Christianity had with its mother church. But it is clear that Christianity did not penetrate the interior of the Arabian peninsula by that route, which is mostly desert in that area. All the sites are on the islands or directly on the coast. The exception is the site of Kilwa in the north of Saudi Arabia, where a church and its monastic cells have been uncovered, a site probably linked with a trade route from modern-day Jordan.

The dating of these archaeological sites, on the basis of ceramic dating, recently raised the question of whether they were founded after the 7th century. But the new dating does not have unanimous support. The contradiction remains in any case that the communities are attested in written texts from the 4th century to the 7th, and that the material remains begin just as the communities disappear from literary sources.

SOUTH INDIA

Missionaries of the Church of the East reached South India by the Persian Gulf, where they founded communities that still flourish today. When and where those missionaries arrived is unclear, however. The local tradition revolves around the evangelization by the apostle Thomas. He disembarked at Cranganore, north of Cochin, and founded seven churches in Kerala, where Christians today still take pride in their prestigious origins. Passing through Ceylon, Thomas then journeyed to southeastern India, where he underwent martyrdom at Mylapore (Mailapuram), near Madras, where his remains are still venerated. However, the *Acts of Thomas* (see chapter 2), a third-century legend account of Thomas's voyage to India, mentions nothing of this: the only historical element that it contains is the name of the king Gondophares,

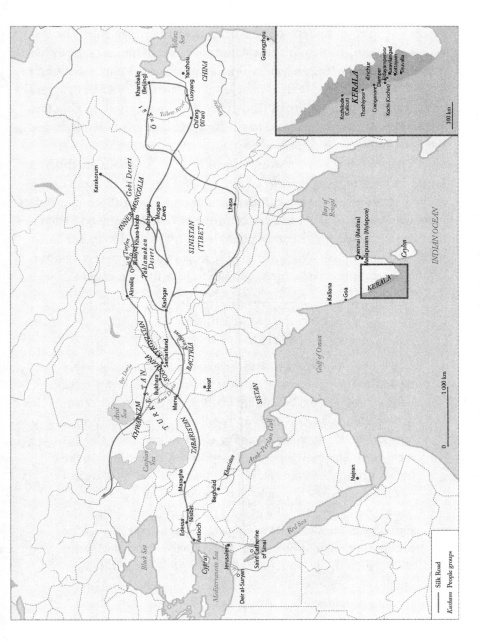

The Greatest Extent of Syriac Influence

which is similar to the king Gudnaphar, a ruler whose appearance is known from coins minted in the 1st century AD and whose place of origin was west of modern-day Pakistan, under Parthian rule. The text does not establish a firm historical link to South India. Local tradition goes on to mention the arrival, in 345, of a man named Thomas of Cana who came from Edessa with a small group of Jewish-Christian believers and founded a community of Christians. A community still exists that claims descent from them and has carved out their own church in the religious landscape of Kerala.

The first verifiably historical mention of Christians in India is found in *Christian Topography* by the traveler Cosmas Indicopleustes, at the beginning of the 6th century, which mentions a diocese in Kalliana whose bishop was consecrated in Persia. The location of Kalliana has been discussed as either being Quilon, north of Cochin in Kerala, or just south of Bombay. Wherever the site might have been, this mention implies a community structured enough to have its own bishop.

COSMAS INDICOPLEUSTES,
CHRISTIAN TOPOGRAPHY

Even in Taprobanê [Socotra], an island in Further India, where the Indian sea is, there is a Church of Christians, with clergy and a body of believers, but I know not whether there be any Christians in the parts beyond it. In the country called Malê, where the pepper grows, there is also a church, and at another place called Calliana there is moreover a bishop, who is appointed from Persia. In the island, again, called the Island of Dioscoridês, which is situated in the same Indian sea, and where the inhabitants speak Greek, having been originally colonists sent thither by the Ptolemies who succeeded Alexander the Macedonian, there are clergy who receive their ordination in Persia, and are sent on to the island, and there is also a multitude of Christians. I sailed along the coast of this island, but did not land upon it. I met, however, with some of its Greek-speaking people who had come over into Ethiopia.

Here as well, it is possible that Christians arrived before the 5th century. A port named Muziris is attested as a place of commerce in the Roman world and is present in Peutinger's Atlas (a 13th-century copy of a Roman atlas), but its exact location is not known for sure, even though it is most likely in the region of Cochin. Roman coins and the remains of amphorae have been found in the area. But there is no tradition of a community founded in earlier times.

Certain documents of the Church of the East mention the ecclesiastical community of India, which relied on the metropolitanate of Fars before gaining its own metropolitan in the 7th century. Several centuries later, Marco Polo lingered on the veneration of Indian Christians for the tomb of St. Thomas of Mailapuram on the east coast of India, but only mentions briefly in chapter 24 the Christians who lived in Malabar, who relied on the "Pope" of Baghdad. Almost no known archaeological traces of this medieval church survive, apart from several East Syrian–style crosses with inscriptions in Pahlavi (Middle Persian), which underscore the importance of this language for the Church of the East. However, no really thorough archaeological study has been done, and such a study might show the earlier phases of the churches that tradition says are ancient but whose extant architecture has been thoroughly influenced by Portuguese trends.

No monastery is known to us from India, nor is any Syriac author originally from there. No Syriac manuscript from before the arrival of the Portuguese survives in India itself. Local tradition says that the Portuguese destroyed massive numbers of manuscripts, and the acts of the Synod of Diamper in 1599 (see page 219) ordered the burning of heretical books. But it is not certain that there were many manuscripts to burn in the first place. The surviving manuscripts, which were transported to Rome and are conserved in the Vatican Library, date to the 14th century. These include fragments of the Bible and liturgical texts related to the daily usage of parochial life, not academic or monastic texts. This contributes to an image of a community of living faith, but one only marginally attached to the East Syrian church and quite distant from an East Syrian community in full decline on the eve of the arrival of Vasco da Gama and the Portuguese colonizers.

Cross from a church in Valliapally. Inscription in Pahlavi around
the arch and in Syriac below. Kottayam, Kerala, India.
Photo by Françoise Briquel Chatonnet.

Land Routes

The third pathway by which Christianity expanded into Asia was the
various land routes that for two thousand years had linked the Near East
to China, generally following a path that curved north of the Himalayas
and relied on the oases that dot Central Asia. These routes are often
called the Silk Road, although other kinds of merchandise traveled on
them as well. As in other contexts, the Christian faith and Syriac culture
took commercial routes and hitched rides with merchant caravans. This
vast region was a crossroads of people, languages, and religions, and
Christianity existed side by side with Manichaeism, Buddhism, Sha-
manism, Confucianism, Taoism, and Islam. Christianity was thus dif-

fused along Central Asia all the way to China. It continued there until the end of the Middle Ages, but its history can be split into two periods, that of the Tang dynasty (ca. 618–907) and that of the Yuan, which is to say the Mongol period.

The expansion eastward was primarily the work of the Church of the East, based in the Persian Empire, but not exclusively. The roads to Asia were also traveled by Syriac Orthodox missionaries, Melkites (Chalcedonians—see chapter 6), and even Armenians and Georgians.

CHRISTIANITY ON THE ROADS TO CENTRAL ASIA, FROM MERW TO XI'AN

Among the oldest references to an eastward expansion of Christianity is an allusion to Bactria (part of modern-day Afghanistan) in the early-3rd-century work *The Book of the Laws of Countries* (see chapter 2). A little later, there were conversions among the Hephthalite Huns and Turkic populations. The Church of the East was increasingly organizing itself in Central Asia during the same era that it was consolidating its hold on the Persian Gulf. A bishop of Merw (modern-day Turkmenistan) and another from Herat (in Afghanistan) were present at the Synod of Dadisho in 424. These two bishoprics, especially Merw, fueled the expansion to the East. They would become metropolitanates, along with Samarkand, and a metropolitanate was later created in China. The church thus adapted itself for far-flung missions abroad. Special rules, for example, allowed officials in "exterior" ecclesiastical provinces to ordain bishops without the presence of a patriarch or metropolitan, which was normally required. The sudden emergence of Arab power in this period did not disrupt missionary efforts; on the contrary, the East Syrian catholicos Timothy I (r. 780–823), who was the head of the Church of the East during the first century of ʿAbbasid rule and who moved the see from Seleucia-Ctesiphon to the newly created capital of Baghdad, was particularly active in sending out missionaries. One of his letters mentions the conversion of a Turkish ruler and assigns a metropolitan for that region. He also proposed consecrating a metropolitan for the Tibetans.

The first phase of Christianity in China extends evenly before and after the Arab Conquest. The arrival of Christianity in the heart of the Chinese Empire, under the Tang dynasty, is documented by an exceptional piece of evidence, a stele discovered at Xi'an, at that time the capital of the Tang kingdom. It was uncovered in 1625, and its discovery had a tremendous effect on the European world by showing that Christianity had spread in China almost a thousand years before the arrival of Latin missionaries. The East Syrian dimension was minimized, since at that time Catholics considered the Church of the East to be heretical. Voltaire even suspected that it was a Jesuit fake. Playing off on the discovery of the stele, he wrote a satirical story called "The White Bull," also supposedly translated from Syriac, which showcased anti-religion themes.

LETTER OF PATRIARCH TIMOTHY I (780–822) TO THE MONKS OF MAR MARON

See that in the lands of Babylon, Persia, and Assyria, in all the places of the East, the regions of the Indians and the Chinese, like those of the Tibetans and the Turks and in all the territory which has submitted to the patriarchal throne, where God has ordained us as servants and ministers, this *Trisagion* is recited without the addition of these words, "Who was crucified for us."

See that in our days . . . the king of the Turks with almost all of his people rejected their old errors of irreligion and converted to Christianity, thanks to an act of great power by Christ, to whom everything is subjected. He asks from us a letter to arrange a metropolitan for all of his royal territory; we have accomplished this with the help of God.

During these days, the Spirit consecrated a metropolitan for the Turks; we are preparing another for the Tibetans.

The stele was mounted on a pedestal in the shape of a tortoise, following Chinese traditional construction, and it reached a height of 2.79 meters and bore writing in both Chinese and Syriac. It features a title in Chinese, "Stele for the Diffusion of the Illustrious Teaching

Stele from Xi'an inscribed in Chinese and Syriac.
© RMN-Grand Palais / Art Resource, NY.

[*jingjao* can also be translated as "radiant teaching"] of Da Qin [the Roman or Byzantine Empire] in the Middle Kingdom." Erected and inscribed in 781, its purpose was to explain the Christian faith (the Christian God is called Aluohe, derived from the East Syriac *Alāhā*), and to record the history of Christianity in China since the arrival of the first missionary, Alopen, in 635. The person who built the stele, Yazd-bozed, a priest with a Persian name, had received the title of magistrate of the first rank, with a gold seal and purple robes. His motivation in erecting such a monument was to underscore the official protection that the emperor had granted his community, in order to strengthen the Christian religion in a context where it remained foreign and where it sometimes had difficulties with Buddhism. The inscription affirms the compatibility of Christian doctrine with the Tao.

XI'AN STELE

Stele [commemorating] the diffusion of the "Luminous" Religion in the Middle Kingdom [China]—a eulogy and preface composed by the monk Jingjing of the *Da Qin* [Roman] Monastery.

Thus the constant and true tranquility, preceding all and without beginning, all-knowing; everlasting and mysterious, the impenetrable core of creation, worthy of utmost reverence among the wondrous host of sages. He is three, yet a single wondrous being, the true lord who has no beginning, Āluóhē [i.e., God, Syr. *Alāhā*].

He determined that the Figure of Ten [i.e., the Cross] should be planted throughout the world. He set the first stirrings in motion and produced the two forces. The dark void was changed and heaven and earth came into existence; the sun and moon began to move, making day and night. He created all things, then he established [i.e., created] the First Man, making everything harmonious for him and giving him charge over land and sea. His original nature was one of contentment, his simple heart had no lustful desires.

Other documents discovered since then complete the picture. Most recently, a funerary pillar was uncovered, erected at Luoyang in 814/815 along the models of Buddhist pillars: it was a private monument built by a son for his mother, with an inscription that contains, besides the funerary context, the "Sutra on the origin of the origins of the Illustrious Teaching of Da Qin," a text that had been known only in manuscript form up until that point. Other Chinese Christian texts were preserved which also date to the Tang period. These are not translations of texts known in Syriac but autonomous compositions, often paraphrastic.

The collection of sources seems to indicate that early Christianity in China was essentially supported by the Sogdians, a merchant people whose language belongs to the Iranian family and who lived in Central Asia. They were neither Chinese nor people who came from the Syriac heartland in Mesopotamia. This means that the East Asian mission was carried out by people who had themselves been missionized, and that by the 7th century previous missionary zones had started to send out missionaries of their own. The sources also give us a sense of a structured community: the stele mentions a bishopric at Xi'an and another at Luoyang, and a slightly later source mentions a metropolitan of China. The community had priests, deacons, archdeacons, and several monasteries, concentrated in the two capitals.

This phase of the history of Christianity in China came to an end in 845 with an edict that was aimed particularly at proscribing Buddhism but which forbade all foreign religions in China. In an empire that controlled everything, the Christian community was able to exist thanks only to imperial approval. Once that was withdrawn, it disappeared.

MULTICULTURALISM AND RELIGIOUS ENCOUNTERS
AT THE OASIS: TURFAN AND TIBET

The Middle Ages in Central Asia was a particularly vibrant period for linguistic, religious, and cultural coexistence. During the course of its expansion, the Church of the East was in contact with multiple languages and its adherents represented a plethora of cultures. If the liturgical language was generally Syriac, and although it spread throughout a vast territory, other languages entered Christian liturgical and intellectual use from the period of the very first evangelization. In the 7th or 8th century, Simeon of Rev Ardashir composed a treatise of canon law on family and inheritance practices in Middle Persian, which was then translated into Syriac by a monk of Beth Qaṭraye. Conversely, the translation of Psalms and hagiographical texts from Syriac into Middle Persian took place in the 5th century.

For the study of the Central Asian world, we have a relatively abundant corpus of texts thanks to several spectacular finds. During an exploratory mission in Chinese Turkestan between 1906 and 1908, the French scholar Paul Pelliot acquired thousands of manuscripts that had been hidden in the caves of Mogao in Dunhuang, a city in the east of the desert of Taklamakan. Written in Chinese, Sanskrit, Tibetan, Khotanese, Sogdian, and Uighur, these manuscripts are mainly Buddhist. Some texts, however, written in Chinese, Sogdian, and Syriac, are Christian. Another important source of manuscripts is the oasis at Turfan, in the north of the same desert, where several text fragments have been uncovered, especially at Bulayiq: in Syriac, Sogdian, Old and Middle Persian, Old Turkic, Uighur, and even Greek. Other texts in Uighur and Syriac, but also in Chinese and Tangut, a language from the Tibeto-Burman group, were found at Qaraqota, today a dead city at the southern edge of the Gobi Desert.

These finds allow us to get a sense of the wide variety of spoken and written languages into which Christian texts were translated. The multiculturalism lies in the myriad combinations of language and writing: Syriac written in Uighur script, Uighur written in Syriac script. The manuscripts are on paper, a Chinese innovation that quickly replaced other methods in the Near East and later in Europe.

Chinese hymn from Dunhuang in praise of the Trinity.
Bibliothèque nationale de France.

The finds include all the usual kinds of texts common to Christian communities, especially the New Testament and Psalms, but also translations of apocryphal texts, canonical works, *Acts* of the martyrs, hagiographies, treatises on asceticism, homilies, and biblical and liturgical commentaries, which all suggest a literature meant for monastic use.

In a later era, a spectacular manuscript, now in the Vatican Library, was written in gold ink (chrysography) on blue parchment for a princess named Sara, the sister of George, the king of the Ongut tribe of the Mongols in 1298. It was probably produced in northern Mesopotamia but follows a model used for copying Buddhist sutras onto manuscripts.

CHRISTIANITY IN THE MONGOL EMPIRE

Another period that is well documented in Syriac history is the beginning of the Mongol Empire. It was a time of tolerance, with the Mongol rulers being open to all the religions of their empire but especially favoring Christianity. As a result, the princes of the West, notably Louis IX of France, hoped that the Mongols would convert and form a grand alliance with Christian Europe against the Muslim powers.

EXCERPT FROM MARCO POLO

Chingintalas is also a province at the verge of the Desert, and lying between north-west and north. It has an extent of sixteen days' journey, and belongs to the Great Kaan, and contains numerous towns and villages. There are three different races of people in it—Idolaters, Saracens, and some Nestorian Christians. At the northern extremity of this province there is a mountain in which are excellent veins of steel and ondanique.

During this time, western travelers circulated along the Silk Road. The most famous, of course, is Marco Polo (1254–1324), a young Venetian who in 1271 accompanied his father and his uncle, both merchants, from Italy to Khanbaliq, modern-day Beijing and the seat of Kublai Khan. He remained in the emperor's service for fifteen years, eventually returning to Europe by the sea route that curves around Southeast Asia: all told, a voyage of twenty-four thousand kilometers and an absence which lasted twenty-four years. Imprisoned for several years upon his return, Marco Polo had ample time to compose an account of his journey, *The Book of the Marvels of the World*, in which he mentions the Christian communities that he encountered during his stops in Central Asia, mostly East Syrian but also some Syriac Orthodox. Other European voyagers, generally religious, such as the Franciscans John of Plano Carpini and William of Rubruck or the Dominican André of Longjumeau were sent by popes or by Louis IX to try to convert the Mongol rulers and to suggest an alliance to them. Their travel accounts are an irreplaceable source for the history of the Mongol Empire. William of Rubruck notes,

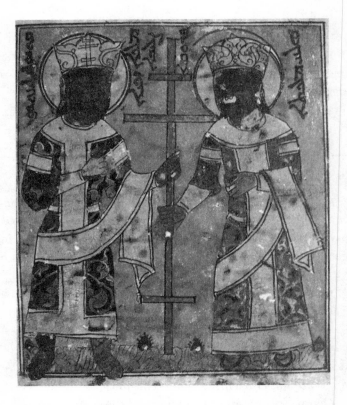

The Mongol emperor Hulegu and his wife Dokuz
Khan as Constantine and Helena. Courtesy of
Wikimedia Commons.

for instance, that Karakorum, the Mongol capital, had two mosques, a "Nestorian" church, and a dozen Buddhist and Taoist temples. The Franciscans Odoric of Pordenone and John of Montecorvino are also worth mentioning. All of their accounts mention Christian communities, often very poor, but in each case centered on a church, stretching all along the roads of Central Asia.

Westerners were not the only ones to travel toward distant horizons. One exceptional travel account in an inverse sense, from east to west, exists. It relates in Syriac the story of a voyage, written in the first person, of a Christian monk, Rabban Ṣauma, who left China in order to travel to Jerusalem with a companion, Rabban Marcos. He traveled across all of Asia, with the goal of going first to Baghdad to meet the East Syrian patriarch, Mar Denḥa. Learning that he was at Maragha, near Lake Urmia in northwestern Iran, he went to go find him. He then returned to Baghdad in order to visit the tomb of Mar Mari, the apostle to Mesopotamia, at Kokhe (see chapter 2). He completed several diplomatic missions for the patriarch, visited Ani and Georgia, but had to give up on traveling to Jerusalem, as the journey was too dangerous. The catholicos named Marcos metropolitan of northern China and the Ongut, and Rabban Ṣauma as an ecclesiastical envoy. However, the war prevented them from returning east, and upon the death of the catholicos Mar Denha, Rabban Marcos was elected patriarch under the name of Mar Yahballaha (Given by God) because his origin made him a good intercessor for his community to the Mongol ruler. Sometime later, Rabban Ṣauma was sent to the West as a messenger for the Mongol king Arghun and Mar Yahballaha. He went to Constantinople first, then to Italy, passing by the foot of Mount Etna, and disembarked at Naples, where he met the king Irid Sharlado (the Syriac rendition of King Charles II, *le roi Charles deux* in French). He then went to Rome, where the pontifical seat was temporarily vacant, and explained his faith to the cardinals there.

HISTORY OF MAR YAHBALLAHA

Rabban Sauma and Rabban Mark one day came up with a plan: "If we left this land for the West, we would have a lot to gain

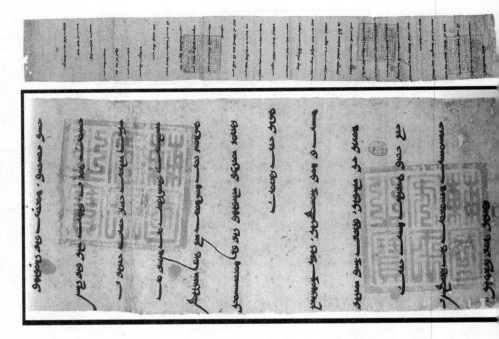

Letter from the Mongol king Argun to Philip the Fair, and a detail.

in receiving the blessing of the shrines of the holy martyrs and the fathers of the Church; then if Christ, the omnipotent Lord, prolonged our lives and sustained us with His grace, we might reach Jerusalem and attain complete atonement for our faults and the remittal of our sins." Rabban Sauma tried to withhold Mark, frightening him with the labors of the journey, the perils of the itinerary, the dangers entailed by the routes, their needs and their foreign status. But Rabban Mark burned with a desire to leave; he felt in his heart that some treasure was in store for him in the West.

MAR YAHBALLAHA IN PARIS

They later came to the place called Paris, before King Francis (Philippe le Bel or Philip the Fair designated by the name of his nation) who sent many people to greet them. [. . .] They remained over a month in that great city Paris, and visited all there was to see.

There are 30,000 scholars, who study both religious and secular disciplines: the interpretation and commentaries to all the Holy Scriptures, and the wisdom, that is philosophy, and rhetoric, along with medicine, geometry, arithmetic and the science of planets and the stars. They are constantly busy writing and receive a stipend from the king. They then saw a great church (the basilica of Saint Denis), in which there are coffins where the dead kings are buried. [. . .] Five hundred monks provide service to the burial site, whose maintenance is paid by the king. [. . .] On the tombs are the crowns and arms of those kings, along with their clothes.

   Then the king sent for them and they went to meet him in the church [Sainte-Chapelle]. [. . .] The king opened a gold tabernacle and extracted a beryl reliquary containing the crown of thorns that the Jews put on the head of Our Lord when they crucified him. So transparent was the beryl that the crown could be seen in the casket without opening it. There was also a fragment of wood from the Cross.

He left for France, where he was received by Philip the Fair at Sainte-Chapelle in Paris; went to meet the English king at Bordeaux; voyaged to the Holy Roman Empire; returned through Rome, where he was received by the newly elected pope; and returned to Maragha. Throughout his travels, he sought out relics. He left a very vivid account of his adventures and his encounters.

   The last witness is that of funerary inscriptions. In China itself, the number of discoveries has multiplied, from Almaliq on the Kyrgyz border to Yanzhou and Quanzhou (Zaitun), the southeastern port of China, passing through Inner Mongolia and the region of Beijing. These inscriptions, on tombs and steles, are in Syriac writing but in the Uighur language, a branch of the Turkic language family, interspersed with Syriac words specific to the Christian religion. This system, similar to *garshuni* in Arabic (see pages 87 and 223), shows the inculturation of Syriac Christianity via Syriac writing, considered a marker of Christian identity. The language used shows that Christianity had especially made headway among Turkic populations. Sometimes a decorative element shows the influence of Chinese culture (angels, dragons, clouds, lotus

Nestorian funerary stone. Musée du Louvre, Paris,
France. © RMN-Grand Palais / Art Resource, NY.

flowers). Their usage shows the axis of Syriac Christianity that linked
Central Asia to the seaports of southern China.

Another group, comprising nearly 650 inscriptions, is that of the
inscriptions of Kyrgyzstan. They date from between the middle of the
13th century and the middle of the 14th, a period when the region was
under Mongol rule. These are simple river stones, smoothed but not
carved, which were planted on their narrowest end in the ground. On
one side, an East Syrian cross is carved. The inscription, generally in
Syriac, sometimes in Turkic, is arranged around this cross, above and
in vertical lines along the sides. The text begins in general with the year,
according to the "Year of the Greeks" that was used in the Syriac world

(see the Note on Terms) and then afterward the Sino-Turkic system of twelve years symbolized by animals (for example, the Year of the Horse), followed by the name of the deceased, which can be followed by his genealogy or his profession.

FUNERARY STONES FROM KYRGYZSTAN

In the year 1618, being the year of the Sheep [January 31– September 30, AD 1307]; this is the tomb of the believer Jeremiah.

In the year 1650, being the year of the Hare [January 31– September 30, AD 1339], in Turkish ṭebiškân, this is the tomb of Šâdikâm, leader of the church, son of Mangu Ṭâš, priest.

A number of priests are mentioned, sometimes still children, which corroborates an observation made by William of Rubruck that since the East Syrian bishop could not come by the area very often, he ordained many children in order to guarantee that there would always be a priest. One finds archbishops, periodeutes, and archdeacons, but also chieftains, *scholastikoi*, and teachers and students. The number of tombstones expanded rapidly during the years 1338–1339, showing a sharp increase in the number of deceased, and then hits its lowest point in 1345. These communities disappeared very quickly, and some inscriptions mention deaths caused by plague. It suggests that there was a violent epidemic, the first wave of the Black Death that reached Europe in 1347. Decimated, the Christian communities of Central Asia were too weak to survive. The inscriptions are the last mention of Christians in Central Asia for a long time.

Separations and Flourishing
5th–9th Centuries

The history of the church from the 5th to the 9th century is one of gradual separation from western Christianity and the establishment of separate Syriac churches with their own hierarchy and geography, competing with one another and expanding toward East Asia. The political history of this era began with a series of conflicts between Rome and the Sasanians, caused by the question of Rome's tribute to Persia. However, the rulers of each empire supported each other in the face of internal challenges: Arcadius (r. 383–408) asked Yazdegird I to be the guardian of his young son Theodosius after his death, while the emperor Maurice helped Khosrow II Parvez (r. 590–628) to retake his throne. The Persians later took the assassination of Maurice by Phocas as a pretext to invade the Roman Empire. At the same time, the cultural history is one of continued production and transmission of knowledge between the 6th and the 9th century, with scholars translating Greek as well as Indian and Iranian works into Syriac and then Arabic.

The Roman Near East was occupied twice in the 7th century, first by the Sasanians, who conquered the territory from Egypt to Constantinople between 602 and 628 and even besieged Constantinople itself in 626 (unsuccessfully), and the second time by Arab Muslims just after the Byzantines counterattacked the Persians under the emperor Heraclius. This time, the conquerors would establish a new state, the caliphate. For the first time since Alexander the Great, the frontier between the "Western" states and Persia disappeared. This period of political disruption obviously affected the population on the frontiers as wars and the changing of administration usually did, but it did not affect the development of churches or the Syriac cultures. The rhythms of cultural, political, and religious history are not the same, and periodizations inevitably conflict with one or the other. The 7th century saw an enormous surge of commentaries and translations from Greek into Syriac as well as the missionary expansion to China (see chapter 5). Although this period was "the Dark Ages" for Byzantium, defeated and shorn of its eastern provinces, it was also a time of flourishing for Syriac culture, which in turn helped preserve the Greek heritage in the Middle East.

During the 8th and 9th centuries, Syriac Christians played a central role in the translation movement that took place in Baghdad under the patronage of the ʿAbbasid caliphs, where scholars of all religions and areas of the empire participated in what is called the ʿAbbasid Renaissance. Although sometimes characterized as a resurgence of ancient Greek culture, it was in reality the extension of a process that had been ongoing since the end of late antiquity, especially in the Syriac world. Greek texts were selected, read, transmitted, and commented on in the Christian circles in which they were circulating. Because of the amount of intellectual activity that took place in the East, it was a period of "light" for the ʿAbbasid world, and only a dark age for the Byzantines. This literary production in Greek and Syriac took place both before and after the arrival of the Arabs, including the Umayyad period, before the ʿAbbasids. Thus, the concepts of an ʿAbbasid Renaissance and a Byzantine Dark Ages do not fit the Syriac world, especially since it was not only Greek but also eastern knowledge that enriched the intellectual world of late antiquity.

The Age of Separations, 5th and 6th Centuries

The 4th and 5th centuries were a period of theological reflection and refined doctrine, marked by the meeting of four ecumenical councils that resulted in the permanent division of the Christian world. These two centuries also saw the restructuring of the church via patriarchates, of which the three main centers were Antioch, Alexandria, and Rome, along with Constantinople, the capital of the empire, which asserted its independence as a fourth patriarchate. Another small patriarchate, which held sway over Palestine and outer Jordan, was created in 451 to honor Jerusalem and its link with Christ. Finally, as we have seen, Seleucia-Ctesiphon established itself as the independent patriarchate of the Church of the East in the same period. Although the Council of Chalcedon established the patriarchate organization, the Church of the East created its own pentarchy, substituting itself for the patriarchate of Jerusalem, which it did not recognize, and claiming to be the head of the other patriarchates.

LETTER OF THE CATHOLICOS TIMOTHY ON THE PRIMACY OF THE CHURCH OF PERSIA

It is for this reason that it is recognized that the honor of precedence legitimately falls to the Easterners, which is due to the honor owed to the region, for the East is the queen of all the regions, because it was crowned by the crown of paradise, because paradise is the model on earth of the Kingdom of Heaven, because of the crown of the earthly kingdom, because it is there that the king Nimrod bound together the first crown, because of the ancestors of Our Lord, because it was there that Abraham was born and the place from which he ventured, because of the absolute antiquity of our faith in Our Lord, because he was two years old when we sent messengers and offerings to His royalty. Thirty years before the rest of the world, we had already confessed His Lordship, and we were prostrate before His divinity.

This was the period that saw the emergence of the bishop as the shepherd and defender of orthodoxy, but also as a new community leader, responsible for organizing the defense of the cities' walls and the construction of churches, hospitals, and bridges, and for conducting the prayers and processions during times of war or natural disasters, as Ephrem shows in his poems on the bishops of Nisibis. The bishop Rabbula of Edessa (d. 435/436), who was renowned for his forceful per-

Lintel of Khirbet Hassan, Antioch, Syria (AD 507). The inscription details the cost of building the church. Photo by Mission inscriptions syriaques de Syrie.

sonality, was an example of these new roles. In addition to his hagiographic *Life*, an inscription about him also survives. It shows that in the 5th century Syriac spread in a Christian environment on the western side of the Euphrates (see Nabgha, page 67) and very quickly around Antioch.

THE LATER ECUMENICAL COUNCILS

In the 5th century, discussions about the nature of the union of the divine and human natures of Christ (known as a "hypostatic union") crystallized a number of tensions between the Christian communities of the Near East, which later resulted in permanent ecclesial division. Two schools of thought emerged: one from Alexandria, marked by its affinity for Neoplatonism, which strongly affirmed Christ's divinity and the unity of his nature after the incarnation, according to the formulation of Patriarch Cyril of Alexandria, "a single nature (*mia physis*) of the

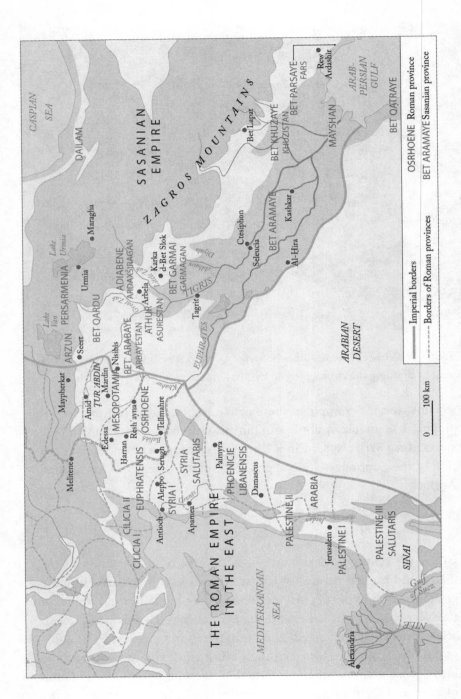

The Syriac Churches in the Roman and Sasanian Empires around 600

Incarnate Word"; and the other from Antioch, which centered on the economy of salvation and insisted on emphasizing the human nature of Christ, by which he won salvation for all people.

LI 'E OF NESTORIUS

Then we came to write the story of the calumny spread against the deceased martyr of Christ, the blessed Nestorius, bishop of Constantinople, and by the insidious pitfalls which were laid for him by the impious Cyril. We need to show before anything else the mode of his conduct, his elevation to the episcopate and the truth of his teaching. This courageous war leader was from Antioch in Syria, a compatriot of Mar Theodore, famous in his works of perfection. This spiritual athlete suckled the intellectual milk from the mouth of the blessed Diodorus and Theodore in the city of Antioch. He was attached above everything to fasting and chastity, and he completely laid aside from himself any idea of marriage; he turned away in his childhood from profane games, as he was sitting at the feet of these saints.

The debate began when Nestorius, a prominent theologian from the Antiochian school, declared that he could not assent to giving Mary the title "Mother of God" (*theotokos*), since she was only the mother of Christ's human nature. He suggested instead that she should be given the name "Mother of Christ" (*christotokos*). A new council to resolve this question was convened by the emperor Theodosius II at Ephesus in 431, but in the absence of the Antiochians, who were prevented by

The word "Nestorian" is written upside down, while the word "Orthodox" is decorated by a cross.

Christological Divisions in the 5th Century

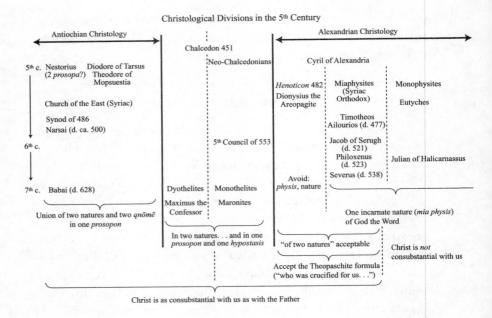

mischance from arriving, the council was dominated by the authority of Cyril of Alexandria and adopted the Miaphysite position. It also explicitly condemned Nestorius and his mentor Theodore of Mopsuestia.

THE INDEPENDENCE OF THE CHURCH OF THE EAST

The Church of Persia, which had established its independence at the beginning of the 5th century, had remained in full communion with the church of the Roman Empire but now found the christological question theologically alienating. By the end of the 5th century, this church, whose theology was thoroughly Antiochian, refused to ratify the 431 Council of Ephesus and its conclusions and rejected the condemnation of Nestorius and Theodore of Mopsuestia. Though it was called "Nestorian" by its detractors because it adopted Nestorius's formulation to speak about Mary, *eme da-mshiḥa* in Syriac, mother of Christ, it considered itself primarily indebted to the thought of Theodore of Mopsuestia instead, to whom it awarded the title of "Interpreter" par excellence of the Scriptures. The bishopric of Nisibis became the most important seat of the Church of the East in the first half of the 5th century. This was the period when it created the School of Nisibis, which would go on to gain great renown (see chapter 4).

NARSAI

A figure with one foot in both Rome and Persia, the East Syrian theologian Narsai (d. ca. 503) was educated at the School of the Persians at Edessa, where he also later taught and eventually became a leader. Just before the closure of the school in 489, he crossed into the Persian Empire after a disagreement with Bishop Cyr of Edessa. He founded the School of Nisibis, where he was followed by some of the students of the School of Edessa, and became its leader. Renowned in the Church of the East, where he became the most famous poet and theologian, known as the "Harp of the Holy Spirit," he penned roughly eighty *memre* about the Old and New Testaments, on subjects such as creation, the flood, Noah, the Tower of Babel, Jonah, Joseph, the revelations made to the prophets, the Virgin, Saint Stephen, the Nativity, Epiphany, the Resurrection, Pentecost, the Eucharist, baptism, martyrs, and many more. According to the history of Barḥadbshabba, he composed a poem for each day of the year, filling twelve volumes. Only one of his *memre* is dedicated to someone outside the Bible: the three doctors of the Church of the East: Diodore of Tarsus, Theodore of Mopsuestia, and Nestorius. Again, according to the history of Barḥadbshabba, Narsai was inspired to begin writing in order to counter the influence of his contemporary, Jacob of Serugh, who defended Miaphysite theology. He hoped to attract believers to his theology by the beautiful sound of his *memre*. This anecdote helps show the importance of liturgy in the culture of different churches and their role in catechizing the faithful.

NARSAI, *HOMILY ON CREATION* VV. 23–32: ON THE CONSTITUTION OF ANGELS

By a sign, he gave a sign to Creation to appear,
And it was suddenly established, though not knowing how it had
   been established,

He spoke suddenly and the mute beings existed at the same time
as those endowed with reason, and they were astonished and
wonderstruck at themselves, seeing how they existed suddenly.

The rational beings marveled especially at their nature, seeing
how it was adapted, and how it dominated the freedom which
remained within it.

Their groups remained in astonishment and stupefaction while
they were being constituted, and they admired the reason which
was within them insatiably.

They were astonished by their sentience, seeing how it was rational,
And how alive was the power of understanding which was within it.

The Church of the East, henceforth absent from the ecumenical
councils, developed independently from the debates held by the "universal" church, though a number of its dogmatic definitions retained the old
vocabulary and manner of understanding Christology before the later re-
finements. This is the case, for instance, with the Syriac anaphora (eucharistic prayer) of Addai and Mari, one of the oldest in Christianity, which
is still in use today in the Assyrian Church of the East and the Chaldean
Church and omits the words of the eucharistic consecration itself.

In the time of Yazdegird I (r. 399–420), Persia was at peace with
the Roman Empire and Christians were generally treated well, until a
persecution was launched in the final years of his reign. Busy with the
Hephthalite Huns who threatened the empire from the east, the Sasanian rulers turned away from Rome.

One of the major figures among the bishops of the Church of the
East was Barṣauma of Nisibis, who deposed the catholicos Babowai during the Council of Beth Lapaṭ in 484, authorized marriage for priests
as well as for bishops even after their ordination, and commanded believers to adopt the theology of Theodore of Mopsuestia under pen-
alty of excommunication. With the support of the king of kings Peroz,
Barṣauma led a violent expedition into Beth Garmai to force local Christians to adopt the decisions of the council. He was accused by his opponents of having "nestorianized" the Church of the East. At this point,
Peroz began a persecution in Beth Garmai, where the catholicos was
martyred. However, the Christians of the Church of Persia were no lon-

name was associated with a twelve-syllable meter, dubbed "the meter of Jacob of Serugh."

Jacob is remembered as a teacher par excellence (a highly prestigious title in Syriac culture, where teaching and schools were so highly praised), thanks to his *mimre* on various subjects from the Old and New Testaments (Jonah, the chariot of Elijah, the Virgin, etc.) or ascetic topics, just at the moment when monasticism was developing. Other *mimre* are linked to the life of the church and the theology of the councils, against Jews, or on the fall of idols. Jacob also touches on events that affected the believers of his time, such as the spectacles of the theater, the taking of Amida by the Persians, and the plague of locusts. He also composed *mimre* on important persons or saints like the emperor Constantine, Ephrem, Stephen, George, and Simeon Stylites. His correspondence with monks of important monasteries, both in his region and in Sinai, or even with the Arab phylarch in al-Hira in Arabia, shows his importance as a figure in the Miaphysite movement.

PHILOXENUS OF MABBUG

The career of the Syriac Orthodox theologian Philoxenus, or Aksanaya in Syriac (440–ca. 523), is symptomatic of the religious controversies of the 5th century in which he was a fervent participant. Born in the Persian Empire, at Tahal, in the region of Beth Garmai (the modern-day region of Kirkuk, Iraq), he completed his studies at Edessa. A partisan of the theology of Cyril of Alexandria, he was a fierce opponent of the Council of Chalcedon (451). He composed thirteen sermons (called *šarbe* in Syriac) on ascetic topics: on faith, simplicity of spirit, the fear of God, renunciation, the battle against gluttony, the ascetic, and the struggle against lust. Translations were made into Greek, Armenian, and Arabic, which show their popularity in the Christian world.

JACOB OF SERUGH, *MIMRO ON THE STRANGER*

Exile, how bitter are your consequences,
In health, sickness, and even death!
On your paths, persecution, pain, vexations,

Scenes from the Old and New Testaments in the Rabbula
Gospels. Courtesy of Wikimedia Commons.

Hunger and thirst, exhaustion, opprobrium, and threat!
The harshness of face and word cruelly wound the heart! [. . .]
The one who loves you has no pause or rest;
When the waves which capsize reach him, he leaves, he goes.
And when other waves buffet him, he leaves again,
And all his days he is tossed about by all these calamities.
Melancholy, dark, screaming with sorrow in the streets,
He lives his life in horror, his heart terrified; he hates himself.
He torments himself, asking himself where he should go, where he
    should rest,
And who will provide for him the daily bread in the name of Our
    Lord.

May they weep over me, those whose loved ones are dead
By the ways and paths of exile!
They know how to frame complaints about exiles.
Who are struck by sickness, laid out by the road,
The kind who have no one of their family or parentage near them.

PHILOXENUS OF MABBUG

The only Son of God became the advocate of our nature and began a suit for all of us against the Enemy, the Father being the mediator and judge. Satan took the defense of death, Christ pleaded for all of us, and the Father was like a judge hearing both parties. The Enemy nevertheless objected to Christ: "Why have you taken the defense of humankind?" Then he saw the physicality of men in his hypostasis . . . the Son became a man from the beginning to make it possible to plead legitimately, as was appropriate for one who shared in human nature. Christ was able to reply to the Enemy: "It is not as God that I begin this suit against you, out of concern that you might worm your way out under the pretext of not being able to enter into a suit with the king. In fact, it is not the king that you see in me, but the image of a servant like the humans."

In this period, the patriarchate of Antioch was being contested by partisans and opponents of the Council of Chalcedon. Peter the Fuller was made the non-Chalcedonian patriarch in 470–471, 476–477, and 485–488 in alternation with Chalcedonian patriarchs. At the third elevation of Peter, Philoxenus was named metropolitan of Hierapolis, known as Mabbug in Syriac. He wrote defenses of Miaphysite ideas: around 480, he composed ten polemical *mimre* titled "On the Member of the Trinity Who Was Incarnated and Underwent the Passion." In 507/508 he ordered the chorepiscopus Polycarp to revise the Peshitta version of the New Testament to align more closely with Greek. This version sought to reconcile Syriac with Greek in order to have a shared base of theological vocabulary for discussions with Chalcedonians in the Greek language. Philoxenus also played a deciding factor in the deposition of the patriarch Flavian II and his replacement by the Miaphysite Severus (in November 512). At the instigation of Justin I, he was driven from his seat and exiled to Philippopolis in Thrace until the end of 519, and then to Gangra, where he died. Between the years 515 and 518, he composed three treatises called *On the Trinity and the Incarnation*. He also composed thirty letters on dogma or the ascetic life. Because of his staunch defense of Miaphysitism, many prayers and liturgical texts in the Syriac Orthodox Church are attributed to him.

THE BIRTH OF THE SYRIAC ORTHODOX CHURCH

An "eternal peace" was signed in 532 during the reign of Khosrow I Anushirvan ("The Immortal Soul"), but in 541–562 and in 572–591, war broke out once again between the two empires. Although the emperor Justinian (r. 527–565) declared his support for the decisions made at Chalcedon, his wife, the empress Theodora, protected major Miaphysites and welcomed them into the palace of Hormisdas in Constantinople. The Miaphysite historian John of Ephesus (ca. 507–585), originally from the region of Amida, was chosen by the emperor despite his theology to lead campaigns to convert the pagans who still lived in Asia Minor. In his *Ecclesiastical History* and *Lives of the Eastern Saints*, he created a memory of anti-Miaphysite persecution by the Chalcedonians who represented the official church. The history of Pseudo-Zachariah the Scholastic, also from the region of Amida, also helped shape the local memory of persecutions. The separation between Chalcedonians and non-Chalcedonians happened slowly. Under the reign of Justin and Justinian, the scattered communities of non-Chalcedonians took shape and formed the church that would later be known as Syriac Orthodox or Syro-Orthodox, because it declared itself to be the only orthodox faith, as opposed to the Roman-Byzantine church, which also labeled itself orthodox, but according to the revisions made at the Council of Chalcedon (both churches retain the label "orthodox" to this day).

THE LIFE OF JACOB BARADAEUS

But, when he had been engaged for a period of about fifteen years in these labors in the same royal city [Constantinople], in his cell, then by the provision and at the instigation of the believing queen [Theodora] he was under great pressure summoned to episcopacy, together with another blessed man from the country of Arabia whose name was Theodore; for the party of the believers had diminished and a deficiency had moreover arisen in the order of the priesthood over all the commonwealth of the party of the believers. And when both had received the high priesthood, that is the blessed James that of the city of Edessa and Theodore that of Ḥirta of the Saracens, then he armed himself with divine strength, and went out to the work of his ministry, while he thenceforth began to pour out the priesthood derived from him copiously over the regions in all the eastern districts, like a great river in the days of Nisan.

The Arab Christian tribes, which were structured with phylarchs at their head (one of whom received the title of king from Justinian I), were won over to Miaphysitism. They played a role in forging a new non-Chalcedonian hierarchy. In 542/543, a phylarch named Ḥarith b. Gabala asked the empress Theodora to send a bishop of his confession. The patriarch of Alexandria, Theodosius, secretly ordained Jacob Baradaeus at Constantinople as the Miaphysite bishop of Edessa (r. 545–578) and Theodore for Ḥirta/al-Ḥira, the capital of the Arab tribes. Jacob fled, hidden under rags (*burdʿoyo* in Syriac, transliterated as Baradaeus in Greek), in order to escape imperial agents, and traveled throughout the Near East, ordaining Miaphysite priests and bishops and building up a new hierarchy after the dismantling of Severus's network under Justin I. He also opposed the Chalcedonian patriarch of Antioch, Paul of Bet Ukkama, as well as tritheism within Miaphysitism itself. It is because of Jacob Baradaeus that the Syriac Orthodox Church and its believers are sometimes called Jacobites.

Another division from within the Miaphysite movement itself came from Julian of Halicarnassus (d. ca. 520), also exiled to Egypt, who opposed Severus in a series of treatises and letters. The "Julian-ists," "Phantasiasts," or even "Aphtartodocetae," as they were called by their opponents, spread throughout Armenia, Egypt, Ethiopia, and Arabia following the persecutions of Justin I in the 520s. It is not

Stele of Bir al-Qantari, which mentions the Phantasiasts.

inconceivable that their ideas about the incorruptibility of the body of Christ before the Resurrection (they were accused of saying that Christ suffered only in appearance) had an influence on the way in which the Qur'an depicts the crucifixion of Jesus (Surah *an-nisā'*, 4:157).

The Council of Constantinople of 536 condemned the Miaphysites, and the subsequent absence of non-Chalcedonians at the council of 553 marks a permanent divide between Miaphysites and Chalcedonians.

THE CONVERGENCE OF THE SYRIAC CHURCHES IN PERSIA

The catholicos Aba I (r. 540–552) is an important figure in the development of the Church of the East in the 6th century. A converted Zoroastrian noble, he studied at Nisibis, traveled in the Byzantine Empire, and eventually returned to Nisibis to teach. He translated texts from Greek into Syriac and wrote biblical commentaries. The traveler and Greek-speaking writer Cosmas Indicopleustes studied under him. Mar Aba founded a school at Seleucia-Ctesiphon and reformed the Church of the East. He, or his disciple Cyrus of Edessa, translated *The Bazaar of Heracleides* by Nestorius into Syriac in 539–540.

In 558/559, Jacob Baradaeus ordained Aḥudemmeh of Beth ʿArabaye as the Syriac Orthodox bishop of Tagrit (modern-day Tikrit in Iraq), establishing a Miaphysite hierarchy in the Persian Empire. The monastery of Mar Mattai was another Syriac Orthodox center in the Persian Empire, where a competition played out between the two churches, including at the court of the shah, often through Christian doctors. The anti-Nestorian controversy was very active in the border regions, as shown by the letters of Philoxenus of Mabbug and the activity of Simeon of Beth Arsham (d. ca. 548), the "Persian Debater," who traveled throughout Persia to defend the Syriac Orthodox faith (see page 115).

HISTORY OF MARUTA OF TAGRIT

The Nestorians of the East, who want to attract the simple to their error and charm the ear of the laypeople who are very easy to deceive by their songs and by their sweet cadences—and also in order to please the world and to rule it, and thus to devour the houses of widows and married women according to the word of the Gospel, under the pretext that they extend their prayers—have taken care to establish a school in each of their towns to speak in this way. They have organized them with chants, canticles, responses, and hymns which are sung in the same manner in every place where they are. The pious believers [Syriac Orthodox], moved by an admirable zeal and in order to obey the apostle Paul who advises and rouses them in saying, "it is good that you should always be full of emulation for the good, and your zeal has reached a great number," began to establish excellent schools, beginning with the land of Bet Nahudrâ.

During the time of Justin II (r. 565–578), the Persians advanced as far as Yemen, and in 572 the war resumed. It persisted under the reign of the king of kings Hormizd IV (r. 579–590) and the emperor Maurice (582–602). In 591, a treaty was put in place. During the 6th century, the western Turks replaced the Hephthalites in menacing the Persian Empire from the east.

A crisis shook Nisibis when Ḥenana of Adiabene, a renowned teacher in the School of Nisibis, criticized the policy of relying only on Theodore of Mopsuestia's writings and advocated using John Chrysostom's, a Chalcedonian bishop. More than three hundred students, including Isho'yahb II of Gdala and Isho'yahb III of Adiabene, two future catholicoi, left the city. At the end of the 6th century, with the reforms of Abraham of Kashkar, monasticism was freshly integrated into the Church of the East (see chapter 4). In 605, a council reasserted the absolute authority of Theodore of Mopsuestia and condemned anyone who did not recognize it as such, putting an end to the Ḥenanian movement.

The good relationships between the emperor Maurice and the king of kings Khosrow II Parvez (590–628), whom Maurice regarded as a son after having helped him regain his throne, ushered in a period of peace, during which Khosrow consolidated his power.

Crisis and Continuity in the 7th Century

After the assassination of Maurice by Phocas (r. 602–610), relations between Persia and Rome deteriorated. Khosrow took Phocas's usurpation as a pretext to renew hostilities. This was the final Romano-Persian war, conducted at the very end of the Sasanian Empire before the profound changes that would reshape the Near and Middle East. In five years, nearly the entire eastern territory of the Byzantine Empire had passed into Sasanian hands; Jerusalem was taken in 614, and in 619 Alexandria, and the rest of Egypt, also fell.

THE PERSIAN OCCUPATION AND THE RIVALRY
BETWEEN THE SYRIAC CHURCHES

In 612, a theological debate between the Church of the East and the Syriac Orthodox Church took place at the court of Khosrow. In 615–616, at Alexandria, Thomas of Ḥarqel (ca. 570–640), who had fled the anti-Miaphysite persecutions of 598–599, produced a new translation of the New Testament in Syriac, and in 616–617 Paul of Tella translated the Syrohexapla. Meanwhile, Paul of Edessa, who fled to Cyprus in 624 during the Persian invasion, translated several works from Greek into Syriac, including the *Hymns* of Severus of Alexandria, the *Hymns* of John bar Aphtonia, and the *Gloria* of Athanasius of Alexandria. The Romano-Persian war did not keep theologians from the different Syriac churches from competing against each other or redefining themselves against each other.

For the Syriac churches, these years were not as dramatic as the politics might suggest—just another episode in a long history of wars. At Edessa, the notables made themselves available to the ruler to collect taxes, just as they had in the time of the Byzantines. The Syriac Orthodox, who had gotten to know the king of kings while he was living in exile in Edessa, obtained the restitution of the churches that had been handed over to the Chalcedonians. The Syriac Orthodox bishops who had come to Persia, where they had taken refuge and where they had encountered the Church of the East, were chosen by the king of kings to replace the Chalcedonian bishops in formerly Byzantine territory whose loyalty was in doubt. Meanwhile, the Christians who were in Persia did not mind having the True Cross at Seleucia-Ctesiphon, where it had been transported after the taking of Jerusalem.

In 626, Constantinople was besieged by the Persians and the Avars, but it did not fall. The emperor Heraclius and his troops launched a counteroffensive in 622 and triumphed in 628, entering the Iranian heartland itself. Thomas of Ḥarqel contributed to dialogue between the Copts and the Syriac Orthodox, both Miaphysites, following a period of schism, at the instigation of the Chalcedonians and with the support of Heraclius, who was searching for religious unity after the reconquest, to the point of forcing Jews to be baptized and trying to bring together all

Christians to imperial orthodoxy. The religious situation became tense once again, culminating in the Syriac Orthodox bishop of Edessa refusing communion to the emperor. Heraclius removed the confiscated Chalcedonian churches from Miaphysite control, a situation that was finally solidified after the Arab conquest in 636, as the victors established a status quo to avoid complications.

In the eastern part of the Christian world, between 620 and 628, Khosrow forbade the Church of the East from naming a new catholicos following complaints by his Christian wife Shirin and his physician Gabriel of Sinjar. Instead, Babai the Great (551–628) played the role of catholicos. In 628, Kawad II Seroe, supported by his nobles, overthrew Khosrow. A final period of instability ensued, with several kings and queens following in quick succession. Isho'yahb of Gdala (r. 628–646) became the new catholicos. He reformed the church and insisted on the importance of teaching theology and pastoral morality. He also reopened several schools.

THE MONOTHELITE CONTROVERSIES

In the West, a new round of christological controversies emerged regarding the wills and energies of Christ. It was this controversy in the 7th and 8th centuries between Monothelites and Dyothelites (one and two wills, respectively, either simply divine or divine and human, after the incarnation) that divided the Melkites and the Maronites, both Chalcedonians. In the 780s, the term *melkite* (from *malka*, "king," in Syriac) emerged to designate the Chalcedonians who took the emperor's side and supported the official doctrine of Dyothelitism but lived outside the empire. The monks of the monastery of Beth Maron rebelled against Dyothelitism, which was supported by the theologian Maximus the Confessor and Patriarch Sophronius of Jerusalem, and refused to accept the results of the Council of Constantinople in 680–681, which formalized it. They continued to chant the *Trisagion* (an ancient "thrice holy" hymn), with the typical Near Eastern addition of "who was crucified for us," which was used by Miaphysites but not by Melkites. The divisions thus took a concrete aspect in liturgical practice.

THE BEGINNING OF ISLAM

The rapid Arab Muslim conquests abolished the borders that had defined the Near East for the first time since Alexander the Great. In 632 the Arabs took the Sasanian capital of Seleucia-Ctesiphon as the king of kings Yazdegird III fled. At the same time, in 635 Syriac Christianity reached China (see page 128). Edessa surrendered in 641. As with the Sasanian invasion earlier, most of the cities of Iraq, Syria, and Mesopotamia chose to negotiate in order to avoid bloody sieges and massacres. Syriac Orthodox and East Syrian Christians were both widespread throughout the Arabian Peninsula, from Yemen at the southern tip to al-Ḥira in the north and the shores of the Persian Gulf in the east, in the same region where the prophet of Islam would appear. Muhammad supposedly concluded a treaty with the Syriac Orthodox bishop of Najran, Abu al-Ḥarith, exempting priests and monks from the payment of tribute. Such treaties were also attributed to the caliphs. The catholicos Ishoʿyahb of Gdala was said to have sent a delegation to Muhammad and obtained privileges for the Church of the East from his successor, later confirmed by the caliphs ʿUmar and Ali, because Christians had fed their troops.

In the 8th century, a story that was to become very popular began circulating about an East Syrian monk named Sergius Baḥira, who supposedly instructed Muhammad in a simplified, heretical form of Christianity and began teaching the Arabs about the existence of only one God. Bahira also appears in biographies of the Prophet in the 9th century. A polemical adaptation in a Christian setting appears in a Syriac apocalypse that circulated in both eastern and western networks and most likely also dates to the 9th century. Bahira is presented there as having received a vision that Muhammad was a new prophet, even before Muhammad had had his first revelation.

SYRIAC INSCRIPTION ON A CHURCH
DEDICATED TO ST. SERGIUS IN EHNESH
(ON THE EUPHRATES, TURKEY)

[Years are given according to the Seleucid era beginning October 1, 312 BC.]
In the year 309 the Messiah came to the world

and in the year 930 the Arabs came to the land

and in the year 968 a battle occurred at Ṣiffin

and in the year [9]95 a great famine occurred

and in the year 1005 a darkness occurred

and in the year 1088 the vale of Mar'ash entered into captivity in
the territory of the Romans on account of our sins

and in the year 342, on 24 March, the 6th day, the Messiah suffered

and in the year 1091 the Commander of the Faithful, al-Mahdi,
came and entered as far as Giḥon and he returned and ordered
the churches to be turned down and the Banū Tanūkh to adopt
Islam.

THE DELEGATION SENT BY THE CATHOLICOS
ISHOʿYAHB TO MUHAMMAD

The catholicos Ishoʿyahb had sent to the Prophet—peace be
upon him—presents and a million staters of silver with Gabriel,
bishop of Maishan, a virtuous and knowledgeable man. He wrote
to him asking him to be charitable towards Christians. The bishop
Gabriel arrived at Yathrib after the death of Muhammad, offered
what he had brought to Abu Bakr and apprised him of the situation
of the subjects of the Persian Empire and what Christians had
suffered at the hands of the Arab army; he made known to him
that Christians were tributaries to the Persian kings, who were at
war with the Greeks. [Abu Bakr] listened to his speech, accepted
the presents, and guaranteed what he had requested. The bishop
returned to the catholicos pleased with the success of his mission.

Though the wars were always traumatic, the new situation did
not overturn the life of the border communities as much as it did the
Chalcedonians who fled to Constantinople and Italy. In particular, the
Syrian elites of Antioch and the coastal cities fled during the civil war
(*fitna*) that took place in the time of the caliph Muʿawiya (r. 661–680)
and rejoined the territory that was under Byzantine control. They were
Chalcedonians, as shown by the existence of the monastery of St. Sabas
in Italy, which was tied to the Chalcedonian community in Palestine,
and by the election of popes of Syrian origin in the second half of the

The monk Sergius Bahira pays homage to Muhammad.
Edinburgh, University Library, Or. 20, f. 43v.

7th century. The Syriac Orthodox, who were now considered heretics by the Byzantines, did not have that option, nor did the East Syrians. Additionally, they did not realize at the time how permanent the new situation would become, treating it instead like the many other wars they had experienced in the past.

As with the Persian occupation, the notables passed into the service of the local emirs and the caliphs. The different churches, as they were in previous periods, were in competition to gain control of, construct, and restore churches and to gain the attention and aid of their new masters. Only at the beginning of the 8th century did new restrictions appear: the use of the *semantron* (the plank of wood that was struck to sound the call to prayer, as bells were not used in the Near East) by Christians was regulated, as were the construction of churches and processions in the streets, though the restrictions were not absolute but varied according to time, place, and local circumstance. The main question had to do with the collection of taxes, for members of the clergy as well as the laity, the first seemingly having the benefit of exemptions, though, as before, to varying degrees. Later, the introduction of the *jizya*, the poll tax paid by Christians, contributed to conversions aimed at avoiding the status of *dhimmi*. Various clothing restrictions, meant to distinguish non-Muslims from Muslims, were also increasingly imposed. The introduction of these measures was not systematic and is difficult to date. It took place over one or two centuries.

Christians were still the majority in this period, and a number of them worked for the Umayyad caliphs (661–750), and later the ʿAbbasids. The family history written by members of the family of the patriarch Dionysius of Tel Maḥre (d. 845) over six generations and partly preserved in medieval Syriac chronicles shows how in the Umayyad period noble Syriac Orthodox Edessans were noted for their culture and multilingualism and were engaged in the service of the caliph, as was John of Damascus on the Chalcedonian side. Athanasius bar Gumoye, a notable Edessan belonging to the family of Dionysius of Tel Maḥre, was the assistant of the brother of the caliph ʿAbd al-Malik (r. 685–705) and continued to work for him when he became governor of Egypt. He thus became one of the foremost figures in the new state as well as considerably rich.

During the transitions between empires, Patriarch Ishoʿyahb III of Adiabene, who had been sent as an emissary to Queen Boran by Heraclius in 630 before his elevation to the dignity of catholicos in 680, moved the patriarchate to the monastery of Beth ʿAbe during the Arab Conquest but continued the scholastic practices of the Church of the East. He founded a school in Adiabene, reformed the statutes of the School of Nisibis, composed the *Life* of the monk Ishoʿsabran, the last martyr of the Sasanian period, and wrote a hundred letters that show the extension of the Church of the East and the difficulty of governing it. It was Ishoʿyahb who composed the *Ḥudra*, the liturgical book and hymn cycle used for various occasions in the East Syrian church to the present day, including on the Malabar coast. His liturgical work contributed to the unification of the Church of the East, which had reached its greatest extent (see chapter 5), even while the bishop of Rew Ardashir on the shores of the Persian Gulf contested the authority of the catholicos. Ishoʿyahb also worked to prevent the Christians of Oman from converting to Islam.

The Continued Transmission of Knowledge

The trend of translating Greek to Syriac took hold in the 6th century and largely continued through the 9th, with the addition of Arabic in the ʿAbbasid period. Between the 5th and the 7th century, a common curriculum founded on the *Organon* of Aristotle and incorporating the study of metaphysics and logic was established throughout the Byzantine world and the Persian Empire. Iranian and Indian influences also entered Syriac culture. This movement included not only translations but also all kinds of lexicographical notes and commentary in Arabic as well as Syriac.

SEVERUS SEBOKHT AND THE INDIAN SCIENCE

I abstain here from speaking about the science of the Indians, who are not Syrians, about their subtle discoveries in this science of astronomy—discoveries which are more ingenious than those even of the Greeks and the Babylonians—and of the rhetorical method of their calculations and of the mode of calculation which surpasses the rhetorical mode, which I want to say has nine signs. If they knew these things, those who imagine that they alone have reached the highest form of knowledge, simply because they speak Greek, will perhaps be convinced, albeit a little belatedly, that there are also others who know something; not only Greeks, but also people of a different language. I do not say this to slight the knowledge of the Greeks [. . .] but to show that knowledge is universal.

THE MONASTERY OF QENNESHRE

The monastery of Qenneshre ("Eagle's Nest") on the east bank of the Euphrates, opposite Europos/Jarabulus, was founded shortly after 531 by John bar Aphtonia and trained generations of brilliant Hellenists. These monks were often called to serve in the highest ranks of the Syriac Orthodox Church (five of the patriarchs who served from 591 to 708 were educated there) and were scholars renowned for their works of translation and commentary in the 7th century. They provided the Syriac Orthodox Church with both sacred and profane Greek literature in the midst of the great political changes caused first by the Persian occupation and then by the Arab Conquest. An exceptional scholarly atmosphere surrounded the monastery and its members who studied and sometimes resided there: Thomas of Ḥarqel; Jacob of Edessa, who was interested in all forms of knowledge (see below); his disciple George, the bishop of the

Arab tribes (d. 724), who worked on the calendar, finished the *Hexamae-ron* of Jacob, revised the translations of Aristotle's *Categories*, composed poems and commentaries, and wrote letters on subjects of philosophy, astronomy, theology, and literary criticism; and the patriarch Athanasius II of Balad (r. 680–686), who revised the translation of Porphyry's introduction to the first books of Aristotle's *Organon*. Qenneshre was simultaneously a center of "Greek learning"—it was where the patriarch Julian (r. 687–707/708) learned the "Attic language"—and a laboratory for translation and commentary. The latter contributed to the Hellenization of the Syriac language with the introduction of Greek phrases and vocabulary. It also permitted the transmission of Greek knowledge into the Syriac and Arab world while keeping the ancient culture alive.

JACOB OF EDESSA

The scholar Jacob of Edessa (636–708) was a giant in Syriac Orthodox history. He wrote on a vast range of subjects: exegesis, liturgy, grammar, history, philosophy, and the relationship between scientific knowledge and the Bible. He completed translations of patristic, theological, and liturgical works from Greek to Syriac, but also the *Categories* of Aristotle. Trained alongside another great scholar, Severus Sebokht, he learned Greek and studied the Scriptures. He pursued further education, as did all learned men of the time, at Alexandria in the 680s, to study philosophy there. He returned again to Syria and was consecrated the bishop of Edessa a little after 684. He left his seat after four years and traveled for several months, teaching Greek in various places. His canon laws are a rich historical source for religious and social history (marriage, death, inheritance, etc.) in the early period of Islam and represent an open window into daily life, which is generally absent from literature. His revision of the translation of some books of the Old Testament is highly learned. He also tried to introduce a system of vocalization in Syriac based on Greek, but it was never adopted. He was a polymath in the truest sense of the word, and his correspondence teaches us about Syriac Orthodox networks of his time and the subjects debated in the circle that centered on him.

LETTER OF JACOB OF EDESSA TO THE STYLITE JOHN OF LITARB

Your Brotherhood asks me if it is true that the Jews were called Hebrews because of the name of Heber and if the Hebrew language is the first of all the languages. I answer that it is true that Jews are called Hebrews from the name Heber, son of Salaḥ, because Abraham, who was chosen by God, was descended from him. [. . .] While as to the Hebrew language, I tell you that it is true that it is the first language, and not the Syriac or Aramaic language as many people wrongly suggest, even remarkable and famous people. This perfect demonstration should satisfy you, from the word of Clement, disciple of Peter who spoke on this subject of the confusion of languages at Babel; there was only one language in the entire world that everyone spoke: the Hebrew that is loved by God. And also from the speech made by Eusebius of Emesa in which he shows and deduces that Hebrew is the first language. He confirms his opinion after the names of the men who came before the deluge and especially by the word spoken by Adam to Eve his wife.

The famous translation movement that took place in Baghdad in the ʿAbbasid period is difficult to understand without this fundamental step: the crucial work at Qenneshre translating from the Greek and Oriental (Iranian and Indian) traditions from the 6th to the 8th century. The Greek knowledge was kept alive by the translation and the copying of manuscripts and by the commentaries that perpetuated an interest in scientific subjects. The first translations in Arabic, among which were the Gospels, took place in a Christian Arab tribal setting, perhaps in the 7th century.

TRANSLATION OF THE GOSPELS INTO ARABIC ACCORDING TO A TEXT OF CONTROVERSY

And ʿAmrou wrote for our patriarch John. And when he entered before him, [the emir] began to say unusual words foreign to the scriptures and he began to ask cunning questions. But the patriarch resolved all of them with arguments from the Old Testament and the New Testament and also from arguments from nature. And when he saw his courage and the extent of his knowledge [the emir] was amazed. And then he commanded him saying: "Translate for me your gospel into the Saracen language, that is, Arabic. Only do not put the name of Christ, that he is God, and baptism, and the cross [in it]." But the blessed one was strengthened by the Lord and said: "[God] forbid that I would remove a yod or character from the gospel, not even if all the arrows and spears in your camp would pierce me." And [the emir] commanded: "Go, write as you like." And he gathered bishops and he sent for and summoned men from the Tanukaye, the Aqulaye and the Tuʿaye who were experts in Arabic and in Syriac. And he commanded that they translate the gospel into Arabic. And he commanded that every word that they translated pass before each translator. And thus it was translated and given to the king [of the Arabs].

The Flourishing of the ʿAbbasid Period

Syriac Christians participated with Jewish, Sabean, Zoroastrian, and Muslim scholars in the cultural movement encouraged by the caliphs and dominant families for the sake of legitimacy as much as practicality (noble families needed to train large administrative staffs). Knowledge from all backgrounds and languages was encouraged and made the object of translation and study into Arabic. The chief astrologer at the court of the caliph al-Mahdi (r. 775–785), Theophilus of Edessa, who gave his son the Greek name Deucalion, shows the emergence of a new class of cultivated laity, fluent in Greek, Syriac, and Arabic, as well perhaps as Persian. A Maronite Christian born circa 695, Theophilus, son of Thomas (d. 785), composed treatises on astrology in Greek, using Sasanian material. He created horoscopes and practiced military astrology during the campaigns with the caliphs. He also completed translations of Aristotle from Greek to Syriac, and possibly Galen and Homer as well. He composed a history in Syriac that is no longer extant, but which was used by Dionysius of Tel Maḥre in his own chronicle and the Syro-Arabic chronicle of Agapius. A generation later, the catholicos Timothy I (r. 780–823), a confidant of the caliphs, especially al-Maʿmun, translated or had translated Greek texts into Syriac or Arabic and wrote on astronomy and astrology. Baghdad during the reign of the first ʿAbbasid caliphs was a place where mathematical, geographical, astronomical, and astrological knowledge from both Greece and the Far East was passed on.

With the establishment of the caliphate at Baghdad by al-Manṣur in 762, new opportunities opened for the transmission of philosophy and the knowledge of Syriac, called "the translation movement," both from Greek into Syriac and Arabic and from Greek to Arabic directly. This setting, centered on Ḥunayn ibn Ishaq, shows the extent of the academic activity in Baghdad. A Christian literature dedicated to Christian apologetics developed at the same time in Syriac and Arabic, with the most famous authors being active around the 10th century, at the moment when conversions from Christianity to Islam were increasing.

HUNAYN IBN ISHAQ

Ḥunayn ibn Ishaq (808–873) is probably the most famous physician of the ʿAbbasid period. An Arab Christian, a member of the tribe of ʿIbad from al-Ḥirta/al-Ḥira south of Baghdad and belonging to the Church of the East, Ḥunayn is known for his works of translation of medical, philosophical, mathematical, and astrological texts from Greek into Syriac, Greek into Arabic, and Syriac into Arabic. When he was invited to convert to Islam, he also composed an apologetic work for Christianity. His own medical contributions had a significant influence on the Latin West as well as the Near East: his commentary on the *Ars parva* of Galen was translated into Latin, as were his works on ophthalmology, which were also influential in Arab medicine. Ḥunayn was a physician first, and it was in this capacity that he was introduced into the court of the caliphs and conducted his life as a practitioner, translator, and commentator. He lived through the reign of ten caliphs as part of their courts, and it was during the reign of the caliph al-Mutawakkil (r. 847–861) that his career was at its apogee. Commissions for his translations came from other Christian scholars and physicians, such as Gabriel bar Bokhtishoʿ and Yuḥanna ibn Musawayh, and from Muslims such as

Muhammad and Ahmad ibn Musa, two brothers who were mathematicians and physicians. High nobles at court also requested translations.

There was a strong milieu of translation in Baghdad during Ḥunayn's time, including his two sons, Dawud and Ishaq, his nephew Ḥubays of Damascus, and his many disciples. Three scholars known as "The Edessans" were active at the ʿAbbasid court as well: Job, Thomas, and Theophilus of Edessa (apparently different from Theophilus the Astrologer). At Baghdad, the East Syrian family of Bokhtishoʿ was known for seven generations for its physicians. Many Christian secretaries are also mentioned as part of the administration.

The intense flurry of translation was accompanied by reflection on language and the composition of indispensable dictionaries, especially for technical terms. Ḥunayn ibn Ishaq made a lexicography and a treatise on homographies, and Ishoʿ of Merw, a lexicography. These works were taken up in an important Syriac-Arabic dictionary by Ishoʿ bar Ali, a student of Ḥunayn ibn Ishaq, during the second half of the 9th century. A physician of al-Muʿtamid (r. 870–892), he composed two works of medicine in Arabic. He was also a copyist but was especially known for his lexicon, which still forms the basis of modern Syriac dictionaries.

SCHOLARS OF THE ʿABBASID PERIOD

A well-known figure in the Melkite Church was Theodore Abu Qurra, who was the bishop of Ḥarran, near Edessa, at the beginning of the 9th century. He wrote in Syriac, but only his Arabic works have come down to us. Of the many Greek works attributed to him, most are pseudonymous. He was one of the first Christian authors to use Arabic in his controversies with Islam. He participated in a theological dispute at the Armenian court with an East Syrian, Nonnus of Nisibis, around 815. He also discussed theological subjects with the caliph al-Maʾmun in 829, but the dialogue that has come down to us is mostly literary. His theological work has a strong polemical bent aimed at explaining and defending the Christian faith against Islam on such topics as the Trinity, the knowledge of God, free will, the veneration of icons, and the true religion. Theodore was a scholar, translating the pseudo-Aristotelian work *On the Virtues of Souls* from Greek into Arabic.

THEODORE ABU QURRA, *REFUTATION OF THE SARACENS*

There was once a debate in Azotus. The Christians there were in distress because of the Saracens and asked the bishop for help. Boldly, the Saracen began:

Saracen: Tell me, bishop, wasn't the world full of idols before Moses preached Judaism?

Theodore: Clearly.

Saracen: When Moses summoned to Judaism, which part of the world seems to you pious, that which accepted Judaism, or that which remained idolatrous and did not obey Moses?

Theodore: That which accepted it.

Saracen: When later Christ came preaching Christianity, which part seems to you pious, that which accepted Christianity, or that which remained fixed in Judaism and did not obey Christ?

Theodore: That which accepted Christianity.

Saracen: When later Muhammad came preaching Magarismos [Islam], which part seems to you pious, that which accepted Magarismos, or that which remained in Christianity and did not obey Muhammad?

Theodore: That which remained in Christianity and did not obey Muhammad.

Saracen: Your last conclusion does not accord with the premises.

Theodore: There is no need for me to draw a conclusion based on false premises. Things are not as you suppose. Moses and Christ were not deemed worthy of belief simply because they preached and taught, such that Muhammad should also be believed because he preached and taught. Let me tell you why each was deemed worthy of belief.

PRAISE OF PAGANISM BY THE SABEAN
DOCTOR ṬĀBIT IBN QURRA IN ḤARRAN
(END OF THE 9TH CENTURY)

This blessed city has never been defiled by the error of Nazareth. We are the heirs and transmitters of paganism which was famed throughout the world. [. . .] Who has peopled the inhabited world and multiplied towns besides the excellent kings from pagan times? Who built the ports and canals? Who revealed the hidden knowledge? To whom has the divinity who attributes destiny and teaches the future shown other than to those who are renowned among the pagans? They explained everything, caused the medicine of souls to shine and showed them salvation. They also caused the medicine of the body to shine and filled the world with excellence in conduct and wisdom which is the summit of virtue. Without these contributions of paganism, the universe would be empty and deficient, enveloped by great poverty.

In the second half of the 9th century, the great mathematician Tābit ibn Qurra edited several mathematical treatises in Arabic and revised several translations of mathematical works. He also composed a book on music in Syriac and on questions of geometry. Writing in Arabic, he composed two treatises on geometry, the theory of numbers, and integral calculus. Bar Hebraeus indicates that Ibn Qurra, who was a Sabean (a category recognized as one of the Religions of the Book), mastered Greek, Syriac, and Arabic, and wrote in Arabic some 150 books on dialectic, mathematics, astronomy, and medicine and sixteen books in Syriac (mostly on topics of religious practice). He translated from Greek to Arabic works of Archimedes, Euclid, Ptolemy, and even Apollonius. The works in Syriac of this non-Christian author have not come down to us but were known to Bar Hebraeus in the 13th century.

Other Syriac authors produced works intended for their communities. Ishoʿ bar Nun (d. 828), who succeeded Timothy I as the next catholicos, promoted ecclesiastical canons on questions of marriage and inheritance law which were integrated into the book of canon law of the Church of the East. He also wrote a brief grammatical treatise on homographs and some homilies and letters. Most famously, he produced a commentary on the Old and New Testaments, *Select Questions*, in a question-and-answer format, most likely for catechesis and to defend Christianity against Islam. This work had a great influence in the Church of the East and was reused by Isho'dnah of Basra. Only a small part of his works has been published and translated today.

In the 850s, the monastic histories of Thomas of Marga and Isho'dnah of Basra repurposed the vast hagiographical literature of the Church of the East (today largely lost) to write the stories of schools and monasteries as they passed through various abbots, thus creating a collective scholastic memory of the Church of the East and delineating its local and ecclesiastical networks. Another important writer, Isho'dad, was originally from Merw (in modern-day Turkmenistan) and was made bishop of Ḥdatta, not far from Mosul. He produced a commentary on the Old and New Testaments typical of East Syrian exegesis, founded on the works of Theodore of Mopsuestia but also enriched by the influence of Ephrem, the Greek fathers, and eastern authors. This commentary had just as great an influence on the Syriac Orthodox Church as it did on the Church of the East. It was the first East Syrian work that included citations of the Syro-Hexapla produced in a Syriac Orthodox environment.

On the Syriac Orthodox side, the scholarly activity that took place east of the Tigris was similar to the west. The Syriac Orthodox patriarch Dionysius of Tel Maḥre (d. 845) and his brother Theodosius (d. 832), the bishop of Edessa, were held in high esteem by the caliph al-Ma'mun and the emir of Edessa, respectively, for their knowledge of Greek and their mastery of Greek, Syriac, and Arabic. Theodosius copied the chronicle of Eusebius of Caesarea into Syriac and translated the poems of Gregory of Nazianzus. Dionysius composed a chronicle in Syriac, today lost, but reused in subsequent chronicles. Dionysius traveled frequently in the course of administering church affairs and was well known in the courts of the caliphs and local emirs. On a diplomatic mission to Coptic Christians in rebellion, he visited Egypt, saw the pyramids and the floods of the Nile, and while in Baghdad met the Miaphysite Ethiopian prince on an ambassadorial mission to the caliphal court. He gives glimpses of daily life in Edessa in his writings as well: around 815, the rich families were compelled to contribute to the reconstruction of the walls by the Muslim authorities. The amount of tax levied in the time of al-Ma'mun was mentioned by the bishop of the city, Theodosius, the brother of Dionysius: the tax was levied on inns, shops, baths, and mills, but when the caliph learned that the tax was too burdensome for a great church that he admired, he declared that it no longer applied to anything with a roof.

A bishop located not far from Tagrit, Moses bar Kepha (d. 903), was an exegete and liturgist of the Syriac Orthodox Church in the east, who had access to a number of sources, both western and eastern, for his

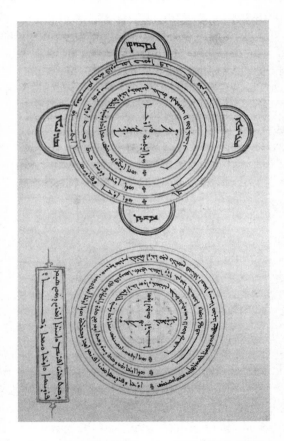

Schema showing the location of Paradise in the commentary of Moses bar Kepha. Bibliothèque patriarcale de Charfet (Lebanon).

Hexamaeron (a commentary on the six days of creation). He also wrote a commentary on Paradise (at a time when Islam had its own concept of paradise) as well as one on the New Testament. His theological treatises are still unpublished, as are at least some of his commentaries on liturgy, especially the feasts and their causes (a genre practiced in the Church of the East), and on *myron*, the oil used for anointing. His other biblical, patristic, and philosophical commentaries (on the *Organon* of Aristotle, for instance) are lost, along with the chronicle that he wrote. His work was extensively translated into Arabic.

Traditions and New Influences
10th–14th Centuries

Although Elias of Nisibis repeated in the 11th century what Ḥunayn ibn Ishaq had said in the 9th to defend the superiority of Syriac over Arabic—namely, that there were no works translated from Arabic whereas they were always translated from Syriac (and Greek, and Persian)—it was no longer true of his time, and his plea was primarily over identity rather than language, as even he himself wrote in Arabic. By the 11th century, Arabic had become the primary language used for communication and, increasingly, for culture throughout the Near and Middle East. Arabic was adopted very quickly in Chalcedonian circles—both Melkite and Maronite—as well as by the Church of the East, though it was not used by the Syriac Orthodox until later, as their identity was closely tied to Syriac, the language of their Syro-Mesopotamia homeland, and they continued to write in Syriac for some time longer. From this point forward, Syriac was largely a literary and liturgical language, known as *ktobonoyo* (from the root word *ktobo*, "book"), and less and less a spoken tongue, replaced by local dialects of Aramaic, Arabic, or in some places Persian (and later Turkish). The exception was a number of high-ranking ecclesiastical officials in the Syriac Orthodox Church, trained in monasteries where they spent virtually their entire lives, who seem not to have spoken Arabic correctly.

SIXTH CONVERSATION OF ELIAS OF NISIBIS WITH
THE VIZIR AL-MAGHRIBĪ ABOUT SCIENCES

[Al-Maghribī] said to me: Do you have sciences like those of the Muslims?

I said: Yes, and much more!

He said: What proof do you have of that?

I said: The proof is that the Muslims have many beneficial sciences that were translated from Syriac, while Syriac has no sciences that were translated from Arabic, because they have no science that would be beneficial if it were translated into another language.

By the 14th century, the use of Syriac had become only residual. The language was used only in ecclesiastical or scholarly circles as a "classical" language. Until recently, it was the obligatory and exclusive language of the seminary of the Syriac Orthodox Church. A lot is still to be done to publish and translate Syriac documents in these periods, still poorly known.

Besides language, the Arabic educational system, literature, and scientific knowledge all exercised an increasing influence on Syriac writers, who trained together with Jewish and Muslim scholars in the same circles and by the same methods. The influence of Greek *paideia* faded in favor of a new dominant Arabo-Persian culture, in which these Syriac writers participated. The writers of this period are often accused of lacking originality, but it is worth mentioning that encyclopedic practices had been popular since antiquity, where the reorganization of existing knowledge was praised, as opposed to innovation, which was considered dangerous. Late antique and medieval literature is primarily a form in which pieces of existing works are rearranged in a new order. Encyclopedism in Latin as well as Arabic characterized all medieval culture from the 12th century onward, and Syriac culture was no exception.

We can use the term "Syriac renaissance" to speak of the 12th and 13th centuries as a time in which there was both a return to classical influences and a series of new beginnings, a period of religious and cultural

The women at the tomb. Manuscript from ca. 1220. The iconography bears
stylistic parallels with Islamic iconography. British Library Add. 7170,
f. 160, / British Library, London, UK / © British Library Board.
All rights reserved / Bridgeman Images.

openness, as opposed to a more traditional analysis that sees this time
as one of slow decadence. However, this choice of periodization and the
concept of renaissance cannot be discussed without raising the question
of whether it was really a return to classical influences or more of a tilt-
ing toward Muslim Arabo-Persian culture. There has as yet been little
study of the art and literature of this period and no general synthesis.
At the same time, we can point to the emergence of new iconographic

programs in the churches and manuscripts that drew from local and Western influences, similar to what one finds in other Christian traditions and Islamic traditions of the time, as a sign of openness.

New Influences of the 10th Century

The 10th century saw the weakening of the 'Abbasids and the emergence of local dynasties who seized some of the caliphal power, resulting in a disintegration of central authority. From 893 to 932, Mesopotamia was ruled by the Hamdanids, who achieved a great degree of independence after the death of the caliph al-Muqtadir in 932. Two members of this family are especially famous: Hasan Nasir al-Dawla ("Defender of the ('Abbasid) Dynasty," 929–964) and Sayf al-Dawla ("Sword of the Dynasty," 940–967), who were the first emirs of Mosul and Aleppo, respectively, while southern Syria remained under the control of the Fatimid dynasty, which came to power in Egypt in 969.

The 10th century also saw the reconquest of lost territories by the Byzantines. The emperors Nicephorus II Phocas (r. 963–969) and John Tzimiskes (r. 969–976) launched land offensives in Armenia, northern Mesopotamia, and Cilicia and naval assaults that reclaimed Cyprus and Crete. In 969 Antioch was retaken.

The Hamdanids were on the front lines in the war against the Byzantines, and a language of holy war developed on both sides. Meanwhile, patronage of scholars, doctors, lawyers, and men of letters helped legitimize the dynasty, and the courts of Mosul and Aleppo played an important role in the preservation of literature. The Shi'ite Buyid dynasty (945–1055) controlled Iraq and western Iran and clashed with the Hamdanids, but this was nevertheless a period in which literature and science flourished.

The different Christian churches (or communities) sought support from the various Muslim powers to settle their disputes and strengthen their influence: in 912, for instance, a Melkite bishop was prevented from being ordained in Baghdad owing to the opposition of the East Syrian catholicos. The East Syrians had essentially gained the foremost position among the other Christian communities of Baghdad, and only a visiting bishop was permitted until the Melkites gained the

upper hand around 960. The Melkite patriarch of Antioch, Christopho-
rus (r. 960–967), on the other hand, was a relative of the emir Sayf al-
Dawla, at a time when Byzantine-Arab relations were tense in northern
Mesopotamia.

It was most likely during this period that murals were painted in
Deir al-Suryan in Egypt, a Syriac Orthodox monastery. Most famously,
there is a mural of King Abgar and the emperor Constantine, today
severely damaged. The abbot Moses of Nisibis was responsible for
the renovations of the monastery and the acquisition of a number of
manuscripts, among which were 250 that he brought from Baghdad and
its surroundings. They are a major source of our knowledge of Syriac
literature.

THE BYZANTINE RECONQUEST AND THE
FLOURISHING OF THE SYRIAC ORTHODOX

With the Byzantine reconquest of 934, Syriac Orthodox communities
returned to Melitene (Eskimalatya, not far from modern-day Malatya
in Turkey), an important town in Greater Armenia situated at the intersection of several roads in the fertile basin west of the Euphrates. The
reconquest of Melitene and much of the Levant is retold by the patriarch Michael the Syrian on the basis of the 11th-century chronicle of
the metropolitan of the city, Ignatius of Melitene, no longer extant, and
from the 12th-century work of Basil bar Shumana, also lost. The Syriac
Orthodox patriarch John VII Sarigta (r. 965–984/985) received an invitation from Nicephorus Phocas to come with his community and settle
in the regained land. As frontier dwellers, the emperor reasoned, the
Syriac Orthodox were accustomed to living between two peoples and
two empires, the Byzantine and the Arabo-Muslim, while the Romans/
Byzantines did not dare to do so "for fear of the Arabs." In exchange, the
emperor guaranteed the Syriac Orthodox religious toleration.

A period of economic and intellectual flourishing thus began for
the Syriac Orthodox communities, and the monasteries around Melitene experienced a golden age between 950 and 1020. Two monasteries
were built, one at Sergisyeh (958/959) and another, called Bar Gagai,
near Melitene. The monasteries of Cursor, Sarigta, and Barid were

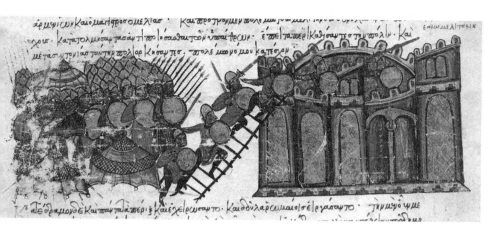

Reconquest of Melitene by the Byzantines. Chronicle of John Skylitzes.
The Picture Art Collection / Alamy Stock Photo.

equally important. The patriarch John Sarigta and his two successors lived at the monastery of Barid (which numbered more than a thousand monks). As the chronicler and metropolitan Ignatius of Melitene underscored, "During this time, religious houses and monasteries multiplied and prospered in the region of Melitene." Joseph Gumoyo, a Syriac Orthodox, was appointed *protospathairos* and governor by Byzantine authorities. After his appointment, it appears that the personnel of the Byzantine administration began to be recruited from among the Syriac Orthodox, a novelty because, as heretics, they had not been able to occupy official positions until that point.

This period was a golden age for the Syriac Orthodox from an economic standpoint as well as a cultural and religious one. At the end of the 10th century, some rich Syriac Orthodox merchants from Tikrit took refuge in Melitene to escape their tax burden and contributed to the construction of some buildings; the Bene Abu Imran of Tikrit, for instance, were famous for their wealth and built churches and monasteries, including convents for women, and distributed money among the poor. They received the duty of minting coins from the emperor Basil II (r. 976–1025) and gave him the funds to finance one of his campaigns. They also redeemed captives from the Turks. As the Syriac chronicle of Bar Hebraeus says, "We have written some words [about this time] in order to know what prosperity we had, and what misery we fell into afterwards."

The patriarchs who reigned in our Orthodox Church since the Arabs ruled in Syria resided in Antioch, Ḥarran, Callinicum, Edessa. Since the Greeks had again seized Syria, the emperor Nicephorus, seeing that Melitene was ruined and devastated, as well as Hanazit, busied himself with restoring its inhabitants. But the Romans were not inclined to live there out of fear of the Tayaye [the Arabs]. Some of his advisors suggested to him to call the Syrians who were accustomed to live and dwell in the midst of these two peoples and two empires.

The Monastery of Saint Sergius and Bacchus of Sergisiyeh

As the monastery became famous, they brought to them Mor John, the disciple of Maron, the great tree of the mountain of Edessa. Besides being very well versed in the teaching of dialectic and secular knowledge and in all the holy books, he was very learned in all kinds of virtue and holiness. Elias [the archimandrite] made progress in his works and the number of monks increased. He demolished the church, enlarged it, and raised it up. He decorated it with ornaments, with wall hangings, with books and gold and silver vases, for Joseph, the governor of the place, gave them presents. The monastery shone through its doctrine, the reading of books, the commentaries and the discussions in the presence of John of Maron. Many people came to be instructed. We found a book in the hands of whoever happened to be in the monastery. There were many scribes in the monastery.

A frenzy of teaching, production, and copying of books took place during this period of toleration by the Byzantines. A man named John of Maron attracted a number of students because of his reputed mastery of both sacred and secular knowledge. One hundred twenty priests flocked to his monastery of Bar Gagai, because it was necessary to train new ecclesiastical students for the reconquered regions where several new dioceses were created. Many manuscripts were copied there, some of which still survive.

At the very end of the 10th century, John, the abbot and bishop of the monastery of Qarṭmin, reintroduced *esṭrangela* script to Ṭur ʿAbdin, which had been forgotten for nearly a century. The region of Melitene was also likely where the five Greek vowel signs were first invented and added to the *serṭo* alphabet as an aid to reading the Ḥarklean version of the New Testament that had been translated in the 7th century (see chapter 4). This academic version, which was modeled closely on the Greek, came to be used for liturgical readings. This new interest in Greek, the language of the Byzantine Empire, can be explained by the dialogue with Melkite communities in the region, largely bilingual (Greek and Syriac) in the context of competition between the Syriac Orthodox and Byzantine churches. Conversion from one Christian community to another—including the very large Armenian community in the region—seems to have had as great a significance as conversion from Christianity to Islam.

The wealth and influence of Syriac Orthodox communities sparked jealousy in the Chalcedonians, who denounced them as heretics. Debates between Chalcedonians and Miaphysites were organized in Constantinople in 969. The Chalcedonian patriarch of Antioch, Athanasius, who noticed with concern how much importance was given to the Syriac Orthodox during the centuries when Antioch was under Muslim rule (since the Syriac Orthodox patriarch had been forbidden to stay in Antioch ever since the exile of Severus of Antioch in 518), tried by all means to convert the nobles and the people to the faith of the Byzantine Church. In 1028–1029, the Chalcedonian metropolitan of Melitene, jealous of and nervous about the influence of the charismatic Syriac Orthodox patriarch Jacob bar ʿAbdun, who was successfully converting Chalcedonians to Syriac Orthodoxy, caused him to be summoned to Constantinople by the emperor Romanos Argyros (r. 1028–1034). His successor, the Syriac Orthodox patriarch Dionysius IV, was forced to flee to Arab territory in order to escape the Chalcedonians who were seeking to arrest him. He moved the seat of the patriarchate

Flabellum from Deir al-Suryan. © Musée du Louvre, Dist.
RMN-Grand Palais / Claire Tabbagh / Art Resource, NY.

Detail of flabellum from Deir al-Suryan. © Musée du Louvre, Dist.
RMN-Grand Palais / Claire Tabbagh / Art Resource, NY.

to Amida and was protected by the Muslim governor, who refused to turn him over to the Byzantines. The renewed persecutions of the Syriac Orthodox were interpreted by Syriac writers as the reason for the defeats that the imperial armies suddenly began to suffer at the hands of the Muslims, a divine punishment of the Byzantines who had dared to take action against other Christians. At the same time, the Turks began to spread throughout the region, taking captives and pillaging, and the emperor Constantine X Doukas (r. 1059–1067) was forced to rebuild the walls of Melitene.

EXCERPT FROM A CHRONICLE ABOUT THE
RELATIONSHIP BETWEEN BYZANTINES
AND THE SYRIAC ORTHODOX

At this time the monasteries multiplied and prospered in the region of Melitene. Virtuous men were found there, both wise and eloquent. This is the reason that they were envied by the heretic Greeks who were in Melitene. As soon as [the Greeks] saw that the patriarch Mor Athanasius was dead and that the ocean of wisdom, Mor John of Maron, was dead also, the accursed leaders seized Mor Iwannis of Melitene and seven righteous and learned monks and sent them in fetters to Constantinople where they spent their lives in prison, in a true martyrdom. The Greeks took the great church called the Cursor.

Despite the renewal of persecutions by the Byzantines from 1004 onward, the Syriac Orthodox community continued to enjoy prosperity and intellectual activity for at least a century around Melitene. Ignatius, who was metropolitan of the city (r. 1063–1094), is a perfect example of a Syriac Orthodox Christian who was educated and trained in Greek. He was compared to Jacob of Edessa and Thomas of Ḥarqel for his translations. He composed a chronicle in two sections, one devoted to secular history and one to ecclesiastical, for which he relied on Greek sources in addition to Syriac and possibly Arabic ones. Under the reign of Constantine Doukas, he was persecuted by Chalcedonian powers and imprisoned for five months in the monastery of Hebdokos. No doubt because he was familiar with Greek, he took part in a debate in front of the Chalcedonian patriarch of Constantinople, after which he was banished to Macedonia. After the death of the emperor, he was able to regain his diocese.

IBN BUTLAN, 11TH CENTURY, DOCTOR AND PHILOSOPHER OF THE CHURCH OF THE EAST, *THE BANQUET OF PRIESTS*, TRANSLATED FROM ARABIC

[The master of the house (i.e., the priest of Mardin)] said to his disciple, "Idiot, don't you know that I saved this wine for people like these pure lords? Until what time will we hold back the clash of glasses in the arena at the hands of priests? Bring back gaiety to us and pass round the wine!" He got up, took a glass, stroked it lovingly, turned back to his companions and began to declaim to them, turning, in the light of day, the wine which was in his hand like a fiery flame:

If wine by essence were able to have an equal,
Or if another drink was able to resemble its subtlety,
Our Lord, cup in hand, would not have said,
"This is my Blood shed for the salvation of creatures."

Then he had the servers pass it round and refilled their glasses, and I was the only one among the priests to abstain from drinking.

EASTERN SYRO-ARABIC CULTURE

In the Church of the East, though Syriac remained a literary language, it was rivaled by Arabic. Emmanuel bar Shabare (d. 980), a monk near Mosul, wrote a commentary on the Hexaemeron, the six days of creation, which incorporated (as was customary) scientific knowledge and which remains untranslated in modern languages. He also wrote a *memra* on baptism and a Marian hymn preserved in the *Ḥudra*, the liturgical book of the Church of the East. Elias of Anbar, in the first half of the 10th century, wrote ten *memre* organized in thirty cycles which aimed to explain the symbols of salvation and which drew from the works of Pseudo-Dionysius the Areopagite.

ELIAS OF NISIBIS (ELIAS BAR SHINAYA)

Elias of Nisibis (975–1046) was one of the major figures of the Church of the East in the 10th and 11th centuries. Together with his brothers and Abu-l-Farag ʿAbdallah ibn al-Tayyib, he was part of a circle of East Syrian writers and scholars at the court of the prince Naṣr al-Dawla, renowned for his magnificence but also for his moderation with respect to taxation and his welcoming of other princes who sought asylum. These East Syrian Christian circles were formed at least as much by Arabic culture as Syriac, if not more. Elias wrote the essential parts of his works in Arabic. His bilingual Syriac-Arabic chronicle used sources from both languages, of which the majority are lost today. Despite his work in Arabic, Elias tried, in a discussion with a minister from the Marwanid court of Amida, to demonstrate the superiority of Syriac over Arabic in terms of lexicography and syntax. He wrote a grammar and a Syriac-Arabic dictionary, which attested to the need to defend and to continue to standardize a language that was not widely spoken and that found itself confronted by a new dominant language. His poetry is partially integrated into later works (such as the book of George Warda), and his canonical work (a Syriac collection in four volumes) has partly been preserved in an Arabic translation.

Elias of Nisibis had two brothers who were doctors; one, Abu l-ʿAlaʾ al-Ṣaʾid ibn Sahl, was a doctor and secretary, while the other, Manṣur ibn ʿIsa, was the physician of the Marwanid prince Naṣr al-Dawla. He reestablished the hospital at Maipherqaṭ/Martyropolis (Mefarkin in Turkey). A specialist in ophthalmology, he wrote five medical books and taught in a hospital, where he held seminars with other doctors and medical students. He had a vast library and was interested in theological and apologetic questions.

Works on Syriac and Arabic grammar and lexicography continued to flourish in the Church of the East, even as Syriac was spoken less and less. Elias of Tirhan (d. 1049) was the first to use the categories of Arabic grammar to compose one of his own. In the middle of the 10th century, Ḥasan bar Bahlul, who came to Baghdad, produced a valuable lexicon of Syriac and Greek terms in transliteration, where the definitions were in Syriac and Arabic. This dictionary did not contain ordinary words, but rather words pulled from the Bible, patristic commentaries, and scientific texts, as well as works like *Kalila wa Dimnah*, or *The Proverbs of the Arameans*. Besides the fact that this work references texts that have disappeared today, it also mentions dialectical differences of Syriac that were spoken in the regions between Bet Qaṭraye to the south and Edessa to the north, on the one hand, and between the Jazira to the west and Bet Aramaye and Bet Garmai to the east, on the other. It is therefore a veritable encyclopedia and today a valuable tool for understanding Syriac language and literature. The *Kitāb al-Dalā'il*, or *Book of the Signs*, by Bar Bahlul is situated in the Syriac tradition of *chronica*, or treatises on the calendar, and notably compares the Jewish, Muslim, and Sabean calendars of Ḥarran. But the "signs" also allow readers to determine the fitness of slaves, of fish, and of physiognomy, and the interpretation of dreams. It partly preserves the work of Ibn Qutayba (828–889), who produced the first Muslim treatise on the interpretation of dreams.

Among the East Syrian writers of the 11th century, it is also necessary to mention those who wrote in Arabic, like Ibn al-Tayyib. The theological encyclopedia *Kitāb al-Majdal*, which dates to the 10th/11th century, is organized by *bab*, "gates," from which two histories (including the chronicle preserved in Seert in Turkey and bearing the title of the *Chronicle of Seert*) were written in Arabic.

The Instability of the 11th and 12th Centuries

The political and military situation of the 11th and 12th centuries is relatively complicated: the forces involved include the Byzantines, who had retaken several of their old territories (in 1050 Edessa was controlled by the Byzantines, for instance); the Seljuk Turks and their *atabegs*, or princes, who took the northern areas of the Buyid and Fatimid kingdoms; and the Franks who arrived with the First Crusade. The crumbling of a central power resulted in instability and a quasi-permanent state of war. The local population bore the cost of sieges and the constant presence of armies.

The Turkish Seljuk tribe gradually seized Iran, Iraq, and Asia Minor. In 1055 they chased the Buyids out of Baghdad; in 1059 they took Isfahan. In 1078 they displaced the Fatimids from Jerusalem, where

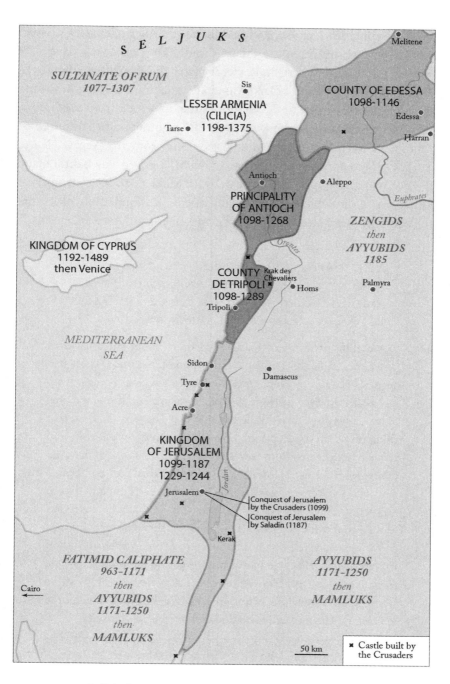

S E L J U K S

SULTANATE OF RUM
1077–1307

Sis

LESSER ARMENIA
(CILICIA)
Tarse ● 1198-1375

Melitene

COUNTY OF EDESSA
1098-1146

Edessa ●

Harran ●

Antioch ●

● Aleppo

Euphrates

PRINCIPALITY
OF ANTIOCH
1098-1268

Orontes

ZENGIDS
then
AYYUBIDS
1185

KINGDOM OF CYPRUS
1192-1489
then Venice

COUNTY
DE TRIPOLI
1098-1289
Tripoli ●

Krak des
Chevaliers
● Homs

Palmyra
●

MEDITERRANEAN
SEA

Sidon ●

Tyre ●

Acre ●

● Damascus

KINGDOM
OF JERUSALEM
1099-1187
1229-1244

Jerusalem ●

Jordan

Conquest of Jerusalem
by the Crusaders (1099)
Conquest of Jerusalem
by Saladin (1187)

Kerak

FATIMID CALIPHATE
963–1171
then
AYYUBIDS
1171–1250
then
MAMLUKS

Cairo
←

AYYUBIDS
1171–1250
then
MAMLUKS

50 km

✖ Castle built by
the Crusaders

Political Fragmentation in the 12th–13th Centuries

they had ruled since 970, and closed the road to Jerusalem to Christian pilgrims, which triggered the First Crusade. They also took control of Armenia and scored a crushing victory over the Byzantine emperor at Manzikert, on the shores of Lake Van, in 1071, taking the emperor Romanus Diogenes prisoner. In the territories that they took from the Greeks, they created the Sultanate of *Rum* (Rome). The other branch of the Great Seljuks, in Baghdad, governed a vast empire from the Aegean Sea to Turkestan and comprising the Iranian world, modern-day Bahrain, and the holy cities of Arabia. After the death of Malik Shah in 1092, a period of decline set in, which was especially due to economic difficulties and the conflicts that pitted the atabegs against the sect of the Assassins.

THE MISFORTUNES OF THE SYRIAC-ORTHODOX
COMMUNITY OF JERUSALEM UNDER THE FRANKISH
KINGDOM: COLOPHON OF MS LYON 1 AND PARIS 51
(JERUSALEM AS THE LATIN KINGDOM)

We think it is useful to say something about the villages of 'Adecieh and Beith 'Arif, which had monasteries once. These had been bought at a very high price, by the elect of God, Thomas, who was at that time the metropolitan of Jerusalem. But during the time of our father, Ignatius, during the year 1448 (AD 1137), a great trial fell upon us [in these villages] through the cruelty of a Frank, who came to be delivered from the fetters of Egypt. It was one of these old Franks who had taken Jerusalem ... [the villages had been confiscated and then recovered at great cost]. But when everything had been finished, perhaps on account of our sins, perhaps because God wanted to test the righteous, the Frank which we have mentioned above was delivered by the intermediary of the Armenian bishop [of Jerusalem]. He came back from Egypt and harassed the whole town, but us more than anyone else because we were weak. First, we were told to leave all the places, in order for the Frank to enter the monastery. Then we had to go find him and begin a lawsuit.

From 1086 to 1099, the First Crusade took place, resulting in the foundation of states in the Near East, of which the County of Edessa was the foremost (Edessa had been taken by the Seljuks in 1087, then by the Franks in 1098, when Baldwin of Boulogne became the first Count of Edessa). The Artuqids, one of the main vassals of the Seljuks, ruled Amida, Harput, Maipherqaṭ, and Mardin between 1082 and 1408, while the Danishmends, another Turkish dynasty, ruled over Anatolia and Melitene (1080–1174). The 12th century saw the atabegs of Mesopotamia establish their own principalities. Zengi, the atabeg of Mosul and Aleppo, took Edessa in 1144.

The dynasty of the Ayyubids, under Saladin, took power in Egypt in 1170 and extended toward Syria in a series of violent confrontations with the Fatimids on one hand and the Franks on the other, and took Jerusalem in 1187.

It is not a coincidence that between the 11th and the 14th century so many Syriac and Arabic chronicles try to understand this complex situation, tracing it back to creation, and lament the often tragic state of the Syriac Christian communities as well as divisions and corruption in the heart of the church. The relationship between the Syriac Orthodox Church and people with the Armenians in Anatolia and northern Mesopotamia was one of the main issues in this period, at a moment when the Byzantine emperor Manual I Comnenus needed an agreement with the Armenians to reunite his empire in the south. As the Armenians and Byzantines exchanged formulas of unification, the Syriac Orthodox sought support from the Franks.

The monastery of the prophet Moses (Deir Mar Musa) that overlooks the plain of Nabk in Syria was important until at least the 6th century. Starting in the 12th century, it took the name of Moses the Ethiopian (Mar Musa al-Ḥabashi), by which it is better known today. It includes a rich iconography made between the 11th century (the time when its church was rebuilt) and the 13th, the most elaborate in the Levant which survives to the present.

DIONYSIUS BAR ṢALIBI ON THE TAKING OF EDESSA BY THE EMIR ZENGI IN 1144

At that time was the lamentable taking of Edessa in Mesopotamia, the famed town of the Christians, which the sword of the Turks ravaged because of our sins, us being justly abandoned by God.

Fresco of the Last Judgment, Deir Mar Musa.

As the inhabitants had been imprisoned for a long time by the Turks and as the town was weakened in this way, Joscelin, the lord of this town, all of a sudden began a war against Zengi, lord of Mosul. As Joscelin, having left for Antioch, was far away, Zengi gave the order to begin the attack from all sides. Seven ballistas threw stones and the troops showered down their arrows like raindrops. What language can recount or what finger can write without trembling the thing that happened at the 3rd hour of Saturday, the 23rd of Kanun [Dec. 23, 1144]? The Turks entered with their swords and blades drawn and spilled the blood of old men and young, men and women, priests and deacons, cenobites and monks, religious, virgins, nursing children, fiancés and fiancées! The Assyrian boar prevailed and trampled the delicious grapes. Ah! What a bitter tale. The city of Abgar, the friend of Christ, was crushed underfoot because of our iniquity! Meanwhile, the Franks did not open the gate to those who fled to the citadel for safety. The Turks spared the lives of all those of our people, the Armenians and Greeks, who survived, but they killed the Franks everywhere where they found them. It is not for us to tell the rest of the calamity, but to the prophet Jeremiah and to those like him to summon the mourners to compose elegies for this unfortunate people.

EDESSA

In the 12th century, the noble family of Shumana gave the city of Edessa a metropolitan, Abu al-Faraj, better known by the name Basil, who wrote a chronicle that was used by Michael the Syrian, *The Chronicle of 1234*, and Bar Hebraeus. His brother Michael was the steward of Count Joscelin when he was prince of Edessa. Michael played an important intermediary role between the Frankish powers and the Syriac Orthodox communities. He intervened with Joscelin to free the patriarch Athanasius, who was being held at Amida. In the story of the second conquest of Edessa by the Turks in 1146, which is reported in the chronography of Basil bar Shumana, the list of treasures in the Syriac Orthodox cathedral reveals that the donors included "kings and other nobles," and that sponsorship of the church was always popular. Bishops and metropolitans suffered the same fate as the local populace when it came to sieges and acts of war: they could be abducted, imprisoned, or ransomed. They wrote books of history but also poems about contemporary circumstances. The capture of the city by Zengi in 1144 sparked discussions about the protection given to the city by Jesus (see the Abgar Legend, page 16).

DIONYSIUS BAR ṢALIBI

Known as "the star of his generation" and "the pride of the Syrians," Dionysius bar Ṣalibi (d. 1171) was educated in Melitene, his native city, where he studied both sacred and secular knowledge. He became a bishop at Marʿash in 1148. He was the victim of an attack launched by a group of Armenian bandits that pillaged Marʿash and expelled the population, forcing Dionysius to take refuge in the monastery of Kasliyud. His commentary on the Bible is the first exegetical collection since the

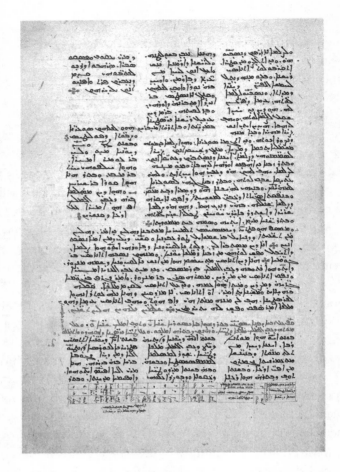

Columns and canons in the *Chronicle* of Michael
the Syrian. The parallel columns present political
events, ecclesiastical matters, and others in a
synchronous format.

11th century to show a new style. Several concurrent commentaries—
the first factual, the rest spiritual—are presented in columns in an order that is still only partially understood, but innovative. As a theologian, Dionysius wrote a book against "all the heresies and beliefs which
increase the pressures on our orthodox faith," which is to say pagans,

Jews, Muslims, the Church of the East, Chalcedonians, and Armenians. Only Latin Christians receive a relatively positive treatment.

MICHAEL THE GREAT

One of the most exceptional figures in the history of the Syriac Orthodox Church was the Syriac Orthodox patriarch Michael—called "the Great" to distinguish him from his nephew, who succeeded him and bore the same name—known in the West as Michael the Syrian (1126–1199). Originally from a family of priests in Melitene, Michael became a monk in the monastery of Mor Barṣaumo, located in the same region, before becoming patriarch in 1166. For the administration of the church, he was in contact with the Armenians and the Copts. With the consent of the Byzantine emperor Manuel I Comnenus, he traveled on a regular basis to Antioch, at that time under Latin rule. He also returned several times to Jerusalem, also under Frankish control. His authority was contested for a time by an antipatriarch who was supported by a faction in the church and by the Latins, and consequently Michael turned to the Seljuk sultan, Kilij Arslan II. He drafted a document (today no longer extant) for the First Lateran Council (1123), which he was invited to attend, but declined. He gathered canons designed to put the church in better order, but they are not preserved either. He organized the hagiography of the Syriac Orthodox Church in order to assure the continued memory of the church's martyrs. Michael is especially known for having composed a universal chronicle, beginning at creation and extending until his own time, which relies on Greek, Syriac, and Arabic sources that are lost today. This chronicle attempts to make sense of the history of the world, especially Michael's own period, which suffered so many ecclesiastical and political difficulties, and adopts an original format that divides history into three columns: civil history, ecclesiastical history, and miscellaneous matters.

Michael lived at the monastery of Mor Barṣaumo and the monastery of Mor Ḥananyo, not far from Mardin. The library of the monastery was nearly entirely destroyed by a fire in 1183. The only books to escape the fire were a breviary in two volumes that he had made and two volumes of homilies by Jacob of Serugh in his own hand. Michael carefully began to restore the library. He dedicated his free days to copying manuscripts and his nights to pastoral writing and the administrative paperwork of the church. Among the manuscripts he copied by hand was an exceptional Gospel with silver bindings, written in gold ink on a silver background and in silver ink on a gold background. It began with an illumination in gold, followed by many colored illustrations of the history of redemption and of religious feasts. It was brought by the patriarch Constantine to Sis in Cilicia at the end of the 13th century but was cut to pieces during the pillage of the monastery where it was found. Michael, who considered the monastery of Mor Barṣaumo to be his home, ended his days there, having enriched the buildings and books of the monastery in all kinds of ways.

The 13th and 14th Centuries

This period was marked by warring Arab dynasties, the presence of the Frankish kingdoms, and the arrival of the Mongols. In 1202 the Fourth Crusade detoured to Constantinople, which it captured in 1204, breaking Byzantine power. Led by Hulegu, the Mongols invaded the Muslim world, taking Baghdad and putting an end to the ʿAbbasid caliphate, then invading Syria and taking Aleppo and Damascus in 1260.

The Syriac Orthodox monastery of Mar Behnam (today Syriac Catholic) in Mosul in Iraq, constructed around the mausoleum of Mar Behnam and his sister Sarah and restored in the 12th century, incorporated exceptional architectural artwork in the 13th century during the reign of Badr al-Din, the atabeg of Mosul. The favorable economic and cultural climate of the region allowed for the addition of several new domes, stuccoes, and bas-reliefs very close to contemporary Islamic style, with Christian motifs taken from the life of Mar Behnam (a warrior saint). Numerous inscriptions can be found on the walls of the church and mausoleum recounting the monastery's history between the 12th and the 20th century.

Ornate niche in Mar Behnam monastery. Photo by Amir Harrak.

AUTHORS OF THE CHURCH OF THE EAST

Grammatical works continued to be produced in the Church of the East: Isho'yahb bar Malkon (d. 1233), who was bishop of Nisibis and Armenia, composed his own bilingual Syriac-Arabic grammar. By arranging it in two columns, following the style of Arabic grammars, he participated in this mixed culture. He composed theological and polemical treatises in Arabic, sometimes introduced in Syriac. John bar Zoʻbi (12th and 13th centuries), who studied with Simeon Shanqlawi, taught at the monastery of Beit Qoqa in Adiabene, where he also attracted Syriac Orthodox students like Jacob bar Shakko. He composed a grammar (still unpublished), which relies on Syriac categories, and wrote on theology and philosophy. Simeon Shanqlawi, in the region of Adiabene, composed a treatise on the calendar (a *chronicon*, still unpublished), formatted as a series of questions and answers with his disciple John bar Zoʻbi. He also wrote a treatise on baptism as a mystical poem.

GIWARGIS WARDA, *HYMN 58*, ON WEDNESDAY OF THE ROGATION

O intender of prayers,
And accepter of rogations
And granter of the requests!
Attend to our prayers and supplications
And turn your ear to our sorrows!

Our Lord, accept the praying
Of the brain and the skull of the Church!
For it stands at the head of the pasture,
Like Moses at the head of Israel!

Our Lord, accept the praying
Of the archpastor and archbishops,
For their glance is directed towards heaven
And they are pleading for mercy in the world.

Our Lord, accept the praying
Of the readers, whose reading is beautiful!
For they sow in the ears of everybody
The seed of Christ's teaching.

Our Lord, accept the praying
Of the scribe and the calligrapher.

Our Lord, accept the praying
Of the hermits and anchorites!

For they are cloistered in their cells,
And have closed the doors behind them.

Our Lord, accept the praying
Of the heads and superiors!
For they are leading along the King's way
Those who wander in ignorance.

The Book of the Rose, most likely dating to the 13th century, is an important liturgical book of the Church of the East, a collection of hymns (for the most part *'onyatha*) on the feasts of the year, attributed to a certain George Warda (Warda meaning "rose"), who is otherwise unknown. Some of these hymns deal with dramatic contemporary events, such as famines or the Mongol raids of the years 1233–1236, others with the celebrations of saints and martyrs. They sometimes rely on apocryphal traditions such as the stories about Jesus's childhood or the wise men. Such poems created and passed down the memory of the Church of the East through liturgical celebrations.

It is worth mentioning as part of the same milieu Khamis bar Qardaḥe, a poet from near Arbela (modern-day Erbil in Iraqi Kurdistan), whose poems were passed down with those of George Warda and who was likely a contemporary. He wrote liturgical poetry, but also on secular subjects like the ignorance of the people of Arbela, the silkworm, or even the letters of the alphabet. More than two hundred epigrams are attributed to him, on subjects such as mystical love, wine, flowers, and more. He achieved great success, and his works were translated into Azeri and Surayt (a modern dialect of Aramaic).

BAR 'EBROYO (BAR HEBRAEUS)

Born in Melitene, Bar Hebraeus passed most of his life in modern-day Iraq and Iranian Azerbaijan, though he also studied in Frankish territory at Antioch and Tripoli. Initially bishop of Aleppo, he saw the city fall to the Mongols in 1260. He was elected *maphrian* in 1264. He lived in Mosul and at the monastery of Mar Mattai, but also traveled with the Mongol court in Maragha and Tabriz. In 1259 Hulegu, the founder of

Celestial globe of Maragha, dating to the time of Bar Hebraeus.
Mathematisch-Physikalischer Salon, Staatliche Kunstsammlungen Dresden,
Photo: Jürgen Karpinski.

the Ilkhanid dynasty, had created an observatory in Maragha (in the province of Azerbaijan, in Iran) under the direction of the great Iranian scholar Naṣir al-Din al-Ṭusi (1201–1274). Bar Hebraeus settled near the court to take advantage of the library, containing more than forty thousand volumes, which was attached to the observatory. It was visited by scholars of all backgrounds and religions.

BAR HEBRAEUS ON THE MONGOLS

At that time a man came who, as I had heard from trustworthy Mongols, had the habit, in the dead of winter, of walking barefoot in the desert and mountain. When he came back, he said, "God spoke to me and said, 'I have given everything on the face of the earth to Temujin and to his children, and I have called him Genghis Khan. Tell him to act with justice.'"

BAR HEBRAEUS ON WEALTH

The advantages of wealth accrue either in this world or in eternity. Those benefits in this world are evident in the eyes of everyone. Those which apply to eternity can be divided into three categories. Essentially, one can spend his wealth either for himself or for other people or for nothing at all. Regarding the first category, if one wants to acquire a moderate subsistence so that one can make a vow of asceticism, this wealth accrues to eternity. The second category has two sides, because someone who lives in the world and is rich can spend his wealth either in alms or for honor, for instance in organizing banquets. And the advantage of this category accrues to eternity if it is without recompense in this world. As the Savior said: "When you organize a feast or banquet, invite the poor, the afflicted, the lame and the blind. Happy are those who will never receive repayment" (Luke 14:12–14). The third category is that of the rich man who comes to the aid of society by building churches, hostels, and bridges or in taking the initiative to arrange water sources, streams, or ponds on dry paths.

BAR HEBRAEUS, *LAUGHABLE STORIES*

Another actor was going about in Sebastia [i.e., Siwas] in the winter season dressed in a new flaxen garment and a certain man said to him, "Give me this tunic of yours and you will still have your cloak, and your Christ commanded that you give both your tunic and your cloak to whosoever asked you for them." And he replied: "Let the mind of Christ be far from me on this matter! For this commandment was not given by Him to the people of Sebastia in the winter season, although it may be given to the people of Palestine in the summer season."

A prolific writer, Bar Hebraeus was the author of more than forty books covering all sorts of topics: exegesis, theology, liturgy, jurisprudence, sciences, poems, and wisdom parables. Medicine and philosophy form the heart of his work, along with two chronicles, one in Syriac, divided into secular and ecclesiastical history, and one in Arabic, most likely intended for Muslims. His works combine the knowledge of Arabo-Persian writers such as Ibn Sina (Avicenna), al-Ghazali, and Nasir al-Din al-Tusi with Syriac sources and works translated from Greek to form a new encyclopedism. Bar Hebraeus considered the knowledge of Arabic to be indispensable, since Muslim culture and forms of knowledge were dominant, and used the paradigm of Arabic grammar to form the foundation of his Syriac grammar. He also demonstrates a softening attitude toward the Church of the East and presents the two churches as branches of the same Syriac tradition.

Another important person in the Syriac Orthodox Church, highly influenced by Arabic literature, is John bar Maʿdani (d. 1263), who was metropolitan of Mardin, *maphrian*, and finally patriarch. John studied Arabic in Baghdad and composed Arabic liturgical works in rhymed prose. He also wrote a collection of Syriac poems, two of which concern the soul (symbolized by a bird), in the vein of the great philosopher and doctor Ibn Sina (Avicenna). He also wrote a poem on the conquest of Edessa. His poems are often transmitted and confused with those of Bar Hebraeus. The anaphora that he composed is still included in the Syriac Orthodox corpus today.

The crowning figure of classical Syriac literature, 'Abdisho bar Brika (d. 1318), known in Latin by the name 'Ebedjesus, became the East Syrian metropolitan of Nisibis and Armenia. He composed a work of theology known as *The Pearl*, an explanation of liturgical services, and a collection of theological poems known as *The Paradise of Eden*. He also gathered together in his *Nomocanon* the synodical canons of the Church of the East. His most valuable work is his catalogue of Syriac authors and works of literature, especially East Syrian, of which there are a great number that are lost today or are known to us only through him.

The second half of the 14th century, known as the "dark night" of the Syriac churches, was defined by the bloody foundation of Tamerlane's (1336–1405) empire in Transoxiana, of which Samarkand was the capital and which encompassed Central Asia, Azerbaijan, Iraq, Syria, and Turkey.

Diaspora and Encounters
with the West
15th–21st Centuries

With the dissolution of the Crusader kingdoms and the Islamization of the Mongol world, Christians in the Near East underwent one of the darkest periods of their history. These events, at the end of the 13th century, resulted in an anti-Christian reaction by the Mamluks (who ruled Egypt and Syria from 1250 to 1517) and marked the beginning of a decline among the churches. This decline was accelerated by the devastation caused by the invasion of the Mongol prince Tamerlane at the end of the 14th century, which destroyed many churches and monasteries. Christian communities, including their most prominent members, took refuge in the mountains: Lebanon for the Maronites (who had already found refuge there during the Arab invasions of the 7th century) and the great mountains of southeastern Turkey, the heart of which was Ṭur ʿAbdin for the Syriac Orthodox and Hakkari for the East Syrians.

The establishment of the Ottoman Empire (born in the 14th century after its victories over the Byzantine Empire and the Seljuk state) and its expansion into northern Mesopotamia at the beginning of the 16th century stabilized the situation, creating a space for peace and cohabitation with the invention of the *millet*, or nation, an administrative grouping centered on confessional identity. Very little information survives from the 15th and 16th centuries. Beginning in the 16th century, relations developed between the Syriac churches and Europe. Factions from the various churches aligned themselves with Roman Catholicism, thus creating Oriental Catholic churches (Chaldean and Syriac Catholic).

Beginning in the 19th and early 20th centuries, the arrival and competition of Protestant and Catholic missionaries, the birth of nationalism, and European orientalism all combined to create a nationalist "awakening" among some Syriac-speaking Christians, who would henceforth call themselves Assyrians or Chaldeans. The creation of an identity-based memory reappropriated imagery from ancient Assyria together with the preservation of writing and classical language.

The Discovery of Syriac in Europe

The study of Syriac in Europe was born in the context of the Renaissance at the beginning of the 16th century, a period marked by openness to the world and intellectual curiosity, during which the invention of the printing press allowed for communication on a new scale. Two elements played a role: the concern for restoring the original language of various texts, and the interest in the text of the Bible that had been stimulated by the controversies around the Reformation. In 1516 Erasmus published the first edition of the New Testament in Greek. The publication process required assembling many manuscripts, and precisely during the fall of Constantinople, Pope Nicholas V had purchased an enormous amount of such manuscripts from the conquerors via secret agents. It was in this humanistic environment that "orientalism" was born. The first books to be printed were Bibles, liturgical books, and grammars. In 1539 the *Introductio in linguam chaldaicum* of Teseo Ambrogio was the first Syriac book printed (in Pavia, Italy), using wooden Syriac letters.

RABELAIS ON THE IDEAL HUMANIST EDUCATION
IN THE FAMOUS CURRICULUM THAT GARGANTUA
PROPOSES TO HIS SON PANTAGRUEL

Now it is that the learned languages are to their pristine purity restored, viz., Greek, without which a man may be ashamed to account himself a scholar, Hebrew, Arabic, Chaldaean [the contemporary term for Syriac], and Latin . . . All the world is full of knowing men, of most learned schoolmasters, and vast libraries; and it appears to me as a truth, that neither in Plato's time, nor Cicero's, nor Papinian's, there was ever such conveniency for studying as we see at this day there is. Wherefore, my son, I admonish thee to employ thy youth to profit as well as thou canst, both in thy studies and in virtue. Thou art at Paris . . . I intend, and will have it so, that thou learn the languages perfectly; first of all the Greek, as Quintilian will have it; secondly, the Latin; and then the Hebrew, for the Holy Scripture sake; and then the Chaldee and Arabic likewise . . . And at some hours of the day apply thy mind to the study of the Holy Scriptures; first in Greek, the New Testament, with the Epistles of the Apostles; and then the Old Testament in Hebrew. In brief, let me see thee an abyss and bottomless pit of knowledge.

In France, the study of Syriac largely developed thanks to royalty, through the foundation of the Collège royal, the ancestor of the modern Collège de France, which was designed to counter what was deemed overly scholastic teaching at the Sorbonne. The new sciences included Greek, Hebrew, and mathematics. A chair of Syriac and Arabic was very quickly added, the first officeholder of which was Guillaume Postel, from 1538 to 1543. Another sign of this new academic interest was the addition of the first Syriac manuscript to the Bibliothèque royale, the predecessor of the Bibliothèque nationale de France, which has a binding with the arms of Henri II and which was probably collected in the time of François I. Today labeled BnF syr. 44, it is a Gospel book according to the Peshiṭta version, copied in 1521 in Rome by Elias, son of Abraham, for the cardinal of Plaisance, Bernardin-Loup Carvajal.

Around the 16th century, the Syriac Orthodox patriarch Ignatius Abdallah I sent the priest Moses of Mardin as a legate to the pope with manuscripts as a gift, with the idea of buying Syriac books or arranging for them to be printed. This initiative shows that the development of the printing press and its potential was known in Ṭur ʿAbdin. Moses was in contact with Guillaume Postel and Andreas Masius, scholars interested in Syriac and Arabic. Chance put him in contact with Widmanstetter (1506–1557), chancellor to the emperor Charles V, and later on with Ferdinand, who was the restorer of the University of Vienna and was enthusiastic about the project. Widmanstetter brought Moses of Mardin to Vienna and obtained financial backing for him from the emperor Ferdinand. Two thousand copies of the first Syriac New Testament were printed in 1555. The font was based on Moses's handwriting, since he had also copied manuscripts during his stay. Moses was also the Syriac teacher of Andreas Masius, who published with his help a Syriac grammar and lexicon, the *Syrorum peculium*, used in the polyglot Bible of Anvers in 1571. Moses continued to copy manuscripts after he returned to the Near East, especially the *Chronicle* of Michael the Great. He returned to Rome after 1578 and copied manuscripts there as well. The costs involved in printing and the low distribution of Syriac books had the result that the tradition of copying manuscripts by hand continued even after the introduction of printing technology.

The work of Moses of Mardin highlights the role that these initial exchanges with the Middle East played in Europe after the end of the Crusades. An archbishop of Edessa was present at the Council of Florence in 1444, which was called to reestablish communion between the Latin Catholics and the Orthodox Greeks and Slavs. Contacts were also established with the Church of the East, with an initial attempt in the 16th century that almost succeeded in achieving union with Rome. But it would be the Maronites who would play an especially decisive role in forging ties between the Syriac world and Europe, owing to the connections that they had formed with the Roman Catholic Church during the Crusades.

Interested in training missionaries to the Oriental churches and in furthering the defense of Christianity against Islam, the Catholic Church created several colleges. At the end of the 16th century, the Maronite College was founded in Rome for young students from the Levant, designed to train them in European science but also in the language and liturgy of their own culture. Over two centuries, this college equipped groups of students in the study of Syriac and Arabic in Europe: one of the most notable was Djibrail al-Sahyouni (or Gabriel Sionite, as he was known in Paris), born in Ehden in northern Lebanon in 1577 and sent

Polyglot Bible of Paris

at the age of seven to the Maronite College in Rome. He was the main architect of *The Polyglot Bible of Paris*, published by Le Jay in seven languages from 1628 to 1645.

The 17th century saw the development of these studies through further missions to the Orient (see more below) to buy and collect manuscripts and enrich European libraries, especially the Vatican Library and the Bibliothèque royale in Paris. The study of Syriac in this period was the work of Maronite scholars who spent their entire lives in

Rome and Paris, such as Abraham Ecchelensis (al-Hakelani) and Jean Hesronite (Yuḥanna al-Hasrouni). Several joined the groups of the Collège royal (modern-day Collège de France) in Syriac and Arabic studies, which were later unified. They created the first tools for working with Syriac in the form of grammars and published texts.

The study of Syriac in the 18th century was defined by the Maronite Assemani family, which searched for Middle Eastern manuscripts for the Vatican collection. Joseph Simon Assemani is the author of the *Bibliotheca Orientalis*, the first magisterial synthesis of Syriac literature and culture, based on the Vatican manuscripts of his time and still valuable today. He also created a catalogue describing the contents of Syriac and Arabic manuscripts and published, among other works, a printed edition of the works of St. Ephrem. His nephew, Étienne Évode Assemani, published a catalogue of Syriac manuscripts in Florence, the *Acts* of the martyrs, and the Latin translation of the works of Bar Hebraeus. Another nephew, Joseph Louis Assemani, published a collection of liturgical texts. The Maronites thus played an essential role as intermediaries between the Syriac world and Europe.

The Birth of Oriental Catholic Churches

Beginning in the 15th and 16th centuries, the churches were split by attempts to unite with Rome, which resulted in the separation of the existing churches into multiple branches. The influence of Western missionaries was particularly felt from the beginning of the 19th century.

THE MARONITE CHURCH

Belonging to the first church that united itself to Rome during the era of the Crusades, the Maronites paid dearly during the first century of Mamluk rule for what was seen as collaboration with the invaders from the West. The Maronites organized themselves to protect against military invasions. The patriarch established himself in the holy valley known as Qadisha, whose very steep sides constituted formidable protection. The monastery of Qannoubin, the seat of the patriarchate, is partly built into the rock. Local society organized itself into a feudal model based on powerful families. The ties with Rome were maintained only through the Franciscans, the only Latins to remain in the Near East after the Crusades. From the 15th century and increasingly during the 16th century, relations grew closer with Rome, culminating at the end of the 16th century with the foundation of the Maronite College at Rome.

In the Ottoman Empire, it was the patriarch who was the civil as well as ecclesiastical head of the community. He exercised real political power over Lebanon along with Arab Druze emirs (the Ma'n) and Sunni Muslims (and the Shihab, who converted to Christianity along

with a number of other Muslims). With the decline of Ottoman influence, the patriarch became the real authority in the region, aligned with
Western powers who did not hesitate to intervene militarily to protect
the Maronites (as demonstrated by a French expedition in 1860 in response to the massacres in Lebanon). This gave the Maronite Church
a role in the formation of Lebanon which has largely given it its shape
today.

CHALDEANS AND ASSYRIANS

The Church of the East entered a period of decline, largely shrinking to
the area in Kurdistan around Lake Van, Urmia, and Mosul, its members
split between the Ottoman and Persian Empires. The Persian Empire
had been dominated since the 16th century by the Safavid dynasty but
transitioned to the Qajar dynasty after 1736. Along the Kurdish model,
the Christian communities were organized into tribes (*ashiret*) ruled by
a *malek* (king or chief). The patriarch believed himself to be the ultimate
head of all parties and factions, as much a temporal ruler as a spiritual
one. Around the 15th century, the office of patriarch became hereditary,
passing from uncle to nephew, sometimes still children, so as to avoid
tribal conflicts. All patriarchs took the name of Shim'un upon ascending to office. The nephew of a patriarch was identified as the successor
even before his birth and prepared for his future role; this preparation
included a very strict dietary regimen that was followed by his mother
while she was pregnant and then by the patriarch himself thereafter.
The future candidate received the title of *naṭar kursya*, "guardian of the
throne." The seat of the catholicos was located, though little used from
the 15th century to 1804, in the monastery of Rabban Hormizd north of
the plain of Mosul. The catholicoi received a firman from the Ottoman
authorities in Istanbul to exercise their authority.

   In the 16th century, after a dispute about the mode of succession
to the patriarchate, one of the candidates, John Sulaqa, the abbot of the
monastery of Rabban Hormizd, sought support from Rome and formalized a union in 1553, receiving a pallium from the pope. He established
himself at Diyarbakır. Again, at the end of the 17th century, an East Syrian priest from Diyarbakır, John, received the assistance of the French

consul in Aleppo—François Piquet, a promoter of union with Rome in
the Near East—in order to receive the money he needed for recognition
by the Ottoman authorities and the Roman church. He was recognized
as the head of the community in Diyarbakır (known as Chaldeans), then
given the title "Patriarch of the Nestorians," and finally "Patriarch of the
Chaldeans of Babylon" (in other words, Baghdad—a reference abandoned in 2021 by the Chaldean Church), under the name of John II. The
liturgy and theology of the new church was strongly Latinized. It was
only in 1828 that this branch of Catholic patriarchs of Diyarbakır came
to an end, though not the Chaldean Church itself, which was centered
in Baghdad from that point on. Formally created in 1831, it endured a
new wave of Latinization in its liturgy and discipline.

The first church from Sulaqa's lineage separated from Rome in
1670. The catholicos Shimʿun III Denha installed himself at Qodshanes
in the lofty Hakkari mountains (a range split between Iran and eastern
Turkey), returning to non-Catholic doctrine and at the same time refusing to recognize the authority of the catholicos of Rabban Hormizd.
Two Assyrian hierarchies thus existed simultaneously.

Persian Christians at the end of the 19th century. Rights reserved.

At the beginning of the 19th century, Protestant missionaries "discovered" the "Nestorians"—already known as Assyrians—and were fascinated by these Christian groups that spoke "the language of Christ" and had a social organization and tribal way of life. Missionary influences were tied to international politics and inevitably had consequences for the life of these communities and their church. Following the arrival of G. Badger, sent by the archbishop of Canterbury in 1843, the local Kurdish emir, with the permission of the Ottoman pasha, massacred a third of the Assyrian population of Hakkari, suspected of being in the pay of the English and of harboring dreams of independence. Evangelical Protestant, Anglican, and Catholic missionaries continued to compete with each other for Assyrian converts. The catholicos also had contact with the Russian Orthodox Church, since the Russians were extending their influence into Persia and considered the Assyrians their allies. In 1898 a number of Assyrians converted to Russian Orthodoxy.

MIRACLE AT MAR GABRIEL MONASTERY IN 1869

By the strength of God, we write a *mimro* spoken by the weak priest Mirza about the miracle which took place through the blessed Mar Gabriel and the monks of the monastery and about the great and unusual miracles which they did, about the young girl who became a young man and about the sicknesses which they healed, about the sight given to the blind and the dead which they raised, in the meter of Mar Jacob the doctor of the faith . . .

O hearers, come to admire this wonder: Mar Gabriel transformed a young girl and she became a boy: this miracle has never happened before in the entire world. No one has ever seen a woman changed into a man.

Brothers, a Roman [i.e., a Turk] witnessed this miracle, and he swore to the people before the judge in the name of the Lord, "I saw that this little girl was indeed a girl, and that she is now a boy"; this man had no fear before God that he might be rejected.

This Roman said to all the people of Midyat, "Great honor to twelve thousand saints; they performed a miracle today that no one

has ever done; I saw the little girl which became a boy, believe it
and affirm it."

Brothers, who among men will not marvel that this pagan who
saw the miracle and said, "This young man was a young girl, affirm
it." The pagan's name was Salam Bayraqdar.

From a doctrinal point of view, it would be necessary to wait for
the 20th century before there would be dialogue between the Church of
the East and the Catholic Church. In 1971 the Austrian Catholic foundation Pro Oriente organized a series of unofficial consultations on christological questions. A common declaration of faith was signed by Pope
John Paul II and Patriarch Mar Dinkha IV in 1994, and in 1997 a formal
accord between the synods of the Chaldean Church and the Church of
the East expressed their desire for complete union.

SYRIAC ORTHODOX AND CATHOLICS

In the 19th century, the Syriac Orthodox Church was mostly confined
to Ṭur ʿAbdin, the "Mountain of the Servants," and Cilicia. Internal
divisions (including two lines of rival patriarchs from the end of the 13th
century until the end of the 15th) aggravated the situation and resulted
in a sharp demographic decline among the community.

By restoring order and by organizing Christian communities into
the *millet* system, the Ottomans introduced stability and a certain level
of protection. However, the Syriac Orthodox were not recognized as a
millet and were instead attached to the Armenian Church, under the direction of the Armenian patriarch of Constantinople. Surrounded as he
was with a wealthy upper and middle class, he barely troubled himself
with the plight of the Syriac Orthodox, who were in a much lower state
as much socio-economic as intellectual.

The biggest threat to the community was proselytization by the
Catholic Church. Although some fruitless efforts at union had been attempted during the Crusades, and although the Council of Florence, in
1442, had blessed the accords of union with various eastern churches, it
was only in the 17th century that a movement toward union took hold
among the Syriac Orthodox Church. Latin missionaries attempted, with

Syriac Catholic monastery of Charfet, Lebanon.
Photo by Françoise Briquel Chatonnet.

the support of the French consul, to recruit various Syriac Orthodox dignitaries to Catholicism. In 1656 a Syriac Orthodox cleric from Mardin, Andreas Akhidjan, was ordained as the first Syriac Catholic bishop of a church that retained the Syriac rite of Antioch in communion with Rome. But this church met with heavy hostility from the Syriac Orthodox and mistrust from Ottoman authorities who were disturbed by its connections to France. It was only at the end of the 18th century that the Syriac Catholic Church truly developed under the guidance of its first patriarch, Michael Jarweh, centered in the Lebanese monastery of Charfet. Since 1783 it has had its own patriarch.

Western Missions and the Construction of Identities
CATHOLIC, PROTESTANT, AND ORTHODOX MISSIONS

Very early on, the Arab Near East had been a target for missionaries of different confessions, who wanted to spread a faith free from doctrinal

errors and to prove the superiority of Christianity over Islam, and European powers, who wanted to use the missionaries as a tool to build
connections with local populations and to spread their influence.

REV. HORATIO SOUTHGATE, *NARRATIVE*
OF A VISIT TO THE SYRIAN [JACOBITE]
CHURCH OF MESOPOTAMIA (1844)

European nations will become more and more deeply interested
in the East by the increase of their trade, the colonizing of their
people in the marts of Turkey, and the visits of their men of science
and religion to those countries. Gradually, by the gentle progress
of civilization and the arts, or more quickly by the shock of some
sudden rupture springing out of the complicated relations of the
states of Europe with the great Mohammedan power of the East,
Christianity will be freed from her bondage of centuries, and the
light of the West will break in upon the Oriental World. Then
will the Churches of the East, remaining still in their present
unprepared state, convulsed by the sudden blaze of free inquiry
and unregulated knowledge, fall into pieces, of which Infidelity will
seize a part, Popery a part, Protestantism a part, and a part will
remain, the only surviving relic of the Ancient Church of Christ in
the East.

These missionaries played an important role in restructuring
communities and the churches, instructing believers and giving them
the tools to better understand their tradition, supporting the printing
of the first books, and building schools in a movement that continued
until the beginning of the 20th century. Manuscripts copied from the
17th century onward show the influence of Western bookmaking traditions, such as the usage of the Christian era (BC/AD) instead of the
Seleucid dating that Syriac communities had traditionally used (which
they called "the years of the Greeks" or "the years of Alexander the
Great"), the numbering of manuscript pages, and the use of catchwords
(putting the first word of the next page in the bottom margin so as to
check the order of the folios).

The Franciscans remained present and active in the mountain ranges of the Levant (Palestine, but also Aleppo) after the end of the Crusades. But it was at the end of the 16th and especially throughout the 17th century that Catholic missions got underway, beginning with Franciscans and Dominicans, and then Jesuits, Capuchins, and Discalced Carmelites, and later Assumptionists. In the 19th century, women's religious congregations created their own institutions. The Catholic apostolate was to reattach the churches to the authority of the pope and to remove any theology judged heretical. They were fully successful only among the Maronites; elsewhere their actions divided the churches in two and created a separate branch subordinate to Rome (see above).

In the 19th century, Protestant missions were sent by the Anglican Church and various American churches. They had a very important role in terms of religious, cultural, and political influence. It is to Robert Payne-Smith that we owe the *Thesaurus Syriacus*, which is still the standard Syriac-Latin reference dictionary. His daughter Jessie Payne Margoliouth published a compendium in English.

Finally, Orthodox missions were sent by the Russians as part of the drive by the empire of the tsars to expand to the south. They were particularly prevalent near the Greek Orthodox, with whom they shared the same Chalcedonian faith, but also in Transcaucasia and in Iran, where the Russian Empire had political ambitions.

MISSIONS AND ORIENTALISM IN THE 19TH CENTURY

The Western missionaries in the Near East were shocked by what they considered to be the intellectual and moral degradation of the local Christians. Their idea that the Eastern churches had declined in comparison to what they defined as a classical period still remains the dominant narrative. As a result, they invested a good deal of their activity and their apostolate in teaching, founding schools where members of the Christian social elite were trained over the decades. Although these schools did not confine their enrollment to Christians, Christians were particularly singled out for recruitment over others and played a role in the birth of a Christian middle class, educated in Western culture and the intellectual trends that were popular in Europe. The schools thus contributed to setting Christians apart from their Muslim social environment. The Dominican minor seminary in Mosul, for example, was the crucible for the education of a sizeable part of the local bourgeoisie.

The 19th century was also the period in which the ancient civilizations of the Near East were rediscovered, as well as the beginning of archaeology in Mesopotamia, which formed part of the program of European expansion. During the missions set up by the French or English, local Christians served as intermediaries, guides, or associates. It was a Christian from the village of Khorsabad who guided Paul-Émile Botta, the French consul and archaeologist, whose excavations in Kuyunjik (Mosul) were unsuccessful, to his own village: during the first week, Botta found an Assyrian palace which was later found to be built by Sargon II (721–705 BC). This was the beginning of the Middle Eastern collection in the Louvre. The most famous archaeologist was Hormuzd Rassam (1826–1910), who began his career as a foreman for Austen H. Layard, the English excavator of Nimrud and Nineveh. Layard sent him to Oxford to study for eighteen months, and Rassam made further discoveries while excavating with Layard; he was notably the discoverer of the tablet that contains the Epic of Gilgamesh and the oldest version of the flood myth. Thanks to Layard's protection, he went on to have a diplomatic career in the service of the English and presented himself as a descendant of the ancient Assyrians.

Aware of the ancient history of the region, the American mission to Urmia was called "The Mission to the Assyrians." Missionaries visited Nineveh, teaching the history of ancient Mesopotamia and tying the biblical stories to the geography. They considered the biblical book of Daniel to be important to the Chaldeans because it showed a knowledge of the ancient history of the Chaldean nation (*melat*), including its ways and customs. Since late antiquity, Syriac Christians had situated themselves and part of their tradition in the Assyrian past as found in the Bible and based on the use of Aramaic. European orientalist discourse reimagined that ambiguous Assyrian past: Assyria was a great civilization that paved the way for other great (Western) civilizations to come, even if it was the ancient foe of Israel and ultimately inferior to Greece. Imagined connections were thus woven between the East Syrians and ancient Assyria. These were taken into account by the communities and developed during the First World War. They are still a form of auto-orientalism today.

On the Syriac Orthodox side, the narrative of an Aramean heritage is very strong, while the Maronites have linked their history to that of the Phoenicians. The idea of a direct descent from the peoples of antiquity, born of Western orientalist research, has given a nationalist form to a culture whose brightest characteristic was its having been shared by several peoples throughout history.

Syriac Christians were not very active in the modern Arab renaissance (*nahda*) and only slightly involved in the cultural movement that aimed to give a sense of nobility to the Arab people. It was instead the members of the Greek Orthodox and Greek Catholic churches, both Chalcedonian, who had been very quickly Arabized. Similarly, the development of a Christian middle class in cities like Beirut, Damascus, or Aleppo was primarily the work of the Greek Orthodox. But Syriac Christians invested more energy in the movement for civil rights and the equality of all citizens before the law, regardless of religion. This was especially the case for Christians in the Persian Empire under the Qajars and those in the Ottoman Empire prior to the revolution of the Young Turks.

The Proliferation of Churches in Kerala

It was with the arrival of the Portuguese at the end of the 15th century—Vasco da Gama reached India at Calcutta in 1498 and died at Cochin in 1524—that the history of the local church began to become better known. The influence of the Roman Catholic Church very quickly became powerful, its missionaries working to separate the local church from the catholicos of the Church of the East so as to enter into the bosom of Catholicism. The process reached its apogee at the Synod of Diamper (Uydayamperoor) in 1599, under the oversight of the archbishop of Goa, Alexis de Menezes. The acts of the synod condemned many Syriac works of liturgy and literature that were considered to be tainted by heresy, but as noted above, the list was most likely theoretical and the actual libraries were probably not very well stocked. However, not a single manuscript dating prior to the 16th century remains preserved in Kerala.

From this official union of the local church with Rome, the Syro-Malabar Church was born, which today includes the largest number of believers among the Syriac Indian churches (approximately three million). Although it is an oriental church whose origin is in the East Syrian tradition, the Latin influence on its liturgy and culture predominates.

It was the weight of this foreign influence that resulted in a faction of the local church trying to reconnect with its Near Eastern roots dur-

Tomb of Alexander de Campo (translation of his name Parampil), implicated in the schism of Matancherry, Kuravilangad. The inscription is trilingual: English, Syriac, and Malayalam, the language of Kerala.
Photo by Françoise Briquel Chatonnet.

ing the following century. A certain number of believers effectively rejected the authority of Rome and the Jesuits and proceeded to choose an archdeacon for all of India, Mar Thomas, with the discreet support of the Dutch, who wanted to erode the connections that the inhabitants of the region had with Portugal. This secession was known as the Schism of Matancherry.

But the Church of the East was at that time sharply divided, and Mar Thomas was unable to reestablish connections with either Mar Elias X, in the monastery of Rabban Hormizd, or with Shim'un XIII Denḥa, at Qodshanes in the mountains of Hakkari, both regions that were difficult to access. The dissidents entered into a relationship with the Syriac Orthodox Church instead and fully adopted the Syriac Antiochian liturgical rite. This resulted in the founding of a Syriac Orthodox church, the Autocephalous Antiochian Church, which is subject to the West Syrian catholicos of Kottayam and which includes around a million and a half believers.

This community knew its share of vicissitudes as well: in 1772 the community of Thozhiyoor, located in the northern part of Christian Kerala, separated and founded its own independent church named the Independent Church of Malabar. It now comprises six thousand believers. In 1875 a reformed church was founded under Anglican influence (India being under British domination at this point), known as the Syriac Church of Mar Thomas, whose see is located at Tiruvalla and which numbers around four hundred thousand faithful. In 1912 a faction of the Syrian Orthodox Church under the authority of Kottayam separated and put themselves under the authority of the Syriac Orthodox patriarch of Antioch; it numbers a million and a half believers. Finally, in 1930, the bishop Mar Ivanios, pressured by the catholicos, decided to side with Rome and join the Catholic Church, founding an Indian Catholic church with an Antiochian rite. But it was only partially successful (the catholicos himself withdrew after second thoughts), and his efforts resulted in the creation of another church, known as the Syro-Malankara Church, with around three hundred thousand believers. The Syriac Christian community of Kerala thus includes five separate Syriac Antiochian churches as a result of the Schism of Matancherry, of which three are Syriac Orthodox, one is Protestant, and one is Catholic.

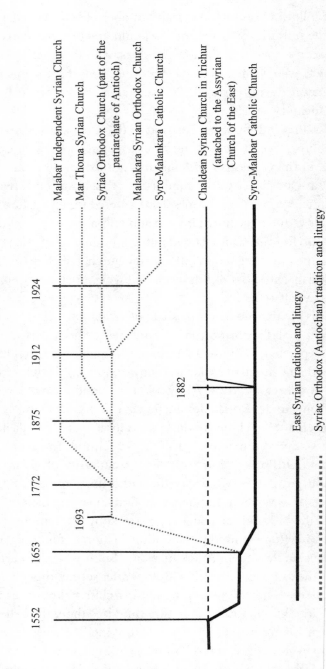

The Churches of India

1552 1653 1772 1875 1912 1924

1693

1882

Malabar Independent Syrian Church

Mar Thoma Syrian Church

Syriac Orthodox Church (part of the
patriarchate of Antioch)

Malankara Syrian Orthodox Church

Syro-Malankara Catholic Church

Chaldean Syrian Church in Trichur
(attached to the Assyrian
Church of the East)

Syro-Malabar Catholic Church

East Syrian tradition and liturgy

Syriac Orthodox (Antiochian) tradition and liturgy

In addition to these five churches, the East Syrian patriarchate of Baghdad replanted itself in India, more than two centuries after the forced Catholicization of the local churches. In 1907 the metropolitanate of the Assyrian Church of the East was founded at Trichur. It is subject to Mar Gewargis III and numbers about fifty thousand members.

Though divided, Syriac Christians form about a quarter of the population of Kerala, where they play an important social, economic, and cultural role. The antiquity of their tradition (reportedly no church was built on top of the ruins of a Hindu temple) and the expansion of the church outside of any kind of colonial context give them a legitimacy in local society that is lacking among Christians of the Latin tradition. Efforts have been made to coordinate the efforts of the various churches and to soothe some of the sensitive issues around schism and competition, as well as to reorient them toward their shared Syriac and Near Eastern heritage. The founding in 1985 of the Saint Ephrem Ecumenical Research Institute (SEERI) in Kottayam, a place of teaching, research, publication, and scholarly exchange, has given a strong momentum to these efforts.

Syriac Language and Writing as Markers of Identity

Starting in the 14th century, Syriac culture entered into a period of decline. It rarely produced new works, and those that it did were infrequent and second-rate. Arabic became all but exclusive in the intellectual and daily life of believers. However, the attachment of Syriac Christians to their culture remained and manifested itself in written form via *garshuni* (an obscure word used only in this one sense), which involved writing the Arabic language in Syriac letters. Although *garshuni* had existed since the 9th century, it began to spread only in the 15th century, particularly among the Syriac Orthodox and the Maronites. Although the similarity between Syriac and Arabic facilitated the transition, Syriac has only twenty-two letters while Arabic, which retained a richer phonological system, has twenty-eight. The *garshuni* writing system is thus defective, reusing the same Syriac letters to represent multiple sounds in Arabic. Sometimes, diacritic marks were used to distinguish these sounds, but they were never employed systematically. The system thus introduced complications and inefficient ambiguities, but justified itself by acting as a way to maintain the Syriac writing system and to affirm the Christian character of texts that were written in Arabic. In other words, it functioned as an identitarian phenomenon.

Beginning in the 19th century, the printing press was introduced as an important aspect of missionary work in order to disseminate knowledge. The missionaries saw education as a means to reform local Christianity and to awaken a "national" consciousness (the term *melat* was used in an ethno-religious sense). In 1841 the press of the American mission at Urmia began to produce thousands of pages, including the monthly periodical *Rays of Light* (*Zahrire d-bahra*), which was published until 1918.

The press of the Dominicans of Mosul was founded around 1857, and in 1877 the Jesuit Catholic press at Beirut was created as well. In India the presses also played an important role in making Syriac literature accessible: the Saint Joseph Press at Mannanam, the Mar Julius Presses at Pampakuda, and the Mar Narsai Presses at Trichur. At Charfet the patriarchal Syriac Catholic presses were founded. The presses of Oxford and Cambridge, the Imprimerie nationale of Paris, and W. Drugulin at Leiden published abundantly between 1848 and 1914. One of the main reference editions of Syriac texts, Corpus Scriptorum Christianorum Orientalium (CSCO), was composed by automation with a type designed by R. Draguet. With the computer revolution, George Kiraz (Piscataway, New Jersey) produced fonts that are still used today and entered them in the international Unicode system (Beth Mardutho: The Syriac Institute), paving the way for all kinds of publications.

As the printing press spread, Justin Perkins developed a written form of Neo-Aramaic based on Classical Syriac, using East Syrian characters, and translated part of the Bible into Neo-Aramaic, thus creating a new literary language. The awakening of a national consciousness paired well with the idea of a decline and corruption of Aramaic dialects following the Muslim conquests, which led to connections with the deterioration of Aramaic as a whole and the loss of autonomy. The idea at the time was one of linguistic decline as compared to Classical Syriac, despite keeping a cultural inheritance intact since the Assyrian period. Language and the construction of identity of an "(As)Syrian nation" were closely connected, as well as the idea that the language of Jesus—and, indeed, the language that Adam used in Paradise with God—gave a sacredness to the nation that still spoke it. A reformation of the Neo-Aramaic language, especially orthographically, was undertaken, because it was seen as a degraded form of Classical Syriac, even though the various dialectical forms had their own complex history. The Chaldean breviary was produced in 1887 by the priest Paul Bedjan in literary Syriac, "recognized as a sacred language," in three volumes "purged of Nestorian errors." He also edited the *Acts* of the saints and the martyrs in seven volumes and the works of Jacob of Serugh in five volumes. The need for a national literature was expressed in the histories of Syriac literature, often indebted to the work of Assemani, that Western scholars produced, and anthologies of classical authors were produced by missionaries.

REV. JUSTIN PERKINS, *A RESIDENCE OF EIGHT YEARS IN PERSIA* (1843)

The press has sometimes been called, "the modern gift of tongues." It is so, but is also much more. It is the gift of tongues stereotyped. Instead of the ephemeral unction of a Pentecost occasion . . . it gives to all the permanent record of those wonderful works to be read and re-read, and transmitted to successive generations. And instead of being limited to Jerusalem, or carried to their respective countries, by the living voice of all those Parthians and Medes and dwellers in Mesopotamia, as was the gospel originally conveyed, the press has the power of *ubiquity*.

THOMAS AUDO, *TREASURY OF THE SYRIAC LANGUAGE* (1897–1901)

That one who discovered the art of writing in the world rendered unto the human race a great favor on account of which he is worthy of continual praise and unceasing thanks. In spite of this, behold, hidden is the name of the one who brought forth this art much value and first introduced it into the world. Nor is it known at what time this was, but certainly it is known which nation [*umtha*] before all first began to write and which race taught writing to the rest of the nations. We shall say then that the Syrian nation has this cause for pride over all the previously known nations ['amme].

THOMAS AUDO, INTRODUCTION TO HIS GRAMMAR OF NEO-ARAMAIC (1905)

We too, the East-Syrians, descend from the aforementioned Assyrians, we are children of the Assyrians or Ashur, son of Shem and on account of this we are also Semites. We have preserved until today the language of our ancestors with of course some changes which have entered it.

LETTER FROM MGR. LAMY, PROFESSOR OF SEMITIC LANGUAGES AT LOUVAIN, TO PAUL BEDJAN, A CHALDEAN PRIEST IN URMIA

The Chaldean breviary, edited in 1865, does not just contain the book of Psalms and the most common prayers. Until now, no one has dared or been able to publish the complete book of Chaldean prayers; the Ḥudra, the Kaskul and the Gaza only exist today in manuscripts. You have endeavored to give to the Chaldean Christians this book which is so important and so fitting, by its beautiful prayers, to give sustenance to faith. It was necessary to prepare the manuscript, edit the texts, correct the vocalization, and refine the proofs with particular care. Nothing at all deterred you, and now we may consider your work complete.

COLOPHON OF A SYRIAC MANUSCRIPT CELEBRATING HENRI POGNON, DIPLOMAT, ARCHAEOLOGIST, AND FRENCH EPIGRAPHIST

This manuscript was completed on 18 Iyyar, the Saturday vigil of the 5th Sunday after Easter, in which the liturgy is without praise, the year 2211 of the Greeks, 1900 of Christ, our Lord, to whom be glory, praise, and honor forever and ever. It was written in the blessed village, powerful in Petrine faith and rich in Pauline preaching, modest, and a place of gathering for strangers, Alqosh, the village of the Hebrew prophet Nahum, where, because of the exile in Assyria, his fathers established themselves and dwelled there. May our Lord reside there and protect its inhabitants. The man who wrote, soiled, and blackened this book is unworthy that his name be remembered; but in order to obtain the prayer of the chaste readers, he writes his name, Abraham, son of the late priest Shim'un, from the ancient family of Israel of Alqosh . . . It was written in the time of the general presidency of our venerable father Mar Joseph of Nisibis, the administrator of the patriarchate of the Chaldeans. For the Church of the Chaldeans was momentarily widowed . . . This book was written for an excellent and renowned man, strong in discipline and knowledge, trained and learned in the ancient Near Eastern languages, especially the languages of the ancient Assyrians and Babylonians, who uncovers the hidden things from the mysteries to the sons of his race in many treasures, who loves our Chaldean community and is attentive to the good of its members, Monsieur Pognon, consul of the prestigious French Republic in the city of Beroe, which is also known as Aleppo.

The efforts to research manuscripts in Classical Syriac and to copy them were closely correlated. The majority of manuscripts preserved in libraries, such as those in Europe, were produced between the 15th and the beginning of the 20th century. It was a period when manuscripts included long colophons that celebrated the merits of copyists and their sponsors, anxious to preserve and spread their culture.

From Genocide (*Sayfo*) to the Diasporas

Emigration to Europe and the United States, which had begun in the 19th century, saw a dramatic surge, with spikes of intensity corresponding to periods of massacre or repression. In certain places, entire communities left and resettled together at places like Detroit in the United States, which was dubbed by Syriac emigrants as "New Tel-Keif" (Tel Keppe, or Tel Kaif, is a town on the outskirts of Mosul).

The massacres that took place in 1915 and the following years in the Ottoman Empire were known as the Armenian Genocide, but to a lesser-known degree also affected Syriac Christians, who called this tragedy the *Sayfo* (in West Syriac) or *Saypa* (in East Syriac), which translates to "the sword." In the Ottoman Empire, the inhabitants of Ṭur ʿAbdin, Hakkari, and modern-day northern Iraq were caught up in the struggle between the Russian and Turkish Empires. They were subjected to deportation in severe conditions and massacres. A number of them escaped to Syria, Lebanon, Palestine, or the West. While the Chaldeans were massacred along with the Syriac Orthodox, Catholics, and Armenians in 1915, the Assyrians of Hakkari took refuge with their coreligionists in Urmia in Iran, where the advance of the Russian forces gave them hope of protection. But, with the retreat of the Russians and the advance of the Turks, they were forced to endure a dramatic exodus to the south. In 1920 only a third of the population reached Iraq, which was at that time under British protection. They had lost many of their high church officials, and the survivors took their positions in refugee camps. Their situation became very difficult in the early 1930s, at the end of the British mandate in Iraq, and a new massacre took place. Some of them went on to take refuge in Syria and settled in Hasakah, in the northeast of the country. Most of them went to the United States, where the patriarch Eshai Shimʿun joined them in 1940, and the seat of the patriarchate moved to Chicago, where it has remained till recently. The current catholicos, Mar Gewargis III, re-established the patriarchate in Erbil (Iraq), a move that has very strong symbolic significance.

After the end of the First World War, France, which had the support of the League of Nations in Syria, and the young Turkish Republic fought over the boundary between Syria and Turkey. France enrolled Christians in its army, and Christian populations endured the repercussions. All the Christians of Edessa (Urfa) had to leave in only a matter of days in 1920, leaving their property and their goods behind. This victory was celebrated by the Turkish government, who ironically renamed Urfa "Şanlıurfa" (Urfa the Glorious) in 1984. Most of the Christians took refuge in Aleppo, where they created the area *Ḥay al-suryani al-qadim*, or Old Syriac Quarter.

REQUEST OF CHALDEAN PATRIARCH
EMMANUEL TOMA TO SPARE THE CHALDEAN
CHRISTIANS OF MOSUL

The patriarchal diocese [of Mosul] and those of Kirkuk, Zakho, Amadia and Akra have, thanks to a miracle of Divine Providence, been able to escape being massacred and, thanks to the good will of the two *valis* of Mosul—I want to say Suleiman Nazif Bey and Haider Bey—who used all their influence to prevent the massacres and to quiet the troublemakers who wanted to imitate the cruelties which took place in other locales . . . The two dioceses of Diyarbakir and Mardin were only partially able to escape the massacres. The diocese of Seert has been totally devastated and ruined: the bishop, the priests, and the people of the town and twenty-six nearby villages were killed horribly; I mention also specifically the rich library and precious manuscripts of the bishopric. The diocese of Djezireh had the same treatment . . . all we know about the situation of Van, Gawar, and Dizza is that the bishop of Van was able to save his life.

When Iraq became independent in 1932, the Chaldeans, whose patriarch was at Mosul, moved to Baghdad, and the patriarchate was transferred there as well in 1947. Embracing their Arab identity, in contrast to their Assyrian brethren, and defending the government against Kurdish demands, the Chaldean Church was treated well by various political authorities. Meanwhile, taking their cue from their leaders in the United States, the Assyrian church established its own Assyrian ethnic identity. The Chaldean Church was associated with this claim of Assyrian roots. In 1968 a schism resulted in the creation of the Ancient Church of the East, centered in Baghdad and enjoying a certain level of support from the authorities, as opposed to the Apostolic Assyrian Church of the East, which was suspected of opposing the Arab ideology of the Iraqi state.

After the Second World War and especially the 1970s, the establishment of socialist-inspired authoritarian regimes in Syria and Iraq weakened the position of the Christian middle class in the economy. Congregational schools, which were still in use, began to close. Although societal problems affected the families of westernized Muslims

Chaldean church in Sarcelles (France) in a Neo-Assyrian style.

just as heavily, Christians, who had more relatives abroad and greater
ability to obtain visas or foreign citizenship, were much more likely to
depart, and little by little those who remained felt themselves to be more
marginalized; although there were more Christians in Aleppo in 2000
than 1900, their proportion of the population had become smaller. In
Iran, the establishment of the Islamic Republic in 1979 did not directly
result in the persecution of Christians, but it imposed a way of life that
did not suit them, limited their possibilities for economic advancement
and participation, and pushed to leave those who dreamed of another
kind of social life for their children.

The Lebanese Civil War, between 1975 and 1990, led to the exodus
of an important part of the population, particularly those who had the
means to finance the costs of emigration. Christians, especially Maronites, made up many of those who chose to leave.

In the 1980s and 1990s, the war between the Turkish government
and the Kurds in Turkey placed Syriac communities in a difficult situa-

tion, as their members were drafted, under pain of retaliation, into one camp or the other. In response, the villages of Ṭur ʿAbdin saw entire communities emigrate to Germany, Sweden, and the United States. The town of Södertälje in Sweden thus came to include a sizable Syriac community, and two local Syriac TV channels were created, along with soccer clubs and all kinds of social groups. The Chaldeans of Turkey also came to comprise an important emigrant group, in their case to France. In 2017 the Turkish government under Recep Tayyip Erdoğan put about fifty churches, monasteries, and cemeteries in the province of Mardin under state control.

The American invasion of Iraq in 2003 and the conflicts that followed destabilized the position of Christians further, as they were accused of collaborating with the enemy, especially since some evangelical American preachers had openly stated that they were coming to their aid. This has been a recurring theme in the history of the Christians of the Near East. The special interest that Western churches have taken in them, from Constantine to the Crusaders to modern evangelical preachers, has often delegitimized them in the eyes of their fellow citizens, even though Christianity has been part of the area since its birth. The protection afforded to Christians by the authoritarian Syrian and Iraqi regimes, who were nominally secular, also rendered them suspicious to those who were opposed to those regimes from all sides. The occupation by the Islamic State, Daesh, of a substantial part of northern Iraq and eastern Syria completed the process of pushing Christians toward exile, whether in their own country or abroad, in Lebanon, Jordan, Turkey, Canada, or Europe.

It is difficult to predict what is to come and whether the Middle East will rebuild itself into a multireligious, multicultural society in the future. But right now it is already clear that emigrant communities are firmly established in various countries in Europe, North and South America, Oceania, and other countries of the Middle East, where they have founded churches, dioceses, seminaries, publishing houses. Along with the Syriac communities in India, they play an essential role in the preservation of Syriac identity, the battle for Syriac culture, and its continued existence.

Glossary

autocephalous—A church that has its own leader (a patriarch or catholicos).

catholicos—The patriarch of the Church of the East.

Church of the East—The term for the Syriac-speaking church that was born in the Persian Empire and rejected the Council of Ephesus. Its believers are known as East Syrians. It refers to itself as the Apostolic Church of the East. It is often referred to as "Nestorian," although this is often considered polemical in modern times.

dhimmi—A non-Muslim "ally" belonging to the category of one of the Peoples of the Book (*ahl al-kitab*). In the Islamic world, *dhimmis* benefit from a 9th-century legal status that establishes their rights and obligations. Most notably, it extends state protection of goods and persons in exchange for the recognition of the supremacy of Islam and the payment of a specific tax, the *jizya*.

Julianism—Sometimes known as aphtartodocetism, the extreme doctrine defended by Julian of Halicarnassus (d. ca. 537) and condemned by the Miaphysite movement. Opposed by Severus, bishop of Antioch, Julian speculated in his *Tome* that the body of Christ was by nature exempt from corruption (*aphtartos*) and thus from suffering. A parallel Julianist hierarchy developed alongside its "orthodox" Miaphysite counterpart in Egypt, Syria, Armenia, and southern Arabia. These ideas found their way into controversial passages within the Qur'an.

Manichaeism—A dualist religion founded in the 3rd century by Mani on the left bank of the Tigris River. Raised among Elkasaite baptizers, he preached his own religion, which aspired to become universal, and presented himself as a new prophet, the successor of Buddha, Zoroaster, and Jesus, as well as the fulfillment of the Paraclete, having received a prophecy from his celestial twin. He sent missionaries to Iraq, Egypt, India, and the Arabian peninsula. He was put to death by order of the Sasanian king of kings Bahram in 277.

Our knowledge of Manichaeism has reached us primarily through its enemies. But the discovery of manuscripts in China and Egypt at the beginning of the last century, as well as several paintings, has created a clearer picture of the religion. Besides Middle Persian—expressed in a specific Manichaean script, based on the Aramaic alphabet used to write Middle Persian—Syriac was also a Manichaean language.

The core doctrine of Manichaeism is based on the idea of the coexistence and antagonism of two equal and eternal cosmic principles: good and bad, light (the soul) and darkness (the physical world, the body). The soul that strives to elevate itself and pass through the cycle of reincarnations would one day reach the kingdom of light. In the Manichaean Church, members are divided into a hierarchy of the elect, or consecrated religious, and the auditors, the laypeople. The church has a leader, apostles, bishops, and priests. The elect wear white clothing and make a vow of honesty, poverty, chastity, and obedience. The auditors serve the religious brothers. They profess five obligations, which include respect for the ten commandments of Mani, the four daily prayers, alms, fasting, and the confession of sins. The main feast of the Manichaeans is the Bema Feast, which commemorates the martyrdom and death of Mani.

maphrian—The second-highest rank in the Syriac Orthodox Church, in charge of the section of the church east of the Tigris.

Marcionism—A belief professed and propagated in Rome by Marcion of Sinope in the 2nd century AD, declared heretical in 144 when Marcion was excommunicated. It was a dualist belief derivative of Gnosticism. Marcion drew a distinction between a demiurge of justice and wrath (whom he rejected), represented in the Old Testament, and the God of love of the New Testament. Marcionism developed primarily in the East, especially in Mesopotamia and Persia.

Mazdaism and Zoroastrianism—Mazdaism, derived from the name that believers gave to their god Ahura Mazda (the Wise Lord), is an ancient Iranian religion whose sacred books, the Avesta, were reformed by the prophet Zoroaster or Zarathustra. Dualist, it holds to the existence of two principle forces who are locked in combat, one good, the god of light and the creator of the world, Ahura Mazda or Ohrmazd, and one evil, Ahriman. Humanity is at stake in this struggle. At the end of time there will be a universal conflagration: the world will be subject to a river of fire, followed by the resurrection of all humanity and the annihilation of evil forces. Other divinities, born from Ahura Mazda, were also venerated, such as Mithra (the god of the sun), Varuna, Mali, Anahita (the fertility goddess), and more.

Fire is considered to be a manifestation of divine omnipresence and must be protected from all impure contact, especially decomposing corpses. The dead are exposed in *dakhmas* (towers of silence), where they are eaten by vultures so as not to pollute the earth, fire, or water. Water is also an object of worship. The purity laws allow humanity to be joined with Ahura Mazda in his unending combat with Ahriman. The religion is known essentially as it was in the late Sasanian period and the first centuries of Islam.

metropolitanate—The main seat of an ecclesiastical province that also houses other bishops, known as suffragans. The bishop who holds a metropolitanate is known as a metropolitan.

Miaphysitism—A Christian doctrine that emphasizes the unity of the divine and human natures of Christ after the incarnation, according to the formula of Cyril of Alexandria, *mia physis tou theou logou sesarkomene*, "One nature of the Incarnate Word." It is also sometimes known as henophysitism. The neologism "Miaphysitism" is preferred today to "Monophysitism," which is reserved for positions judged heretical even within the Miaphysite movement. The term "Monophysite" is used today for the extreme positions defended by Eutyches and Dioscorus of Alexandria, who believed that the Son had only one nature after the incarnation—the divine—which had absorbed and extinguished his human nature entirely.

Monothelitism—A doctrine where Christ had only one, exclusively divine will, which became the object of controversy for the Byzantine Church for the better part of the 7th century. The doctrine of a single operation (monoenergism) of Christ was discussed at the beginning of the 7th century by Chalcedonians and anti-Chalcedonians as a possible framework for compromise and reunification, but the doctrine of Monothelitism only affected the Chalcedonian church. It was an internal evolution of neo-Chalcedonian doctrine. It was first proposed by the patriarch of Constantinople, Sergius, in 616, with the support of the emperor Heraclius. It was finally condemned by the imperial church in the Third Council of Constantinople in 680, but preserved by the monks of the monastery of Bet Maron. It resulted in the origin of the Maronite Church, which finally rejected the doctrine upon its admittance to communion with Rome in 1182.

Oriental Orthodox churches—While not "orthodox" from the point of view of Greek and Slavic (Eastern) Orthodox churches, who usually represent Orthodoxy in the West, they often refer to themselves as Orthodox. They include the Armenian Apostolic Church, the Syriac Orthodox Church, the Malankara Syriac Orthodox Church, the Coptic Orthodox Church, the Ethiopian Orthodox Tewahedo Church, and the Eritrean Orthodox Tewahedo Church (as well as the British Orthodox Church, which was previously part of the Coptic Orthodox Church until 2015).

Sons and Daughters of the Covenant—The original form of male and female ascetic consecration in the Syriac world. They took a vow (or made a covenant) of celibacy and were dedicated, sometimes in childhood, to the service of the church, to the liturgy of five daily prayers, and to the service of the poor and the sick.

Syriac Orthodox—The term for the Syriac-speaking church, as well as its believers, that rejected the Council of Chalcedon and retained Miaphysite theology. It was also called "Jacobite" by its opponents, after Jacob Baradeus, a bishop who ordained the Miaphysite hierarchy. It is also known as Syrian Orthodox.

tritheism—A dissident doctrine within Miaphysitism in the 6th century that recognized only one nature of the Incarnate Word in Christ but persons, natures, and gods in the Trinity, which resulted in the accusation of worshiping three gods.

Syriac Churches by Christology

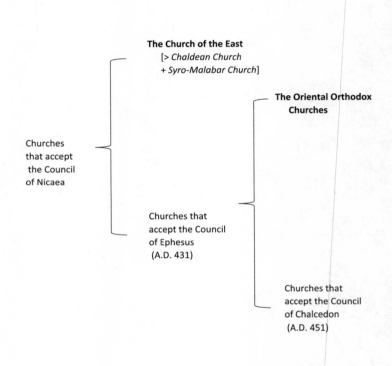

The Church of the East
  [> *Chaldean Church*
  + *Syro-Malabar Church*]

**The Oriental Orthodox
Churches**

Churches
that accept
the Council
of Nicaea

Churches that
accept the Council
of Ephesus
(A.D. 431)

Churches that
accept the Council
of Chalcedon
(A.D. 451)

Catholic
Protestant
Independent
> = Offshoot

The Coptic Orthodox Church
    [> *Coptic Catholic Church*
    + Evangelical Coptic Church]

The Ethiopic Orthodox Church
    [> *Ethiopic Catholic Church*]

The Armenian Apostolic Church
    [> *Armenian Catholic Church*
    + Evangelical Armenian Church]

The Syriac Orthodox Church
    [> *Syriac Catholic Church*
    + *Syro-Malankara Church*
    + Orthodox Malankara Syrian Church
    + Mar Thoma Syrian Church]

The Roman Catholic Church
    [> Reformed/Protestant Churches]

***The Maronite Church** (after a period of independence)*

The Eastern (Byzantine) Orthodox Churches

The Greek Orthodox Church

The Orthodox Church of Antioch (uses both Syriac and Greek in its liturgy) [> *The Catholic Melkite Church*]

The Russian Orthodox Church

The Georgian Orthodox Church, etc.

Chronology

	Edessa	History of the Roman Empire
3rd century BC		
2nd century BC	Ca. 135–130 BC: Birth of the kingdom of Oshroene	
1st century BC		65 BC: Pompey conquers Syria and organizes the administration of the Roman East
		53 BC: Defeat of Crassus at Carrhae (Ḥarran) at the hand of the Parthian general Surena
1st century AD	4 BC–AD 7, then AD 13–50: Reign of Abgar V Ukkama, "the Black"	
2nd century AD	154–222: Bardaisan of Edessa 177–212: Reign of Abgar VIII	193–211: Reign of Septimius Severus
3rd century AD	202: Flood of Edessa 212–213: Edessa becomes a Roman colony	238–244: Reign of Gordian III 244–249: Reign of Philip the Arab 253–260: Reign of Valerian 282–283: Reign of Carus 284–305: Reign of Diocletian 288: Treaty between Diocletian and the king of Persia, Bahram II

Christianity in the Roman Empire	History of the Persian Empire	Christianity in the Persian Empire
	Ca. 247 BC: Beginning of the Parthian Empire	
	54–38 BC: Reign of Orodes II	
Ca. AD 30: Death of Jesus Around the middle of the 1st century, the believers of Christ in Antioch are called "Christians"		"Parthians, Medes, and Elamites, inhabitants of Mesopotamia" are present at the Pentecost in Jerusalem (Acts 2:9)
254: Burial of the Christian house at Dura Europos	224: Revolt of Ardashir, the end of the Parthian Empire, and the beginning of the Sasanian Empire 224–240: Reign of Ardashir I 239–270: Reign of Shapur I; Shapur campaigns in the Roman East 271–274: Reign of Bahram I 274–291: Reign of Bahram II	Deportation of Christians from Syria and the Roman East into the Persian Empire

	Edessa	History of the Roman Empire
4th century AD	After 363: Ephrem of Nisibis (d. 373) takes refuge in Edessa	306–337: Reign of Constantine the Great
		361–363: Reign of Julian the Apostate
		363: Defeat of Julian; Nisibis is handed over to the Persians
		383–408: Reign of Arcadius
5th century AD	411–435: Episcopate of Rabbula of Edessa	450–457: Reign of Marcian
	411: Date of the oldest extant Syriac manuscript, copied at Edessa	
	489: Closure of the School of the Persians and the flight of its director, Narsai, to Nisibis	

Christianity in the Roman Empire	History of the Persian Empire	Christianity in the Persian Empire
303–313: The Great Persecution of the Christians	303–309: Reign of Hormizd II	337–344: Demonstrations of Aphrahat
313: Edict of Milan, issued by Constantine, permits the practice of the Christian religion	309–379: Reign of Shapur II	
	399–420: Reign of Yazdegerd I	
325: Council of Nicaea, which condemns the doctrine of Arianism		
381: Council of Constantinople Maruta of Maypherqaṭ (fl. late 4th–early 5th c.)		
390–459: Life of Saint Simeon Stylites		
428–431: Episcopate of Nestorius in Constantinople	488–496/498–531: Reign of Kavad I	410: Synod of Mar Isaac: the Church of Persia affirms its independence
431: Council of Ephesus		424: Synod of Dadisho, which includes participants from Herat and Merv
451: Council of Chalcedon		484: Synod of Bet Lapaṭ: the Church of Persia refuses to recognize the Council of Ephesus and the condemnation of Nestorius
		486: Council of Acacius, which abolishes celibacy
		489: The famous School of Nisibis founded by Narsai

	Edessa	History of the Roman Empire
6th century AD	544: Siege of Edessa by the Persians	503–506: Capture and occupation of Amid by the Persians
		518–527: Reign of Justin
		527–565: Reign of Justinian
		565–578: Reign of Justin II
		582–602: Reign of Maurice
7th century		602–610: Reign of Phocas
		602–628: Occupation of the Roman East by Persian forces
		610–641: Reign of Heraclius
		636: Victory of Arab Muslims over the Byzantine army at the Battle of Yarmouk; most of Palestine and Syria is conquered

Christianity in the Roman Empire	History of the Persian Empire	Christianity in the Persian Empire
507–586: John of Ephesus	531–579: Reign of Khosrow I Anoshiravan	536: Death of Sergius of Resh'aina
512–518: Episcopate of Severus of Antioch	579–590: Reign of Hormizd IV	500–588: Abraham of Kashkar, reformer of Persian monasticism
518: Severus is sent into exile		540–552: Catholicos Aba I
521: Death of Jacob of Serugh		
523: Death of Philoxenus of Mabbug		
524: Massacre of Christians at Najran in South Arabia		
545–578: Episcopate of Jacob Baradaeus, founder of the Syriac Orthodox hierarchy		
580–662: Maximus the Confessor, defender of Dyothelitism	590–628: Reign of Khosrow II Parviz	Ca. 550–628: Babai the Great
632: Death of Muhammad	628: Kavad II Seroe ascends the throne; beginning of period of instability	628–646: Catholicos Isho'yahb of Gdala
666/667: Death of Severus Sebokht	637: Capture of Seleucia-Ctesiphon by Arab Muslim forces and the flight of Yazdegerd III	635: Arrival of the missionary Alopen to Xi'an, capital of the Chinese Empire

	Political History	**The Chalcedonian Churches**	
7th century	632–661: Reigns of the first caliphs 661–750: The Umayyad dynasty	680: Third Council of Constantinople: condemnation of Monothelitism	
8th century	750–1258: The ʿAbbasid dynasty	Ca. 780: Appearance of the term "Melkite"	The monastery of Beth Maron refuses to condemn Monothelitism; the Maronite Church comes into being as a result
9th century		843: End of the iconoclastic crisis, which marks the reestablish- ment of icons in the Byzantine Church	
10th century	893–932: Mesopotamia under the control of the Ḥamdanids 934–969: Byzantine reconquest of Melitene and Antioch 945–1055: Iraq and western Iran under the control of the Shiʾite Buyids		

The Syriac Orthodox Church	The Church of the East	Notable Writers
		Jacob of Edessa (West Syrian, 636–708)
		Isaac of Nineveh (East Syrian, ca. 640–700)
		John of Damascus (Melkite, ca. 676–749)
	Timothy I (b. 727/728, catholicos from 780 to 823); he moves the patriarchal see to Baghdad, the new capital	Theophilus of Edessa (Maronite, d. 785)
		Theodore bar Koni (East Syrian, late 8th c.)
		Theodore Abu Qurrah (Melkite, 750–820)
Dionysius of Tel Maḥre, patriarch from 818 to 845		Ḥunayn ibn Ishaq (East Syrian, 808–873)
		Thomas of Marga (East Syrian, born around 810)
		Moses bar Kepha (West Syrian, born 9th c.)
		Isho'dnah of Baṣra (East Syrian, born 9th c.)
		Isho'dad of Merv (East Syrian, born ca. 850)
		Moses of Nisibis (West Syrian, 9th–10th c.)
Period of florescence for the monasteries in the reconquered Melitene region		Elias of Nisibis (East Syrian, 975–1046)

	Political History	**The Chalcedonian Churches**
11th century	1055: The Buyids are displaced by the Seljuk Turks 1096–1099: The First Crusade	1054: First schism between the Byzantine Church and the Church of Rome
12th century	1098–1146: County of Edessa 1099–1187: Frankish Kingdom of Jerusalem	1182: The patriarch of the Maronite Church rejects Monothelitism and unites with Rome
13th century	1170–1260: Ayyubid dynasty in Syria, founded by Saladin 1206–1227: Reign of Genghis Khan 1250–1517: Mamluk sultanate in Egypt and Syria 1260–1294: Reign of Kublai Khan	To escape Mamluk reprisals, the Maronites take refuge in the Qadisha valley and move the patriarchal see to the monastery of Qannoubin
14th century	1370–1405: Reign of Tamerlane	
15th century	1498: Vasco da Gama reaches Calcutta in southwestern India	
16th century	1502: Beginning of the Safavid dynasty in Persia	1583: Founding of the Maronite College in Rome
17th century	1516–1918: The Ottoman Empire rules the Near East	1687–1768: Joseph Simon Assemani

The Syriac Orthodox Church	The Church of the East	Notable Writers
1166–1199: Patriarchate of Michael the Great		Dionysius bar Ṣalibi (West Syrian, d. 1171)
	1281–1317: Yahballaha III is patriarch 1286–1288: Mission of Rabban Sauma to Europe	Gregory Barhebraeus (West Syrian, 1226–1286) ʿAbdisho bar Brika (West Syrian, 1250–1318) Khamis bar Qardaḥe (East Syrian, 13th c.) George Warda (East Syrian, 13th–14th c.)
	1553: First union with Rome (Yohannon Sulaqa) 1599: Synod of Diamper at Malabar; birth of the Syro-Malabar Church	Moses of Mardin (West Syrian, 16th c.)
1656: André Aqidian, first Syriac Catholic bishop	1653: Schism of Mattancherry; rebirth of the Syrian Orthodox Church in India	

	Political History	**The Chalcedonian Churches**	
18th century	1794–1927: The Qajar dynasty in Persia	1724: Union of Byzantine-rite Christians with the Catholic Church, resulting in the Melkite Church, separated from the Orthodox Antiochian Church	1790: The Maronite patriarchate moves to Bkerke, where it is still located
19th century			
20th century	1918: Founding of the Turkish Republic 1920: British Mandate in Iraq; Iraq gains independence in 1932 1920: French Mandate in Syria; Syria gains independence in 1946 1928–1979: Pahlavi Dynasty in Iran 1979: Beginning of the Islamic Republic of Iran		
21st century	2011: Beginning of the Arab Spring 2014: The fall of Mosul and the Nineveh Plains to Daesh (ISIS)		

The Syriac Orthodox Church	The Church of the East	Notable Writers
1772: Birth of the independent Malabar Church in the north of Kerala		
1783: Michael Jarweh, first patriarch of the Syriac Catholic Church		
1875: Birth of the Syriac-speaking Mar Thoma Church (Anglican) in Kerala	1831: Formal creation of the Chaldean Church (Catholic) in India	
1912: The believers of the Syriac Church in India reunite with the patriarch of Antioch and rejoin the Syriac Orthodox Church	1915–1920: *Saypa*: the massacre of Chaldean and Assyrian Christians in Hakkari and Urmia	
1915: *Sayfo*: the massacre of the Syriac Orthodox in Tur 'Abdin	1994: Declaration of common faith between the Assyrian Church of the East and the Roman Catholic Church	
1920: Expulsion of the Syriac Orthodox from Urfa (Edessa)		
1931: Part of the Syriac Orthodox Church in Kerala joins with Rome: the Syro-Malankara Church		
June 2017: The Turkish government nationalizes fifty Syriac churches and monasteries		

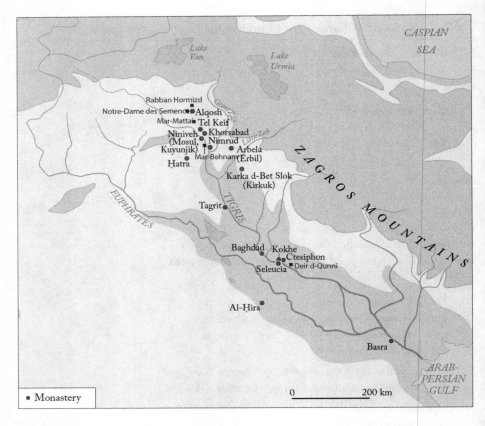

Syriac Centers in the Sasanian Empire

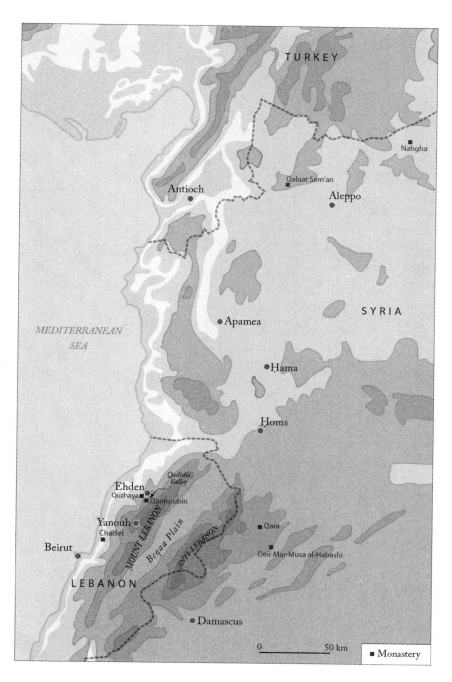

TURKEY

Nabgha

Qalaat Sem'an

Antioch

Aleppo

MEDITERRANEAN
SEA

Apamea

SYRIA

Hama

Homs

Qadisha
Valley

Ehden
Quzhaya
Qannoubin

Yanouh
Charfet

Beirut

MOUNT LEBANON

Beqaa Plain

ANTI-LEBANON

Qara

Deir Mar-Musa al-Habashi

LEBANON

Damascus

0   50 km

■ Monastery

Lebanon and Western Syria

From Edessa to Lake Urmia

■ Monastery

Lake Urmia

Urmia

Hakkari

Alqosh

Mosul

Great Zab

Little Zab

TIGRIS

0   50 km

Secrt

Lake Van

Maypherkat
(Martyropolis)

Amid

Midyat   Mor-Abrohom
         ■ Mor-Gabriel
TUR ABDIN Mor-Abraham
Mardin   Mar-Awgen ■ Mor-Yuhanon
Mar-Hananyo Nisibis
(Deir al-Za'faran)

Hassakah

Khabur

Edessa

Harran

Balikh

EUPHRATES

Bibliography

General Introduction to Near Eastern Christianity (Including Copts, Armenians, and Ethiopians)

Bailey, Betty Jane, and J. Martin Bailey. *Who Are the Christians of the Middle East?* Grand Rapids: Eerdmans, 2003.

Tannous, Jack. *The Making of the Medieval Middle East: Religion, Society, and Simple Believers.* Princeton: Princeton University Press, 2018.

Valognes, J. P. *Vie et mort des chrétiens d'Orient: Des origines à nos jours.* Paris: Fayard, 1996.

Walters, J. Edward, ed. *Eastern Christianity: A Reader.* Grand Rapids: Eerdmans, 2021.

General Introduction to Syriac Studies

Brock, Sebastian. *The Hidden Pearl: The Aramaic Heritage.* Piscataway: Gorgias Press, 2001.

———. *An Introduction to Syriac Studies.* Piscataway: Gorgias Press, 2006.

Brock, Sebastian, Aaron Michael Butts, George Kiraz, and Lucas Van Rompay, eds. *The Gorgias Encyclopedic Dictionary of the Syriac Heritage.* Piscataway: Gorgias Press, 2011.

King, Daniel, ed. *The Syriac World.* London: Routledge, 2018.

Books about the Syriac Churches

Baum, W., and D. W. Winkler. *The Church of the East: A Concise History.* London: Routledge-Curzon, 2003.

Baumer, Christoph. *The Illustrated History of the Church of the East.* New York: I.B. Tauris, 2006.

Collection Fils d'Abraham (Turnhout: Brepols).

Sélis, C. *Les Syriens orthodoxes et catholiques*. 1988.

Teule, H. *Les Assyro-Chaldéens: Chrétiens d'Irak, d'Iran et de Turquie*. 2008.

Mouawad, R. J. *Les Maronites: Chrétiens du Liban*. 2009.

Naaman, Paul. *The Maronites: The Origins of an Antiochene Church*. Collegeville: Liturgical Press, 2011.

Suermann, H. *Histoire des origines de l'Église Maronite*. Kaslik: Presses de l'université du Saint-Esprit Kaslik, 2010.

Wilmshurst, David. *The Martyred Church: A History of the Church of the East*. London: East and West, 2011.

The Études Syriaques Collection (Paris: Geuthner)

Vol. 1: Briquel Chatonnet, F., M. Debié, and A. Desreumaux, eds. *Les inscriptions syriaques*. 2004.

Vol. 2: Debié, M., A. Desreumaux, C. and F. Jullien, eds. *Les apocryphes syriaques*. 2005.

Vol. 3: Cassingena-Trévedy, F., and I. Jurasz, eds. *Les liturgies syriaques*. 2006.

Vol. 4: Gonnet, D., and A. Schmidt, eds. *Les Pères grecs en syriaque*. 2007.

Vol. 5: Briquel Chatonnet, F., and Ph. Lemoine, eds. *L'Ancien Testament en syriaque*. 2008.

Vol. 6: Debié, M., ed. *L'historiographie syriaque*. 2009.

Vol. 7: Jullien, F., ed. *Le monachisme syriaque*. 2010.

Vol. 8: Desreumaux, A., ed. *Les mystiques syriaques*. 2011.

Vol. 9: Binggeli, A., ed. *L'hagiographie syriaque*. 2012.

Vol. 10: Briquel Chatonnet, F., ed. *Les églises en monde syriaque*. 2013.

Vol. 11: Villey, É., ed. *Les sciences en syriaque*. 2014.

Vol. 12: Borbone, P. G., and P. Marsone, eds. *Le christianisme syriaque en Asie centrale et en Chine*. 2015.

Vol. 13: Ruani, F., ed. *Les controverses religieuses en syriaque*. 2016.

Vol. 14: Haelewyck, J. C., ed. *Le Nouveau Testament en syriaque*. 2017.

Vol. 15: Farina, M., ed. *Les auteurs syriaques et leur langue*. 2018.

Vol. 16: Fiori, E., ed. *La philosophie en syriaque*. 2019.

Vol. 17: Heyberger, B., ed. *Les chrétiens de tradition syriaque à l'époque ottomane*. 2020.

Vol. 18: Berti, V., and M. Debié, eds. *Le droit en syriaque*, 2022.

Books on Syriac Literature

Brock, Sebastian. *A Brief Outline of Syriac Literature*. Moran Etho 9. Piscataway: Gorgias Press, 2011.

Penn, M. P., S. F. Johnson, C. Shephardson, and C. M. Stang, eds. *Invitation to Syriac Christianity: An Anthology*. Oakland: University of California Press, 2022.

Wright, William. *A Short History of Syriac Literature*. London: Adam, Charles, and Black, 1894.

Digital Resources

http://bethmardutho.org/: an online portal to resources for Syriac studies.

http://syri.ac/: an online annotated bibliography of resources for Syriac studies.

http://syriaca.org/: an electronic portal for the study of Syriac history, literature, and culture.

http://syriac.msscatalog.org/: an online database of Syriac manuscripts.

https://syriaccorpus.org/index.html: Digital Syriac Corpus.

http://dash.stanford.edu/: Digital analysis of Syriac handwriting.

Chapter 1

Briquel Chatonnet, F. *Les Araméens et les premiers Arabes: Des royaumes araméens a la chute du royaume nabatéen.* Encyclopedie de la Mediterranee. Aix en Provence: Edisud, 2004. https://cnrs.academia.edu/FrancoiseBriquelChatonnet.

Drijvers, H. J. W., and J. F. Healey. *The Old Syriac Inscriptions of Edessa and Osrhoene: Texts, Translations and Commentary.* Handbuch der Orientalistik I.42. New York: Brill, 1999.

Gzeller, H. *Aramaic: A History of the First World Language.* Grand Rapids: Eerdmans, 2021.

Lipiński, E. *The Arameans: Their Ancient History, Culture and Religion.* Orientalia Lovaniensia Analecta 100. Leuven: Peeters, 2000.

Niehr H., ed. *The Aramaeans in Ancient Syria.* Handbook of Oriental Studies I.106. Boston: Brill, 2014.

Ross, S. K. *Roman Edessa: Politics and Culture on the Eastern Fringes of the Roman Empire, 114–242 CE.* New York: Routledge, 2001.

Sartre, M. *D'Alexandre à Zénobie: Histoire du Levant antique: ive siècle avant J.-C.-iiie siècle après J.-C.* Paris: Fayard, 2001.

Chapter 2

Debie, M. "L'empire perse et ses marges." In *Histoire générale du christianisme,* vol. 1, edited by J.-R. Armogathe et al., 610–46. Paris: Presses Universitaires de France, 2010.

Debié, M., A. Desreumaux, C. Jullien, and F. Jullien, eds. *Les apocryphes syriaques.* Paris: Geuthner, 2005.

Jullien, C., and F. Jullien. *Les Actes de Mar Mari, l'apôtre de la Mésopotamie.* Turnhout: Brepols, 2001.

———. *Apôtres des confins: Processus missionnaires chrétiens dans l'empire iranien.* Res Orientales XV. Paris: Groupe Pour L'Étude de la Civilisation du Moyen-Orient, 2002.

Murray, R. *Symbols of Church and Kingdom: A Study in Early Syriac Tradition.* London: Cambridge University Press, 1975.

Phillips, George. *The Doctrine of Addai, the Apostle.* London: Trübner, 1876.

Poirier, P. H. "Les actes de l'apôtre Thomas." In *Écrits apocryphes chrétiens*, edited by F. Bovon and P. Geoltrain, 1331–470. Bibliotheque de la Pleiade. Paris: Gallimard, 1997.

Poirier, P. H., and E. Cregheur. *Le Livre des lois des pays. Un traité syriaque sur le destin de l'"école" de Bardesane.* Bibliothèque de l'Orient chrétien. Paris: Les Belles Lettres, 2020.

Chapter 3

Le monachisme syriaque (ed. Jullien) and *Les mystiques syriaques* (ed. Desreumaux), in the collection "Études syriaques" (see the general bibliography).

Brock, S. P. *Spirituality in the Syriac Tradition.* 2nd ed. Kottayam: St. Ephrem Ecumenical Research Institute, 2005.

———. *The Syriac Fathers on Prayer and the Spiritual Life.* Kalamazoo: Cistercian Publications, 1987. (French translation, *Spiritualité orientale* 90, 2011.)

Guillaumont, A. *Aux origines du monachisme chrétien: Pour une phénoménologie du monachisme.* Spiritualite orientale 30. Begrollesen-Mauges: Abbaye de Bellefontaine, 1979.

Jullien, F. *Le monachisme en Perse: La réforme d'Abraham le Grand, père des moines de l'Orient.* Corpus Scriptorum Christianorum Orientalium 622, vol. 121. Leuven: Peeters, 2008.

Peña I., P. Castellana, and R. Fernández. *Les cénobites syriens.* Studium Biblicum Franciscanum. Collectio minor 28. Milan: Franciscan Printing Press, 1983.

———. *Les reclus syriens.* Studium Biblicum Franciscanum. Collectio minor 23. Milan: Franciscan Printing Press, 1980.

———. *Les stylites syriens.* Studium Biblicum Franciscanum. Collectio minor 16. Milan: Franciscan Printing Press, 1975.

Chapter 4

Becker, A. H. *Fear of God and the Beginning of Wisdom: The School of Nisibis and the Development of Scholastic Culture in Late Antique Mesopotamia.* Divinations: Rereading Late Ancient Religion. Philadelphia: University of Pennsylvania Press, 2006.

Briquel Chatonnet, F. "La Bible dans la littérature syriaque." In *La Bible dans les littératures du monde*, edited by Sylvie Parizet, 2080–86. Paris: Cerf, 2016.

Brock, S. P. *The Bible in the Syriac Tradition.* Piscataway: Gorgias Press, 2006.

———. *The Luminous Eye: The Spiritual World Vision of Saint Ephrem.* Kalamazoo: Cistercian Publications, 1992.

Debié, M. *L'écriture de l'histoire en syriaque: Transmissions interculturelles et constructions identitaires entre hellénisme et islam.* Leuven: Peeters, 2015.

Gutas, D. *Greek Thought, Arabic Culture: The Graeco-Arabic Translation Movement in Baghdad and Early ʿAbbasid Society (2nd–4th/8th–10th Centuries).* London: Routledge, 1998.

Chapter 5

Le christianisme syriaque en Asie centrale et en Chine, in the collection "Études syriaques" (see the general bibliography).

Beaucamp, J., F. Briquel Chatonnet, and Ch. Robin. "La persécution des chrétiens de Najran et la chronologie himyarite." *ARAM* 11–12 (1999–2000): 15–83.

———, eds. *Martyrs en Arabie: Regards croisés sur les sources*. Monographies 31. Le massacre de Najran II. Paris: Centre de recherche d'Histoire et Civilisation de Byzance, 2010.

Borbone, P. G. *History of Mar Yahballaha and Rabban Sauma: Edited, Translated, and Annotated*. Translated by Laura E. Parodi. Hamburg: Tredition, 2020.

Briquel Chatonnet, F., A. Desreumaux, and J. Thekeparampil. "Introduction historique." In *Recueil des inscriptions syriaques*, vol. 1, *Kérala*, 21–24. Paris: Academie des Inscriptions et Belles-Lettres, 2008.

Carter, R. A. "Christianity in the Gulf during the First Centuries of Islam." *Arabian Archaeology and Epigraphy* 19 (2008): 71–108.

——— "Christianity in the Gulf after the Coming of Islam: Redating the Churches and Monasteries of Bet Qatraye." In *Les préludes de l'Islam. Ruptures et continuités dans les civilisations du Proche-Orient, de l'Afrique orientale, de l'Arabie et de l'Inde à la veille de l'Islam*, edited by C. J. Robin and J. Schiettecatte, 311–30. Paris: De Boccard, 2013.

Colin, G. *Saints fondateurs du monachisme éthiopien: Frumentius, Garimā, Takla-Hāymānot et Ēwosṭātēwos*. Bibliotheque de l'Orient chrétien 1. Paris: Les Belles Lettres, 2017.

Debié, M. "Les controverses religieuses en Arabie et le Coran." In *Les controverses religieuses en syriaque*, edited by F. Ruani, 137–56. Études syriaques 13. Paris: Geuthner, 2016.

Kennet, Derek. "The Decline of Eastern Arabia in the Sasanian Period." *Arabian Archaeology and Epigraphy* 18 (2007): 86–122.

Kozah, M., A. Abu-Husayn, S. S. Al-Murikhi, and H. Al-Thani, eds. *The Syriac Writers of Qatar in the Seventh Century*. Piscataway: Gorgias Press, 2014.

Salles, J. F. "Chronologies du monachisme dans le Golfe arabo-persique." In *Monachisme d'Orient: Images, échanges, influences*, edited by F. Jullien and M. J. Pierre, 97–111. Turnhout: Brepols, 2011.

Chapter 6

Cormak, R., J. F. Haldon, and E. Jeffreys, eds. *The Oxford Handbook of Byzantine Studies*. Oxford: Oxford University Press, 2008.

Donner, Fred. *Muhammad and the Believers: At the Origins of Islam*. Cambridge: Harvard University Press, 2010.

Eddé, A. M., F. Micheau, and Chr. Picard. *Communautés chrétiennes en pays d'Islam du début du viie siècle au milieu du xie*. Paris: SEDES, 1997.

Frend, W. H. C. *The Rise of the Monophysite Movement: Chapters in the History of the Church in the Fifth and Sixth Centuries*. Cambridge: James Clarke, 1972.

Griffith, Sydney H. *The Church in the Shadow of the Mosque: Christians and Muslims in the World of Islam.* Princeton: Princeton University Press, 2010.

Kennedy, Hugh. *The Great Arab Conquests. How the Spread of Islam Changed the World We Live In.* London: Weidenfeld and Nicolson, 2007.

Meyendorff, John. *Imperial Unity and Christian Divisions: The Church, 450–680 AD.* Crestwood: St. Vladimir's Seminary Press, 1989.

Payne, R. *A State of Mixture: Christians, Zoroastrians and Iranian Culture in Late Antiquity.* Oakland: University of California Press, 2015.

Chapter 7

Asbridge, T. *The Crusades.* London: Simon & Schuster, 2012.

Eddé, A. M., and F. Micheau. *L'Orient au temps des croisades.* Paris: Flammarion, 2002.

Fiey, J. M. *Chrétiens syriaques sous les Abbassides surtout à Bagdad (749–1258).* Leuven: Secrétariat du Corpus SCO, 1980.

———. *Chrétiens syriaques sous les Mongols: Il-Khanat de Perse xiiie-xive siecles.* Corpus Scriptorum Christianorum Orientalium 362, no. 44. Leuven: Secrétariat du Corpus SCO, 1975.

Garcin, J. C. *États, sociétés et cultures du monde musulman medieval: xe–xve siècle.* 3 vols. Paris: Presses Universitaires de France, 1995–2000.

Hayek, I. A. *Le relazioni della Chiesa siro-giacobita con la Santa Sede dal 1143 al 1656.* Cahiers d'études syriaques 3. Paris: Geuthner, 2015.

Kaplan, A. *Le lectionnaire de Dioscoros Theodoros (Mardin syr. 41/2): Calligraphie, ornementation et iconographie figurée.* Brussels: Editions d'Antioche, 2013.

Teule, H., C. Fotescu Tauwinkl, R. B. ter Haar Romeny, and J. J. van Ginkel. *The Syriac Renaissance.* Eastern Christian Studies 9. Leuven: Peeters, 2010.

Chapter 8

Gaunt, D., N. Atto, and S. O. Barthoma. *Let Them Not Return: Sayfo—The Genocide against the Assyrian, Syriac, and Chaldean Christians in the Ottoman Empire.* New York: Berghahn, 2017.

Hellot-Bellier, Fl. *Chroniques de massacres annoncés: Les Assyro-Chaldéens d'Iran et du Hakkari face aux ambitions des empires (1896–1920).* Cahiers d'études syriaques 2. Paris: Geuthner, 2014.

Heyberger, B. *Hindiyya (1720–1798), mystique et criminelle.* Paris: Aubier, Collection historique, 2001.

———. *Les chrétiens du Proche-Orient.* Paris: Presses Universitaires de France, 2017.

Larsen, M. T. *The Conquest of Assyria: Excavations in an Antique Land, 1840–1860.* New York: Routledge, 1996.

Murre-Van den Berg, H. *Scribes and Scriptures: The Church of the East in the Eastern Ottoman Provinces (1500–1850).* Eastern Christian Studies 21. Leuven: Peeters, 2015.

Raphael, P. *Le rôle du Collège maronite romain dans l'orientalisme aux XVIIe–XVIIIe siècles.* Beirut: Université Saint Joseph, 1950.

Strothmann, W. *Die Anfange der syrischen Studien in Europa.* Göttinger Orientforschungen I.1. Wiesbaden: Harrassowitz, 1971.

References for Excerpts

Inscription of Zakkur. Edward Lipiński, *Studies in Aramaic Inscriptions and Onomastics*, vol. 1 (Leuven: Leuven University Press, 1975).

Inscription of Tell Fekheriye. Edward Lipiński, *Studies in Aramaic Inscriptions and Onomastics*, vol. 2 (Leuven: Leuven University Press, 1994).

The Story of Ahiqar, according to the Aramaic version. James Moore, "'I Am Unable to Do My Job': Literary Depictions of the Scribal Profession in the Story of Ahiqar and Jeremiah 36" (PhD diss., Brandeis University, 2017).

The Wisdom of Ahiqar, according to the Aramaic version: from the maxims of wisdom. Bezalel Porten and Ada Yardeni, *Textbook of Aramaic Documents from Ancient Egypt*, vol. 3, *Literature, Accounts, Lists* (Jerusalem: Hebrew University, 1993).

The Chronicle of Michael the Great (The Edessa-Aleppo Syriac Codex) Books XV–XXI, from the Year 1050 to 1195 AD, trans. Amir Harrak (Piscataway: Gorgias Press, 2019).

Excerpt from the anonymous *Chronicle of Edessa* up to 540: the flood of AD 202. Judah Benzion Segal, *Edessa: "The Blessed City"* (Oxford: Clarendon, 1970).

Beginning of the text on the parchment found in Dura-Europos (AD 243). H. J. W. Drijvers and J. F. Healey, *The Old Syriac Inscriptions of Edessa and Osrhoene: Texts, Translations and Commentary* (New York: Brill, 1999).

History of Abgar and Jesus. *The Teaching of Addaï*, trans. G. Howard (Chico: Society of Biblical Literature, 1981).

Cults in Edessa. *The Teaching of Addaï*, trans. G. Howard (Chico: Society of Biblical Literature, 1981).

Message of Jesus to Abgar. *The Teaching of Addaï*, trans. G. Howard (Chico: Society of Biblical Literature, 1981).

Acts of Mar Mari. Amir Harrak, *The Acts of Mār Mārī the Apostle* (Atlanta: Society of Biblical Literature, 2005).

Hymn of the Pearl (from the *Acts of Thomas*). William Wright, *Apocryphal Acts of the Apostles* (London: Williams and Norgate, 1871)

Another excerpt from the *Acts of Thomas*. Albertus Frederik Johannes Klijn, *The Acts of Thomas: Introduction, Text, and Commentary*, Supplements to Novum Testamentum 5 (Leiden: Brill, 1962).

The letter of Patriarch Timothy I (ca. late 7th or 8th century). "Lettre du patriarche Timothée à Maranzekhâ, évêque de Ninive," trans. Françoise Briquel Chatonnet et al., *Journal asiatique* 288, no. 1 (2000): 1–13.

Bardaisan. H. J. W. Drijvers, *The Book of the Laws of Countries: A Dialogue on Fate of Bardaisan of Edessa* (Assen: Van Gorcum, 1965).

Odes of Solomon 11, "Paradise." *The Odes of Solomon, Syriac Text and English Translation*, trans. Gie Vleugels with Martin Webber, Mōrān Ethō 41 (Kottayam: SEERI, 2016).

Kirdir's inscription. Georgina Herrmann, D. N. MacKenzie, and Rosalind Howell Caldecott, *The Sasanian Rock Reliefs at Naqsh-I Rustam: Naqsh-I Rustam 6, the Triumph of Shapur I (Together with an Account of the Representations of Kerdir): Description and Commentary* (Berlin: Reimer, 1989).

Cave of Treasures. Alexander Toepel, "The Cave of Treasures: A New Translation and Introduction," in *Old Testament Pseudepigrapha: More Noncanonical Scriptures*, vol. 1, ed. Richard Bauckham, James R. Davila, and Alexander Panayotov, 531–84 (Grand Rapids: Eerdmans, 2013).

Syriac *Sogitha* celebrating the cathedral church of Edessa. Kathleen Elizabeth McVey, "The Domed Church as Microcosm: Literary Roots of an Architectural Symbol," *Dumbarton Oaks Papers* 37 (1983): 91–121.

Ephrem, *Hymns on Paradise* 5.2. Sebastian P. Brock, *The Luminous Eye: The Spiritual World Vision of St Ephrem* (Rome: Center for Indian and Inter-Religious Studies, 1985).

Ephrem, *Letter to Hypatius*. Sebastian P. Brock, *The Luminous Eye: The Spiritual World Vision of St Ephrem* (Rome: Center for Indian and Inter-Religious Studies, 1985)

Ephrem, *Paschal Hymn* 9. Ephrem, *Hymnes pascales*, trans. François Cassingena-Trevedy, Sources chrétiennes 502 (Paris: Cerf, 2006).

The Persian martyrs. *History of Karka d-Bet Slok*. Translated by D. G. K. Taylor.

Aphrahat about the Sons and Daughters of the Covenant. Aprahat, *Demonstration* 6:8. Translated by Adam Isaac Lehto. *The Demonstrations of Aphrahat, the Persian Sage*, Gorgias Eastern Christian Studies 27 (Piscataway: Gorgias Press, 2010).

Theodoret of Cyrrhus, *Life of Symeon* (*History of the Monks of Syria/Historia religiosa* 26.12). Robert Doran, *The Lives of Simeon Stylites*, Cistercian Studies Series 112 (Kalamazoo: Cistercian Publications, 1992).

Inscription of Nabgha. Translated by Françoise Briquel Chatonnet and Alain Desreumaux.

Book of Steps, *Mēmrā* 1.9. *The Book of Steps: The Syriac Liber Graduum*, trans. R. A. Kitchen and M. F. G. Parmentier (Kalamazoo: Cistercian Publications, 2004).

266

REFERENCES FOR EXCERPTS

The Life of Maruta of Tagrit. *Vie d'Ahudemmeh*, trans. François Nau, Patrologia Orientalis 4.1 (Paris: Firmin-Didot, 1909), 70–71.

The Life of Abraham of Kashkar. *The Book of Governors: The Historia Monastica of Thomas Bishop of Marga A.D. 840*, trans. E. A. W. Budge, vol. 2 (Piscataway: Gorgias Press, 2003).

Thomas of Marga. *The Book of Governors: The Historia Monastica of Thomas Bishop of Marga A.D. 840*, trans. E. A. W. Budge, vol. 2 (Piscataway: Gorgias Press, 2003).

Simeon of the Olives. Robert Hoyland, Sebastian P. Brock, Kyle B. Brunner, and Jack Tannous, *The Life of Simeon of the Olives: An Entrepreneurial Saint of Early Islamic North Mesopotamia*, Texts from Christian Late Antiquity 66 (Piscataway: Gorgias Press, 2021).

Excerpt from al-Shabushti's *Book of Monasteries* (*Kitab al-Diyarat*). Al-Shabushti, *Kitab al-Diyarat*, trans. Saba Farès (Beyrouth: Dār ar-Ra'd al-'arabī, 1986).

Colophon of Ms. Paris BnF syr. 27B, f. 93r. Translated by Lucas van Rompay. In Françoise Briquel Chatonnet and Muriel Debié, eds., *Manuscripta Syriaca* (Paris: Geuthner, 2015).

The Teaching of Addaï, trans. G. Howard (Chico: Society of Biblical Literature, 1981).

Request to find manuscripts for Patriarch Timothy I. Vittorio Berti, *Vita e Studi di Timoteo I, patriarca christiano di Bagdad*, trans. Françoise Briquel Chatonnet (Paris: Association pour l'avancement des études iraniennes, 2009).

Ephrem, *Hymns on Paradise* 6.1. Sebastian P. Brock, *The Luminous Eye: The Spiritual World Vision of St Ephrem* (Rome: Center for Indian and Inter-Religious Studies, 1985).

Barḥadbeshabba 'Arbaya, *Cause of the Foundation of Schools*. Translated by Adam H. Becker. In *Sources for the Study of the School of Nisibis* (Liverpool: Liverpool University Press, 2008).

The Book of Chastity by Isho'dnaḥ of Baṣra. *Livre de la chasteté par Jésusdenah évêque de Baçra*, trans. J. B. Chabot (Rome: École Française de Rome, 1896).

Regulations of the School of Nisibis. Arthur Vööbus, *The Statutes of the School of Nisibis* (Stockholm: The Estonian Theological Society in Exile, 1961).

Kalilah and Dimnah. I. G. N. Keith-Falconer, *Kalilah and Dimnah or the Fables of Bidpai* (Cambridge: Cambridge University Press, 1885).

Odes of Solomon 19, "Cup." James H. Charlesworth, ed., *The Odes of Solomon* (Oxford: Clarendon, 1973).

Jacob of Serugh, *On the Pearl*. Jacob of Serugh, *Mimro* I.3. Translated by Boulos Sony. *Parole de l'orient* (1979–1980): 85.

Ephrem, *Hymn on Resurrection* 2:1; 2:6. Ephrem the Syrian, *Select Poems: Vocalized Syriac Text with English Translation, Introduction and Notes*, ed. Sebastian P. Brock and George Anton Kiraz, Eastern Christian Texts 2 (Provo: Brigham Young University Press, 2006).

Ephrem, *madrasha* on Mary and Eve. *Ecclesiastes* 37:1. Ephrem the Syrian, *Select Poems: Vocalized Syriac Text with English Translation, Introduction and Notes*, ed.

Sebastian P. Brock and George Anton Kiraz, Eastern Christian Texts 2 (Provo: Brigham Young University Press, 2006).

Cave of Treasures. Alexander Toepel, "The Cave of Treasures: A New Translation and Introduction," in *Old Testament Pseudepigrapha: More Noncanonical Scriptures,* vol. 1, ed. Richard Bauckham, James R. Davila, and Alexander Panayotov (Grand Rapids: Eerdmans, 2013), 531–84.

Jacob of Serugh, *On Biblical Exegesis.* Translated by Boulos Sony. "La méthode exégétique de Jacques de Saroug," *Parole de l'orient* 9 (1979–1980): 67–103.

Sergius of Resh ʿaina. Henri Hugonnard-Roche, "Aux origines de l'exégèse orientale de la logique d'Aristote: Sergius de Reš ʿaina († 536), médecin et philosophe," *Journal asiatique* 277 (1989): 1–17.

Letter of Simeon of Beth Arsham on the Martyrs of Najrân. Irfan Shahid, *The Martyrs of Najrân: New Documents,* Subsidia hagiographica 49 (Brussels: Société des Bollandistes, 1971).

The Life of Mar Yonan, 7th or 8th century. Translated by Richard Payne. *Arabian Archaeology and Epigraphy* 22 (November 2011): 97–106.

Cosmas Indicopleustes, *Christian Topography,* book 3. Translated by John Watson McCrindle (Hakluyt Society, 1897). *The Christian Topography of Cosmas, an Egyptian Monk* (Cambridge: Cambridge University Press, 2010).

Letter of Patriarch Timothy I (780–822) to the monks of Mar Maron. Raphaël Bidawid, *Les lettres du patriarche nestorien Timothée I* (Vatican City: Biblioteca Apostolica Vaticana, 1956).

Xi'an Stele. *Stele on the Diffusion of the Luminous Religion of Da Qin (Rome) in the Middle Kingdom.* Translated by L. Eccles and Sam Lieu of the SERICA Team. https://www.mq.edu.au/__data/assets/pdf_file/0007/55987/Xian-Nestorian-Monument-27-07-2016.pdf.

Excerpt from Marco Polo. *The Travels of Marco Polo,* trans. Henry Yule (London: Murray, 1903).

History of Mar Yahballaha. *History of Mar Yahballaha and Rabban Sauma,* ed. and trans. Pier Giorgio Borbone (Hamburg: Tredition, 2021).

Mar Yahballaha in Paris. *History of Mar Yahballaha and Rabban Sauma,* ed. and trans. Pier Giorgio Borbone (Hamburg: Tredition, 2021).

Funerary stones from Kyrgyzstan. Translated by Alain Desreumaux.

Letter of the catholicos Timothy on the primacy of the Church of Persia. Translated by Françoise Briquel Chatonnet et al.

The Life of Nestorius. Barḥadbeshabba ʿArabaya, *Histoire ecclésiastique,* trans. François Nau, Patrologia Orientalis 9.5 (Paris: Firmin-Didot, 1913), 517.

Narsai, *Homily on Creation* vv. 23–32: *On the Constitution of Angels,* trans. Philippe Gignoux, Patrologia Orientalis 34 (Paris: Firmin-Didot, 1966–1968), 639–41.

Jacob of Serugh, *Mimro on the Stranger.* Translated by Paul Mouterde. "Deux homélies inédites de Jacques de Saroug," *Mélanges de l'Université Saint-Joseph* 26 (1944–1946): 15–22.

Philoxenus of Mabbug, *Sur le Christ avocat.* Translated by André de Halleux. *Philoxène de Mabbog: Sa vie, ses écrits, sa théologie* (Leuven: Imprimerie orientaliste, 1963).

The Life of Jacob Baradaeus. Ernest Walter Brooks, ed., *John of Ephesus: Lives of the Eastern Saints*, Patrologia Orientalis 18.4 (Paris: Firmin-Didot, 1924), 490.

History of Maruta of Tagrit. *Histoire de Marouta de Tagrit sur la concurrence par les chants*, trans. François Nau, Patrologia Orientalis 3.1 (Paris: Firmin-Didot, 1909), 65–66.

Syriac inscription on a church dedicated to St. Sergius in Ehnesh (on the Euphrates, Turkey). Andrew Palmer, *The Seventh Century in the West-Syrian Chronicles* (Liverpool: Liverpool University Press, 1993).

The delegation sent by the catholicos Isho'yahb to Muhammad. *Chronique nestorienne de Séert*, vol. 2, trans. Addai Scher, Patrologia Orientalis 7.2 (Paris: Firmin-Didot, 1919), 619.

Severus Sebokht and the Indian Science. Translated by Henri Hugonnard-Roche. "Mathématiques en syriaque," in *Les sciences en syriaque* (Paris: Geuthner, 2014).

Letter of Jacob of Edessa to the stylite John of Litarb. Translated by François Nau. "Traduction des lettres XII et XIII de Jacques d'Édesse (exégèse biblique)," *Revue de l'Orient chrétien* 10 (1905): 197–208, 258–282.

Translation of the Gospels into Arabic according to a text of controversy. Michael Philip Penn, "John and the Emir: A New Introduction, Edition and Translation," *Le Muséon* 121, no. 1–2 (2008): 65–91.

Theodore Abū Qurrah, *Refutation of the Saracens.* Translated by John C. Lamoureaux. *Theodore Abū Qurrah* (Provo: Brigham Young University Press, 2005).

Praise of paganism by the Sabean doctor Ṭābit ibn Qurra in Ḥarran (end of the 9th century). Bar Hebraeus, *Chronique civile.* Translated by Muriel Debié.

Sixth conversation of Elias of Nisibis with the vizir al-Maghribī about the sciences. Translated by David Bertaina. "Science, Syntax, and Superiority in Eleventh-Century Christian-Muslim Discussion: Elias of Nisibis on the Arabic and Syriac Languages," *Islam and Christian-Muslim Relations* 22, no. 2 (2011): 197–207.

Chronicle of Michael the Syrian on the golden age of monasteries. *Chronique de Michel le Syrien*, MS XIII, 4. Translated by J. B. Chabot (Paris: Leroux, 1899).

Excerpt from a chronicle about the relationship between Byzantines and the Syriac Orthodox. *Chronique de Michel le Syrien*, MS XIII, 6. Translated by J. B. Chabot (Paris: Leroux, 1899).

Ibn Butlan, 11th century, doctor and philosopher of the Church of the East, *The Banquet of Priests*, translated from Arabic. Gérard Troupeau, *Le banquet des prêtres* (Paris: Geuthner, 2004).

The misfortunes of the Syriac-Orthodox community of Jerusalem under the Frankish kingdom: Colophon of MS Lyon 1 and Paris 51 (Jerusalem as the Latin Kingdom) and excerpt of colophon on MS Paris BnF 51. Translated by Jean-Pierre Martin. "Les premiers princes croisés et les syriens jacobites de Jérusalem," *Journal asiatique* (1888–1889): 33–79.

Dionysius bar Ṣalibi on the taking of Edessa by the emir Zengi in 1144. *Chronique de Michel le Syrien*, MS XVII, 2. Translated by J. B. Chabot (Paris: Leroux, 1899).

Giwargis Warda, *Hymn 58*, on Wednesday of the Rogation. Translated by Anton Pritula. *The Wardā: An East Syriac Hymnological Collection; Study and Critical Edition*. Göttinger Orientforschungen, I. Reihe: Syriaca 47 (Wiesbaden: Harrassowitz, 2015).

Bar Hebraeus on the Mongols. Translated by Denise Aigle. "Actes du colloque Bar Hebraeus et la renaissance syriaque," *Parole de l'orient* 33 (2008): 19–198.

Bar Hebraeus on wealth. Gregory Barhebraeus, *Ethicon (Mēmrā III)*, ed. and trans. H. G. B. Teule, Corpus Scriptorum Christianorum Orientalium 534, 535, Syr. 218, 219 (Leuven: Peeters, 1993).

Bar Hebraeus, *Laughable Stories*. Ernest A. Wallis Budge, ed., *The Laughable Stories Collected by Mâr Gregory John Bar-Hebrǣus, Maphrian of the East from A.D. 1264 to 1268*, Luzac's Semitic Text and Translation Series 1 (London: Luzac, 1897).

Rabelais on the ideal humanist education in the famous curriculum that Gargantuan proposes to his son Pantagruel. François Rabelais, *Gargantua and Pantagruel, Complete: Five Books of the Lives, Heroic Deeds and Sayings of Gargantua and His Son Pantagruel* (Glasgow: Maitland Club, 1838).

Miracle at Mar Gabriel monastery in 1869. Translated by Françoise Briquel Chatonnet. Ms. BnF syr 375.

Rev. Horatio Southgate, *Narrative of a Visit to the Syrian [Jacobite] Church of Mesopotamia: with statements and reflections upon the present state of Christianity in Turkey and the character and prospects of the Eastern Churches* ([1844] New York: Dana, 1856), 17.

Rev. Justin Perkins, *A Residence of Eight Years in Persia* (1843). Justin Perkins, *A Residence of Eight Years in Persia, among the Nestorians, with Notices of the Muhammedans* (Andover: Allen, Morrill, and Wardwell, 1843).

Thomas Audo, *Treasury of the Syriac Language* (1897–1901). Thomas Audo, *Dictionnaire de la langue chaldéenne* (Mosul: Imprimerie des Pères Dominicains, 1897–1901). Reprinted as *Treasure of the Syriac Language* (Losser: St. Ephrem the Syrian Monastery, 1985). Translation from Adam H. Becker, *Revival and Awakening: American Evangelical Missionaries in Iran and the Origins of Assyrian Nationalism* (Chicago: University of Chicago Press, 2015).

Thomas Audo, introduction to his grammar of Neo-Aramaic (1905). Thomas Audo, *Grammaire de langue chaldéenne moderne: dialecte d'Ourmiah* (Ourmiah: Imprimerie des Lazaristes, 1905). Translation from Adam H. Becker, *Revival and Awakening: American Evangelical Missionaries in Iran and the Origins of Assyrian Nationalism* (Chicago: University of Chicago Press, 2015).

Letter from Mgr. Lamy, professor of Semitic languages at Louvain, to Paul Bedjan, a Chaldean priest in Urmia. LII, Mgr Lamy, Louvain, January 28, 1887. In Florence Hellot-Bellier, *Chroniques de massacres annoncés: Les Assyro-Chaldéens d'Iran et du Hakkari face aux ambitions des empires (1896–1920)* (Paris: Geuthner, 2014).

Colophon of a Syriac manuscript celebrating Henri Pognon, diplomat, archae-ologist, and French epigraphist. Translated by Françoise Briquel Chatonnet. Ms. Paris BnF 406, f.178–r.179.

Request of Chaldean patriarch Emmanuel Toma to spare the Chaldean Christians of Mosul. AMFAE, Levant 1918–40, Irak, IL, Patriarche chaldéen, Baghdad, January 29, 1919. In Florence Hellot-Bellier, *Chroniques de massacres annoncés: Les Assyro-Chaldéens d'Iran et du Hakkari face aux ambitions des empires (1896–1920)* (Paris: Geuthner, 2014).

Index

Page numbers in *italics* indicate illustrations. Authored works will be found by name of author.